THE HISTORY OF ATLANTIS

ATLANTEAN ARMOUR (MEXICAN TYPE)
(From a figure found in a Mexican grave).

THE HISTORY OF ATLANTIS

by

LEWIS SPENCE

Foreword by

LESLIE SHEPARD

WITH SIXTEEN FULL-PAGE PLATES

BELL PUBLISHING COMPANY
NEW YORK

TO MY DAUGHTER RHODA

Copyright © MCMLXVIII by University Books Inc.
Library of Congress Catalog Card Number: 67-26623
All rights reserved.
This edition is published by Bell Books
a division of Crown Publishers, Inc.
by arrangement with University Books Inc.
   b c d e f g h
Manufactured in the United States of America

FOREWORD

There can be few more romantic legends than the story of the rise and fall of ancient Atlantis.

Over the centuries folklore embroidered the main theme with beautiful traditions of mysterious islands in the western sea—the Greek Isles of the Blest, the Fortunate Islands, the lovely land of Avalon, and many others. In the fifteenth century some of these wistful paradises were even marked on maps, and inspired voyages of discovery.

It all started with Plato's *Timaeus,* a dialogue circa 600 B.C., which told a complex series of stories within a story like those ivory boxes of the Chinese.

Critias tells *Timaeus* and *Socrates* that his great-grandfather *Dropidas* knew the traditions of the earliest Athenians, which he had received from the wise Greek priest Solon, who in turn learnt them from an Egyptian priest of the goddess Net at Säis. This goddess was the same as the Greek Pallas Athene, and Solon claimed that she founded Athens nine thousand years earlier (i.e. about 9,600 B.C.). According to the Egyptian priest, this ancient Greek city was invaded by the people of a great island in the Atlantic.

Additional circumstantial details of this story, including the dramatic rise and fall of Atlantis, were continued in Plato's *Critias,* which told of the way of life of the ancient Atlanteans, their religion, cities and social customs, and how their country sank beneath the waves because of the evils of the people.

Ever since Plato men have speculated whether these accounts were legendary, allegorical, or variants of the Flood stories found in the mythologies of pagan races all over the world as well as in the Christian scriptures. Was there really a great civilization in ancient times on a vast land mass now many thousands of fathoms under the Atlantic Ocean? Obviously it is not an easy task to sift the great mass of fact and speculation in various fields of mythology, comparative religion, geography, geology and archaeology. Much scholarship is needed, as well as the ability to see the ancient past with fresh and imaginative vision instead of stereotyped dry-as-dust pedantry.

The author of this book was well equipped for this work, as writer, folklorist, scholar and poet.

JAMES LEWIS THOMAS CHALMERS SPENCE, who wrote as Lewis Spence, was born November 25, 1874 in Forfarshire, Scotland. He married Helen Bruce of Edinburgh in 1899; one son, three daughters. Spence was educated privately and at Edinburgh University before commencing a journalistic career. Between 1899 and 1906 he was Sub-Editor of the important newspaper *The Scotsman*, Editor of *The Edinburgh Magazine* 1904-5, and Sub-Editor of *The British Weekly* 1906-9. About this time he took to the serious study of mythology and folklore, with special reference to Mexico and Central America. He published a number of important books on the subject, including *The Popul Vuh* (1908)—the sacred book of the ancient Quiché Indians of Maya, and *A Dictionary of Mythology* (1910). Subsequently he published more than forty important books dealing with mythology, folklore and the occult, including the splendid *Encyclopaedia of Occultism* (reissued University Books, New York, 1960). He contributed to *19th Century & After, Hibbert Journal, Glasgow Herald,* and *The Times*. An ardent Scottish Nationalist, he contested North Midlothian as a candidate January 1929. He also found time to write poetry. He was a Fellow of the Royal Anthropological Institute of Great Britain and Ireland, and Vice-President of the Scottish Anthropological and Folklore Society. He received a D.Lit., and in 1951 was awarded a Royal pension for Services to Literature. He lived for many years in Edinburgh, and his unusual combination of scholarship and romantic interests was perhaps typically Scottish. He listed his recreations as "wandering about Edinburgh and studying types, collecting

FOREWORD

Edinburgh folklore, verse-writing, listening to music, and collecting books on old America and the mysterious." He died March 3, 1955.

His early studies of the mythology of Mexico, Peru, Babylonia and Assyria formed an excellent preparation for the present book. In addition, by 1920 he had completed his fine *Encyclopaedia of Occultism* in which there is a first cautious entry on the Atlantis question. He soon became more firmly partisan.

Four years later he published the first of five books dealing specifically with Atlantis—*The Problem of Atlantis* (London, 1924). In the following year he published *Atlantis in America,* dealing with the evidences of Atlantean civilization on the American continent.

Clearly the subject of Atlantis increasingly gripped his imagination, and these two books were soon followed by the present work, first published London, 1926. It is the best basic work for study of the Atlantis question.

Here Spence examines the sources of Atlantean history, evaluates the writings of Plato, and discusses the geological, archaeological and anthropological evidence, as well as the myths, religions and traditions from many cultures which bear upon the subject. With a scholar's skill he assembles a proposition which he interprets with the insight of a poet. He concludes that there is a strong case for the reality of the Atlantis tradition. Later, in 1932, he edited a journal *Atlantis Quarterly*.

Spence also corresponded with that great explorer Colonel Fawcett, who afterwards vanished without trace in the mysterious jungles of Brazil in 1925. Fawcett believed that Brazil might be part of the lost Atlantis, and this theory also provided the basis of the wonderful romance of the late Sir Arthur Conan Doyle—*The Lost World* (1912). Doyle had corresponded with Spence on the Atlantis question and it was Spence who advised him on *The Maracot Deep,* Doyle's thrilling story of a fictional Atlantis miraculously preserved beneath the ocean. Spence suggested, not unnaturally, that

FOREWORD

the Atlantis of Doyle's romance should be sited where Plato had said it was to be found.

After *The History of Atlantis* Spence wrote a number of books on other mythological, folklore and occult subjects, but fifteen years later in 1942 he returned to the question of Atlantis with a new book *Will Europe Follow Atlantis?* Writing during the period of the Nazi excesses in the last war, his style was now somewhat apocalyptic, as he speculated whether Europe might share the fate of the wicked Atlantis, but his factual and scholarly material was firm and skillful. Since the earlier books his case had been strengthened by the support of other writers on Atlantis, and it is surprising how many esteemed scholars had given qualified support to the general theory. In *Homeric Essays* (1935) Professor Alexander Shewan pointed out that although it used to be fashionable merely to jeer at the existence of Atlantis, "that can hardly continue, now that Mr. Lewis Spence has examined the evidence at length in *The Problem of Atlantis, Atlantis in America*, and *The History of Atlantis.*" Geographers, seismologists, archaeologists, paleontologists and explorers have added supporting evidence for the reality of the main outlines of the Atlantis story.

We need not go the whole way with the later Spence in his colorful prophecies about Europe suffering a similar cataclysm to Atlantis through falling away from moral and religious virtue. Fundamentalist ideas about divine wrath have changed radically in the last few decades, but all the same it is necessary to reexamine the religious teachings of old as much as the scientific and scholarly assessments of the past. This is just what Spence did in his studies of Atlantis.

At all events, Spence is the best guide to the strange enthralling story of Atlantis, one of the most fascinating mysteries of the ancient world.

London   LESLIE SHEPARD

PREFACE

The History of Atlantis may, in the light of our present knowledge of Plato's sunken island, appear as a somewhat presumptuous title for a work, the object of which is to present a general outline of what is known concerning Atlantean civilisation. But it is my earnest wish to place the study upon a scientific basis, and in so doing I attach the description of "history" to this work in the hope that the mere invocation of such a name will endow it with the spirit which should inspire all histories—a desire to arrive at fundamental truth by every available means.

The volumes which I have already published on the subject have met with such widespread acceptance, and for the most part with such kindly and catholic criticism, that I am emboldened to proceed a step farther, and to attempt to cast the evidences of Atlantean civilisation, which I have already gathered into something resembling a historical narrative. Such an account, I am the first to admit, must have as many lacunæ as it has facts, and must rely in large measure upon analogy and often upon pure surmise. But in the first chapter of this volume I have explained my reasons for employing certain methods of approach which may seem too unfamiliar to the historian to meet with his ready acceptance.

In the present volume I have arrived at many conclusions, and have brought forward much evidence which did not appear in my former works on the subject of Atlantis. For example, I have shown that the story of Atlantis, as painted upon the peplum of Pallas at the

Preface

Athenian festival, has a very definite bearing upon the credibility of Plato's narrative, pre-dating it as it did by more than a century. I have also demonstrated that, so far from being mythical, the Egyptian sources from which Plato drew his material were very real indeed, and that he himself visited Egypt.

Again, I have, I think, thrown much new light on the character of the Atlantean invasion of Europe, on the exact site of Atlantis, and especially on the great amount of evidence for the former existence of the island-continent which survives in British and Irish folklore and tradition. British tradition, indeed, is the touchstone of Atlantean history, and the identification of Lyonesse with Atlantis, and the grouping of Atlas with the British gods, Albion and Iberius, should go far to prove the ancient association of our islands with the sunken continent.

But it is from the acceptance of my theory of the existence of a definite Atlantean culture-complex, embodying certain peculiar and associated customs, that I hope to gain converts to the belief in a former widespread Atlantean civilisation having cultural outposts in Western Europe and Eastern America, and connected with the motherland by way of the intervening islands. It is in this theory, I feel, that the strongest case for the pre-existence of Atlantis resides, and I confidently present it to my readers in the certainty that they will favourably consider a hypothesis which I devoutly believe approaches within measurable distance of the truth.

LEWIS SPENCE.

66 *Arden Street*,
Edinburgh.

LIST OF ILLUSTRATIONS

CONTENTS

CHAPTER I

INTRODUCTORY

CHAPTER II

THE SOURCES OF ATLANTEAN HISTORY

I. The Writings of Plato

CHAPTER III

THE SOURCES OF ATLANTEAN HISTORY

II. From the Fourth Century B.C. Onwards.

Contents

CHAPTER IV

ATLANTEAN HISTORICAL SOURCES EXAMINED

CHAPTER V

THE GEOGRAPHY OF ATLANTIS

Contents

CHAPTER VI

THE RACES OF ATLANTIS

CHAPTER VII

THE STONE AGE IN ATLANTIS

Contents

CHAPTER VIII

THE KINGS OF ATLANTIS

CHAPTER IX

ATLANTIS IN BRITAIN

Contents

CHAPTER X

THE TRADITIONS OF ATLANTIS

CHAPTER XI

LIFE IN ATLANTIS

CHAPTER XII

THE ATLANTEAN STATE AND POLITY

Contents

CHAPTER XIII

THE RELIGION OF ATLANTIS

Contents

CHAPTER XIV

ANIMAL LIFE IN ATLANTIS

CHAPTER XV

THE COLONIES OF ATLANTIS

Contents

CHAPTER XVI

THE ATLANTEAN CULTURE-COMPLEX

THE
HISTORY OF ATLANTIS

CHAPTER I

INTRODUCTORY

A HISTORY OF ATLANTIS must differ from all other histories, for the fundamental reason that it seeks to record the chronicles of a country the soil of which is no longer available for examination to the archæologist. If, through some cataclysm of nature, the Italian peninsula had been submerged in the green waters of the Mediterranean at a period subsequent to the fall of Rome, we would still have been in possession of much documentary evidence concerning the growth and ascent of the Roman Empire. At the same time, the soil upon which that empire flourished, the ponderable remains of its civilisation and its architecture, would have been for ever lost to us save as regards their colonial manifestations. We should, in a great measure, have been forced to glean our ideas of Latin pre-eminence from those institutions which it founded in other lands, and from those traditions of it which remained at the era of its disappearance among the unlettered nations surrounding it.

But great as would be the difficulties attending such an enterprise, these would, indeed, be negligible when compared with the task of groping through the mists of the ages in quest of the outlines of chronicle and event which tell of a civilisation plunged into the

abysses of ocean nearly nine thousand years before
the foundation of the Eternal City. Before a task
so stupendous the student of history might well stand
dismayed. A sunken Rome, an earthquake-shattered
Athens, would have bequeathed a thousand corroborative
documents. Had Babylon or the entire Egyptian valley
sunk out of sight a thousand years before the birth of
Christ they would still have left behind them the witness
of their trade with the Mediterranean, their pottery and
other artifacts would have been found in Crete and
Cyprus. Even so, let it be remembered, that the very
site of Nineveh was forgotten, that until a century ago
only the barest outlines of Babylonian and Egyptian
history were known to us, that their written hieroglyphs
were undecipherable. Is it too much to expect, then,
that an archæology which has been equal to the task of
reconstructing the details of civilisations over which time
had cast a depth of shadows profound as that of ocean,
should not be competent to approach the discussion of
the more tangled problems connected with the reconstruction of the history of a continent which has been
submerged for twice as long as ancient Egypt endured?

It is here that it becomes necessary to say something
regarding the writer's own views on the subject of historical science. It must be manifest how great a part
inspiration has played in the disentangling of archæological problems during the past century. By the aid of
inspiration, as much as by that of mere scholarship, the
hieroglyphs of Egypt and the cuneiform script of Babylon were unriddled. Was it not inspiration which unveiled
to Schliemann the exact site of Troy before he excavated
it? Inspirational methods, indeed, will be found to be
those of the Archæology of the Future. The Tape-
Measure School, dull and full of the credulity of incredu-
lity, is doomed.

Analogy is the instrument of inspiration, and, if wielded truly, is capable of extraordinary results. Even now Archæology and Folklore are almost entirely dependent for their results upon analogy. Only by comparison can we cast light upon the nature of unexplained customs and objects, and in this volume the analogical method will be largely employed because it provides us with a fitting probe by whose aid we may pierce the hard crusts of oblivion which have gathered around the facts of Atlantean history.

Facts! Are we in possession of any facts relating to Atlantis? Is the very title, *A History of Atlantis*, not an insult to the intelligence of most readers? If, on coming to the end of this book—should he reach the end—the reader cannot agree that a very fair case has been made out for the former existence of Plato's island-continent, he will at least admit that the mere interest of the subject is sufficiently intriguing to permit of hypotheses being erected in its favour. But that a basis of indisputable fact lies at the roots of the Atlantean theory the writer stoutly maintains, and he pleads that in face of such an array of testimony as he has brought together it is merely childish to refuse belief to the main details of Plato's story.

For that it is founded on material, historical or traditional evidence, of still more ancient provenance is manifest from the possibility of equating the statements made in it concerning the geography, customs and religion of Atlantis with those of neighbouring regions. It is possible to take Plato's account of Atlantis, piece by piece, and compare the statements made therein with similar historical and archæological data, to the complete vindication of his narrative.

And let it be said at once that Plato did not intend his account of Atlantean affairs as allegorical or mythical. That ancient plea is completely disposed of elsewhere in this book. There is reason to regard his narrative as more definitely related to fact than, say, Geoffrey of Monmouth's *Historia Britonum*, in which the pure ore of history is mingled with tradition. That he received it from an Egyptian source is undoubted, and there is no more reason to suspect the bona fides of his narrative than there is to doubt those of any other account of antiquity in which history shades off into tradition.

Tradition, it is now being recognised, is, if used with sufficient safeguards, quite as capable of furnishing the historian with trustworthy data as the best attested documentary evidence. Within recent years we have seen the figure of our British Arthur, once dim and mysterious, slowly emerge from the mists of legend and take on the qualities and appearance of humanity. The writer can remember when Menes, the first King of the First Dynasty of Egypt, was regarded as purely mythical, whereas he is now known to have existed and to have had fairly numerous forerunners. Even in the month in which these lines are written comes extraordinary evidence from Syria of the discovery of a sculptured head of Christ dating from the second century, and of the finding in the Russian Cyrillic versions of Josephus of a pen-picture of the great Founder of Christianity, which together completely destroy the arguments of those who have sought to prove the mythical character of our Redeemer. During this month, too, it has been conclusively proved that the bodies of Peter and Paul actually rest beneath the pavement of St. Peter's at Rome. We all recall the manner in which we laughed at Sir Harry Johnstone's "mythical" okapi, before it was found, killed and stuffed for exhibition, and how we sneered at Mr. Hesketh Pritchard's giant sloth until that notable traveller discovered its stable and a large piece of its skin in Patagonia. All these were "traditions" to some, truths to others.

Introductory

The bare idea of an Atlantis as described by Plato has been met with derision by generations of archæologists, simply because no direct documentary evidence relating to its existence survived. But can one reasonably expect direct documentary evidence of a civilisation which totally disappeared more than eleven thousand years ago? It is manifest that another kind of proof than the documentary must be drawn upon to justify the existence of such a culture. Do we find in the countries which must have been contiguous to Atlantis the vestiges of such civilisation as Plato only too briefly outlines? It is the purpose of this book to try to prove that we do. In the final chapter it will be shown that what the writer has called "the Atlantean complex" displays an association of custom, rite and tradition which, as regards its amalgam of peculiar conditions, is displayed in no other part of the globe save that which stretches between the shores of Western Europe and Eastern America. On the coastal tracts of these countries and in their insular outposts can be traced a cultural complex, the separate existence of which clearly demonstrates that it must have emanated from some region in the Atlantic which now no longer exists.

It is, the writer is convinced, by such a treatment of the Atlantis tradition that its verity will ultimately be justified. The Atlantean theory has received considerable damage from the wild assertions of enthusiasts, and perhaps from the frequently over-enthusiastic efforts of the writer himself. But to approach it as certain archæologists approach, say, the problems of pre-history, is to adopt a method extraordinarily vain and futile, for, as has already been said, it is only by the aid of imagination and inspirational processes that a problem of such peculiarity and extraordinary complexity can ever be unravelled. Great archæological discoveries on land are frequently made by accident, as in the case of the epoch-making finds at Crô-Magnon and

Mas d'Azil.   But to wait upon the ocean to disgorge her secrets is to wait upon eternity.   Let not the archæologist then, professional or otherwise, look with too unfriendly an eye upon a quest which has yet to grope among methods, and hazard many a folly and many a piece of empiricism ere it discover the instruments peculiarly applicable to its needs.   No scientist now sneers at what may seem the crazy methods by which generations of alchemists built up chemical science and steered it to a safe haven among the exact sciences, and it is freely admitted that we are still in the "alchemical" stage of Atlantean archæology.   The professional archæologist may encounter a hundred things he dislikes and contemns in this history.   He may, and probably will, deny it the very name of history.   If he does so, I will not feel at all discountenanced, because I am persuaded that the wildest guess often comes as near the target as the most cautious statement when one is dealing with profundities.   Not that I desire to multiply or encourage the haphazard method in the particular sphere of Atlantean archæology, but that I greatly sympathise with that friend of Edison's who, on being told by the inventor that there was no solvent for uric acid, returned to his laboratory, mixed all the drugs it contained with the obnoxious poison—and found that eleven of them *did* dissolve it!

So much for method.   We have now to consider the narrative of Plato concerning Atlantis, and then to compare it with other and later classical allusions to the mysterious island-continent in the Atlantic.

CHAPTER II

The Sources of Atlantean History

I—THE WRITINGS OF PLATO

THE *Timæus* and *Critias* of Plato constitute not only the fullest, but by far the most important body of historical evidence regarding Atlantis which we possess. As the available translations of those passages in Plato's works which have reference to Atlantis seem to leave a good deal to be desired, I have carefully compiled a new version of them, basing my account of the *Timæus* on the translations of Jowett (*The Dialogues of Plato*), and of R. D. Archer-Hind, and founding my version of the *Critias* on that of the Abbé Jolibois (*Dissertation sur l'Atlantide*, Lyons, 1846) and the excellent French translation of P. Negris (*La question de l'Atlantis de Platon*, Congres internat. d'archéol. Athens, 1905). By a careful collation of these translations I believe I have produced an account which will prove of greater general use to students of the Atlantean problem than any at present existing in English. This account must not be regarded as a translation, but rather as a compilation of translations of the Platonic account of Atlantis. At the same time I have taken all due care to avoid doing violence in any way to the original, which, in the following pages, is not rendered in its entirety, though very nearly so, no fact of importance having been omitted.

Plato's account of the *Timæus* is in dialogue form. Socrates, Hermocrates, Critias and Timæus have fore-gathered for the purpose of philosophical debate, and

7

Socrates reminds Critias that he promised them a tale which might prove acceptable "for the festival of the goddess."

Hermocrates : Indeed, Socrates, as Timæus said, we will do our utmost, nor can we excuse ourselves from the promise. Yesterday, indeed, on leaving this place, when we reached the guest-chamber at the house of Critias, where we are staying, we were discussing this very matter. Critias then told us a story from old tradition, which you had better repeat now, Critias, to Socrates, that he may help us to judge whether it will answer our purpose.

Critias : Agreed, if Timæus is pleased.

Timæus : I quite agree.

Critias : Listen then, Socrates, to a tale which, strange though it be, is yet perfectly true, as Solon, the wisest of the seven, once said. He was a relation and friend of Dropidas, my great-grandfather, as he tells us himself in his poems, and Dropidas assured my grandfather, Critias, who, when an old man, repeated it to us, that there were great and marvellous exploits achieved by Athens in the days of old, which, through lapse of time and in the course of generations, have vanished from memory. The most remarkable is one which it would be fitting for us to narrate, and so at once discharge our debt of gratitude to you and also praise the goddess at the time of her festival by a pæan in her honour.

Socrates : A capital proposal. But what was this feat which Critias described on the authority of Solon as actually performed of old by this city, though unrecorded in history?

Critias : I will tell you an old story which I heard from an aged man, for Critias was then nearly ninety years of age, while I was about ten. It happened to be the "children's day" of the Apaturia,[1] and, as was customary,

---

[1] A festival in honour of Dionysius, held in October, at which the young were enrolled in their clan.

the boys enjoyed their pastime, our fathers giving us rewards for declaiming poetry. Much poetry by several authors was recited and, since that of Solon had the virtue of novelty, many of the children sang his poems. Then one of the kinsmen remarked (whether he believed so or merely wished to please Critias) that he considered that Solon was not only the wisest of mankind, but also the greatest of all poets. The old man was gratified, and said smiling: "Yes, Amynandros, if he had not regarded poetry merely as a side-issue, but had addressed himself seriously to it, and if he had completed the account which he carried from Egypt, instead of being compelled to leave it unwritten by reason of the troubles which he found here on his return, I am of opinion that neither Hesiod nor Homer nor any other poet would have enjoyed so much fame as he."

"What account was that, Critias?" asked Amynandros.

"It referred to a mighty achievement," he replied, "and one which deserved to be exalted throughout the world, a great deed which our city actually performed, but, owing to time and the destruction of the doers thereof, the story has not come down to our days."

"Tell us from the beginning," said the other, "the tale that Solon told, and how and from whom he received it as true."

"There is in Egypt," said Critias, "in the Delta, at the head of which the river Nile divides, a province called Sais, and the chief city of this province is also Sais, the birthplace of Amasis, the king. The founder of this city is a goddess whose name in the Egyptian tongue is Neith, and in Greek, as the Egyptians say, Athena. The people of Sais are great lovers of the Athenians and claim a certain kinship with us. Now when Solon sojourned in this city he was most honourably entreated by its people, and when he inquired concerning ancient things of the priests who were most learned therein, he found that neither he nor any other Greek knew anything about such matters. And when he wished to lead them on to talk of ancient times, he told them of the oldest legends of Greece, of Phoroneus, who was called the first man, and of Niobe, of the tale of Deucalion and Pyrrha, how they survived after the deluge, and he reckoned up their descendants, and tried, by calculating the periods, to count up the number of years that passed during the events he related.   Then said one of the priests, a man well stricken in years: "O Solon, Solon, ye Greeks are but children, and there is no Grecian who is an old man."   And when Solon heard this, he said: "What mean you by this?"   And the priest said: "Ye are all young in your souls; for ye have not any old tradition, any ancient belief nor knowledge that is hoary with age.   And the reason of it is this: many have been the destructions of mankind, and many shall be.   The greatest are by fire and by water, but besides these there are lesser ones.   For, indeed, the tale that is also told among you, how that Phaethon yoked his father's chariot, and, for that he could not drive in his father's path, he burnt up all things upon earth and was himself smitten by a thunderbolt and slain; this story has the air of a fable; but the truth concerning it is related to a deviation of the bodies that move round the earth in the heavens, whereby at long intervals of time a destruction through fire of the things that are upon earth occurs.   Thus do those who dwell on mountains and in high places and in dry perish more easily than those who live beside rivers and by the sea.   Now the Nile, which is our preserver, saves us also from this distress by releasing his springs, but when the gods send a flood upon the earth, lustrating her with waters, those in the mountains are saved, the neatherds and shepherds, but the inhabitants of the cities in your land are swept by the rivers into the sea.   But in this land at no time does water fall upon the fields, but the reverse occurs, and all rises up by nature from below.   Wherefore the legends preserved here are the most ancient on record. The truth is that in all places, where great cold or heat does not forbid, there are ever human beings, now more, now fewer. Now whether at Athens or in Egypt, or in any other known place anything noble or great or otherwise notable has occurred, we have written down and preserved an account of it from ancient times in our temple here. But with you and other nations the commonwealth has only just been discovered, the use of letters and the other commodities that cities require, and after the wonted term of years, like a recurring sickness, comes rushing on them the torrent from heaven, and it leaves only the unlettered and untaught among you, so that, as it were, ye become young again with a new birth, knowing nought of what happened in ancient times either in our country or in yours.[1]

"For example, these genealogies, Solon, which you just now recounted of the people of your country, are little better than children's tales. For in the first place ye remember but one deluge, whereas there had been many before it; and again ye know now that the fairest and noblest race among mankind lived once in your country, whence ye sprang, and all your city which now is, from a very little seed that of old was left over. Ye know it not, because the survivors lived and died for many generations without utterance in writing. For, once upon a time, Solon, far back beyond the greatest destruction by waters, that which is now the city of the Athenians was foremost both in war and in all besides, and her laws were exceedingly righteous above all cities. Her deeds and her government are said to have been the noblest whereof the report has come to our ears."

---

[1] The priest means to say that the destruction of ancient records is due to seismic causes or to floods, and that as the Egyptians are preserved from both by the Nile and the absence of rainfall, their population is continuous and their monuments and records escape destruction. This, of course, could not refer to Greece.

And Solon said that on hearing this he was astonished, and used all urgency in entreating the priest to relate to him from beginning to end all about these ancient citizens.

So the priest said: "O, Solon, I will tell it for thy sake and for the sake of thy city, and for the honour of the goddess who was the owner and nurse and instructress both of your city and of ours, for she founded yours earlier by a thousand years, having taken the seed of you from Earth and Hephaistos, and ours in later time. And the date of our city's foundation is recorded in our sacred writings to be eight thousand years ago. But concerning the citizens of Athens nine thousand years ago, I will briefly inform you of their laws and of the noblest of the deeds which they performed. The precise truth concerning everything we will examine in due order hereafter, taking the actual records at our leisure.

"Regard the Hellenic laws in comparison with those of Egypt, for you will find here at the present day many examples of the laws which then existed among you:—first the separation of the priestly caste from the rest; next the distinction of the craftsmen, that each kind plies its own craft by itself and mixes not with another; and the class of shepherds and hunters and of husbandmen are set apart; and that of the warriors, too, you have surely noticed, is here sundered from all other classes; for they are expected to study the art of war, and nothing else. Again there is the custom of their arming with spears and shields, wherewith we have been the first men in Asia [1] to arm ourselves, for the goddess taught this to us, as she did first to you in that country of yours. Again as regards knowledge, you see how cautious our law is in its underlying principles, examining the laws of nature till it arrives at divination and medicine, the object of which is health, drawing from these

---

[1] In Plato's time Egypt was regarded as a part of Asia. Indeed, all Africa was sometimes spoken of as a part of Asia.

divine studies, lessons useful for human requirements and adding to these all the allied sciences. Thus the goddess established you when she founded your nation first, fixing the spot in which ye were born, because she saw that the equal temperament of its seasons would render its people most intelligent. As the goddess was a patroness of war and erudition, she selected the place that should produce men resembling herself, and in it she planted your race. Thus, then, did ye dwell governed by such laws as I have described, and even better still, surpassing all men in excellence.

"Many and mighty are the deeds of your city set down for the admiration of humanity. And there is one which for greatness and nobility surpasses all the rest. For our chronicles tell of a great adversary your city conquered of old, a power which advanced in wanton insolence upon all Europe and Asia together, issuing yonder from the Atlantic Ocean. For in those days the sea there could be crossed, since it had an island before the mouth of the strait, which is called, as ye say, the Pillars of Hercules. Now this island was greater than Libya and Asia together;[1] and, therefrom, there was passage for the seafarers of those times to the other islands, and from the islands to all the opposite continent which bounds that ocean truly named. For these regions that lie within the strait aforesaid seem to be but a bay having a narrow entrance; but the other is ocean verily, and the land surrounding it may with fullest truth and fitness be named a continent. In this island, Atlantis, arose a great and marvellous might of kings, ruling over all the island itself, and many other islands, and parts of the mainland; and besides these, of the lands east of the strait they governed Libya as far as Egypt, and Europe to the borders of Etruria. So all this power gathered itself together, and your country and ours and the

[1] Plato here means, of course, North Africa and Asia Minor.

whole region within the strait it sought with one single swoop to enslave. Then, O Solon, did the power of your city shine forth in all men's eyes, glorious in valour and strength. For, being foremost upon earth in courage and the arts of war, sometimes she was leader of the Hellenes, sometimes she stood alone perforce when the rest fell away from her; and after being brought into the uttermost perils, she vanquished the invaders and triumphed over them, and the nations that were not yet enslaved she preserved from slavery; while the rest of us who dwell this side the Pillars of Hercules, all did she set free with ungrudging hand. But in later time, after there had been exceeding great earthquakes and floods, there fell one day and night of destruction; and the warriors in your land all in one body were swallowed up by the earth, and in like manner did the island Atlantis sink beneath the sea and vanish away. Wherefore to this day the ocean there is impassable and unsearchable, being blocked by very shallow shoals, which the island caused as she settled down.

"You have heard this brief statement, Socrates, of what the ancient Critias reported that he heard from Solon, and when you were speaking yesterday about the constitution and the men whom you described, I was amazed as I called to mind the story I have just told you, remarking how by some miraculous coincidence most of your account agreed unerringly with the description of Solon. I was unwilling, however, to say anything at the moment, for after so long a time my memory was at fault. I conceived, therefore, that I must not speak until I had thoroughly gone over the whole story by myself. Accordingly I was quick to accept the task you imposed on us yesterday, thinking that for the most arduous part of all such undertakings, I mean supplying a story fitly corresponding to our intentions, we should be fairly well provided. So then, as Hermocrates said, as soon as ever I departed hence yesterday, I began to repeat

the legend to our friends as I remembered it; and when I
got home I recovered nearly the whole of it by thinking it
over at night.   How true is the saying that what we learn
in childhood has a wonderful hold on the memory.   Of
what I heard yesterday I know not if I could call to mind
the whole; but though it is so very long since I heard this
tale, I should be surprised if a single point in it has escaped
me.   It was with much boyish delight that I listened at the
time, and the old man was glad to instruct me (for I asked
a great many questions); so that it is indelibly fixed in my
mind, like those encaustic pictures which cannot be effaced.
And I narrated the story to the rest the first thing in the
morning, that they might share my affluence of words.
Now, therefore, to return to the object of all our conversa-
tion, I am ready to speak, Socrates, not only in general
terms, but entering into details, as I heard it.   The citizens and the city which you yesterday described to us as
in a fable we will transfer to the sphere of reality and to
our own country, and we will suppose that ancient Athens
is your ideal commonwealth, and say that the citizens
whom you imagined are those veritable forefathers of ours
of whom the priest spoke.   They will fit exactly, and there
will be nothing discordant in saying that they were the
men who lived in those days.   And dividing the work
between us, we will all endeavour to render an appropriate
fulfilment of your injunctions.   So you must consider,
Socrates, whether this story of ours satisfies you, or whether
we must look for another in its stead."

Socrates : How could we change it for the better, Critias?
It is specially appropriate to this festival of the goddess,
owing to its connexion with her; while the fact that it is no
fictitious tale, but a true history, is surely a great point.
How shall we find other such citizens if we relinquish
these?   It cannot be; so with Fortune's favour do you
speak on, while I, in requital for my discourse of yester-

day, have in my turn the privilege of listening in silence." [1]

So far the *Timæus*.

The next passage in Plato's works which has reference to Atlantis is his *Critias*, which purports to be an account by a person of that name of the circumstances of life in Atlantis, as recounted by Solon to Dropidas, the speaker's great-grandfather.[2] Nine thousand years before Solon's day, or about 9600 B.C., war broke out between the nations within the Pillars of Hercules and those beyond them. Athens placed herself at the head of the Eastern peoples, and the Kings of the isle of Atlantis led the Western races. Atlantis was an isle greater than Asia (Asia Minor) and Lybia (North Africa) together, but it was swallowed up by a convulsion of the earth, and its site is now marked by dangerous quicksands which render the sea-routes in that region unnavigable.

At this early period Athens was possessed of extensive territories, her lands were fertile, and her inhabitants numerous. As regards the Atlanteans, Critias explains to his hearers that he must render the names of their heroes into Greek. Solon, who had written an account of their history in verse, found that the priests of Sais had already given these names an Egyptian aspect. He would thus take a similar liberty, but would retain their significance. His ancestor had possessed an account of these things in writing, but he, Critias, was compelled to rely on his memory for the facts, which he had heard in childhood, and which had deeply impressed themselves on his mind.

[1] Critias means to say that he was struck by the similarity of the ideal state as described by Socrates, to Athens, as shown in Solon's story. He, therefore, made an effort to recall every circumstance of that story in the hope that it would serve Socrates' purpose to illustrate his imaginary commonwealth. After this, Critias proceeds to expound the order of the universe before the creation of mankind.

[2] It is, indeed, an amplification of Critias's account of Atlantis in the *Timæus*.

The gods divided the earth into portions, both great and small, and to Poseidon or Neptune, god of the sea, had been awarded the isle of Atlantis, where he begat children by a mortal woman. The island, which was not mountainous near the sea-coast, had in its midst a plain, which is said to have had no equal for beauty and fertility. About six miles from this plain stood a low mountain, where dwelt an aboriginal inhabitant or aŭtochthone, called Evenor, who, by his wife, Leucippe, had a daughter called Cleito. This girl, after the death of her parents, was espoused by Poseidon, who environed the mountain with mounds and ditches. The mounds were two in number, and the three ditches, which were filled with water from the sea, were placed at an equal distance one from the other, and rendered access to the mount impossible. The art of navigation was at this time unknown. Poseidon also set in the island two currents of water, one hot, the other cold, which assisted its fertilisation exceedingly.

The god reared in this enchanted place five pairs of male children, twins, of whom he was the father. He divided Atlantis into ten parts. He bestowed on his eldest born the maternal domain, which was the largest and best situated, and established the remaining princes in the other regions of Atlantis as chiefs of different nations. The name of the eldest son was Atlas, who was king of the entire island, and from him the Atlantic Ocean takes its name. His twin brother was called, in the Atlantean language, Gadir, and in the Greek Eumolus. He had for his portion the extremity of the island near the Pillars of Hercules, and that part of it has since borne the name Gadiric. The next pair of twins were called Amphisus and Eudemon, and the others respectively Mneseus, Aŭtochthonus, Elassippus, Mestor, Azaes and Diaprepus. These princes reigned in prosperity in the island for several centuries, and established a supremacy in the midst of the ocean over

many other islands, as well as over those which are near
Egypt and Tyrrhenia.

The posterity of Atlas maintained the sovereign power
during several centuries in uninterrupted succession.
Their riches were so great that they surpassed those of the
kings who lived in the centuries preceding their own, and
no monarch of the succeeding ages could in this respect
compare with them. By their wise industry they filled
the capital city and the country with everything that was
useful and agreeable to existence. Their power procured
them all the productions of foreign lands. Their island
furnished them with all kinds of stones and minerals, and,
above all, with that mineral known as orichalcum (mountain copper) the most precious, next to gold, of all the
metals. The island also produced in abundance all kinds
of timber suitable for building construction. It
nourished numerous herds of animals, both domestic and
wild, and large numbers of elephants. These found plenty
of food in the marshes, lakes and rivers, in the plains and
the mountains. The soil also produced a wealth of roots,
wood, gums, flowers and fruits, the sweet juice of the grape,
and corn, all desirable viands, and vegetables in their season.
Shady trees sheltered its happy people, and divers fruits
appeased their hunger and thirst, especially one with a hard
rind, affording both meat, drink and ointment. In a
word, there was to be found in this island, which has so
unhappily disappeared, everything which could satisfy
the body, the spirit, and engender piety towards the gods.

By means of these natural riches the Atlanteans built
temples, palaces, bridges, directing the waters, which
flowed in a triple circle around their ancient metropolis, in
a useful manner. They began by constructing bridges
over the zones of sea, and another leading to the royal
palace. They greatly increased this building in size and
beauty with each successive reign, and drove a canal

through the zones of land three hundred feet in width, about a hundred feet deep, and about sixty miles in length. At the landward end of this waterway, which was capable of navigation by the largest vessels, they constructed a harbour. The two zones of land were cut by large canals, by which means a trireme, or three-decked galley, was able to pass from one sea-zone to another. The bridges by means of which communication was had between the land-zones were sufficiently high to permit of the passage of vessels, and these were roofed over. The first sea-zone was about 1,800 feet wide, the second about 1,200 feet, and the third, which immediately encircled the island, was about 600 feet in width.

The diameter of the island on which the palace stood was five stadia, or about 1,000 yards. The isle and each zone were enclosed by stone walls. At the entrance to the bridges were gates, surmounted by defending towers. The bridge at the principal entrance was about 100 feet wide. The stone of which these immense piles were constructed was quarried from the island, and was black and black and red in colour. The walls which encircled the outward zone were covered with a light coating of brass, those of the interior had plates of tin, and the walls of the citadel were coated with orichalcum.

The palace within the citadel was planned as follows: In the middle and most inaccessible part was the Temple of Cleito and Poseidon, glittering with gold. Here the descendants of the first Atlanteans gathered each year to offer pious sacrifices to the gods. The Temple of Poseidon was about 600 feet in length, 3 acres square, and of a height proportionate to its length and breadth. But its architecture was barbaric. The whole of its exterior was garnished with silver, its pinnacles glittered with gold, and the interior was roofed with ivory, gold, silver, and the flashing orichalcum. But orichalcum prevailed on the decoration of the interior walls, panels and statues, although there were also statues of the purest gold. Poseidon was here represented standing in his chariot, grasping the reins of winged coursers. Around him were grouped a hundred Nereids borne by dolphins, and other contiguous sculptures represented the princesses and princes of the royal line, and other effigies or votive gifts of the kings and people of the Atlantean Empire. The sacrificial altar, by its grandeur and beauty, was worthy of the magnificence of the Temple, as indeed was the remainder of the royal edifice.

In various parts of the city were situated hot springs and fountains of cold water, both of which flowed in abundance. Great baths were constructed, some open others walled and roofed in, as hot baths for use in winter are. These were baths for the royal family, others were reserved for women, and even horses and other domestic animals had bathing-pools of their own. Each bath was constructed with due regard to decency and the convenience of the several classes which it served.

Each of the two zones of the city was filled with temples, shrines, groves and gymnasiums. Near the midst of the central island stood a large circular hippodrome, 600 feet in diameter. Round this hippodrome were arranged the dwellings of the court officials and guards. The soldiers of the royal guard were lodged near the castle, around the mountain which it crowned, but those most trusted had their abode within the castle itself, near the apartments of the princes. The docks were filled with triremes, and well equipped with everything necessary to seafaring.

On passing the gates of the outward zone one came to a wall which commenced at the sea-shore, and encircled the island and its zones for a distance of 9,000 feet until it joined the wall at the other side of the communicating canal. All the enclosed space was cultivated. The part which faced the sea was covered with villas and storehouses. The gulf was dotted with vessels, and the quays crowded with merchants from all parts, who came and went within the port, making a continual clamour.

Landward, the island presented a mountainous aspect, especially on that side of it which looked seaward. Around the royal city stretched a level plain, likewise circled by mountains, except on the coast. The island looked southward.[1] The most elevated sites were the only parts of it exposed to the ravages of the wind. Our mountains give only a feeble idea of the mountains of that island. Their majestic height, their continuous chain, the thick and tangled forests which covered them excited the liveliest admiration. Their slopes were covered with small towns, wealthy and populous, and diversified by rivers, lakes and prairies, furnished with abundant nourishment for an infinite number of wild beasts. In these forests all kinds of useful woods were to be found.

The island had, coastwise, a lengthy aspect, but the canal and the ditches caused it to lose somewhat of this appearance. The canal had an incredible depth, length and width. When one compares this work with other evidences of human industry the mind refuses to believe that it was the handiwork of man. It flowed through the country for a distance of more than 1,000 miles, and received all the streams which descended from the mountains, traversing the city by way of several lesser canals, where it reached the sea. Its affluents served for the transport of timbers and harvests, and afforded countless inland communications. The soil bore two harvests yearly of all descriptions of fruits and cereals.

[1] Plato probably means that its most thickly inhabited part had a southerly aspect.

In winter, through the protection of the gods, the soil was sheltered from rains and floods.

The plain country furnished 60,000 men-at-arms. The country was divided into cantons, each about twelve square miles, and each canton furnished an armed contingent and appointed its own leader. The mountain country supplied an innumerable host of warriors. It was established by law that the chief of each canton must furnish ten chariots, each with two horses and two cavalrymen, with a driver, to permit the riders to fight on foot if necessary. He must also enlist ten heavily-armed foot-soldiers, two archers, two slingers, three stone-shooters and four sailors, the last as a contribution towards the manning of a fleet of 20,000 vessels. This applied only to the royal portion of Atlantis. The nine other parts of the empire (the islands?) had a separate military economy.

As regards the government, each of the twelve kings was absolute in his own island. But their administration and the dealings between them were governed by the ordinances of the ancient Atlantean rulers, and engraven on a column of orichalcum situated in the midst of the island, in the Temple of Poseidon. Once in six years they assembled therein to deliberate on public affairs and examine all pressing matters with pious attention, judging and condemning the wicked. Before commencing the assize they brought ten bulls into the sacred zone. Each king made a vow to offer up one of these bulls to Poseidon without employing the agency of iron. Having taken the animals, they brought them to the graven column and there immolated them. The ceremony over, the kings passed the members of each bull through the fire, making a libation of the blood, and drenching the column with it, afterwards totally consuming the victims with fire. Later they placed the remainder of the blood in small vases of gold and splashed it on the fire, making at the same time a solemn vow to judge according to the laws graven on the column, and to punish those who had violated them, in conformity with the precepts of their sire Poseidon.

They then drank some of the remaining blood and consecrated the golden vase which held it to Poseidon. Night having fallen, they returned to the temple, each wearing a rich blue robe, and sat in council, which terminated with sunrise. They then engraved the sentences which they had pronounced on a tablet of gold, which they suspended in the temple, along with the vestments they had worn, for the behoof of future generations.

They were not permitted to take up arms against one another, and the children of Atlas were invariably given the leadership in all military expeditions. Nor were they allowed to put any member of their family to death unless a majority of six votes of the Council gave them power to do so.

For many centuries they did not lose sight of their august origin, they obeyed all the laws, and were religious adorers of the gods their ancestors. Sincerity reigned in their hearts. Moderation and prudence directed their conduct and their relations with foreign nations. So long as they behaved in this manner, all was well with them. But in the course of time the vicissitudes of human affairs corrupted little by little their divine institutions, and they began to comport themselves like the rest of the children of men. They hearkened to the promptings of ambition and sought to rule by violence.

Then Zeus, the King of the gods, beholding this race once so noble, growing depraved, resolved to punish it, and by sad experience to moderate its ambition. He convoked a council of the gods in Olympus, and addressed them as follows:

Here Plato's account ends, and it is believed that death interfered with its conclusion.

CHAPTER III

THE SOURCES OF ATLANTEAN HISTORY

II. FROM THE FOURTH CENTURY B.C.

DIODORUS SICULUS, a historian, of Agyrium, in Sicily, who flourished contemporaneously with Julius Cæsar and Augustus, has vouchsafed us nearly as much information regarding Atlantis and its history as did Plato himself. His *Historical Library* is a general history of the world as known in his time, from the earliest ages to Cæsar's conquest of Gaul. If Diodorus was essentially a compiler, he was also a great traveller, and traversed a large part of Europe and Asia for the purpose of collecting materials for his work. Dealing with the geography of the eastern Atlantic region in the fourth chapter of his third book, Diodorus asserts that the Amazons of Africa were much more ancient and famous than those of Pontus in Asia Minor. But they were not the only race of warlike women inhabiting African soil, the Gorgons being nearly as celebrated for courage and valour. The Amazons inhabited an island called Hesperia (the Hesperides, or island of Hesperus, the evening star, son of Atlas, where grew the famous golden apples or oranges, guarded by a dragon) lying to the west, near to the morass named Tritonides, a fen so called from the fact that it was traversed by the River Triton. This morass borders upon Ethiopia, under Mount Atlas, which itself extends to the ocean. (I follow Diodorus in his use of the present tense).

The island Hesperia, he says, is very large, abounding in all sorts of fruit trees, herds of cattle and flocks of sheep and goats. But corn is unknown to its inhabitants. The Amazons, inspired by war-like ambition, subdued all the cities of this island, with the exception of one called Mena, accounted sacred, and now inhabited by the Ethiopians called Ichthophages, or fish-eaters. It is frequently scorched by eruptions of fire, which break out of the earth, and is rich in precious stones.

Having subdued many of the neighbouring African and Numidian tribes, the Amazons founded a great city in the morass of Triton, which, from its shape, they called Chersonesus, or the City of the Peninsula. But, not content with their numerous conquests, they invaded Mount Atlas, a rich country, full of great cities, where the gods had their origin in those parts bordering upon the ocean. Led by Merina, their queen, an army of 30,000 foot and 2,000 horse, clad in serpent skins, and armed with swords, javelins and bows, with which they were most expert, hurled itself upon the country of the Atlantides, and routed those which dwelt in the city of Cercenes. They pursued them so closely that they entered the town at their heels, and took it by storm, putting the men to the sword and carrying off the women and children as captives. The remaining Atlantean communities, stricken with panic fear, submitted incontinently, whereupon Merina made a league with them, built another city in place of Cercenes, calling it by her own name, and peopled it with the captives and other Atlanteans.

The Atlanteans, who appear to have entertained a wholesome dread of the warrior-queen, showered rich gifts and honours upon her, and this treatment seems quite to have won her heart. Shortly afterwards, the Atlanteans, being attacked by the Gorgons, Merina, at their request, invaded the country of the Gorgons, slaying large numbers of them and taking 3,000 prisoners. The rest fled to the forests, which Merina tried to set on fire.

But, baulked in this amiable intention, she returned to her own country.

Both Amazons and Gorgons were subsequently conquered by Perseus and Hercules. "It is reported likewise, that by an earthquake the tract towards the ocean opened its mouth and swallowed up the whole morass of Triton." Merina during her reign, however, extended her conquests to Asia Minor and the Mediterranean Islands, and formed a league with Horus, King of Egypt.

Diodorus then proceeds to give a more particular account of the Atlanteans, and the fabulous statements they made of the genealogy of the gods, which, he says, do not differ much from the fables of the Greeks.

The Atlanteans, he tells us, inhabited a rich country bordering upon the ocean, and were notable for their hospitality to strangers. They boast that the gods were born among them, and say that the most famous poet among the Greeks confirms this assertion when he makes Hera say:

" The utmost bounds of earth far off I see
  Where Thetys and old Ocean boast to be
  The parents of the gods."

They assert[1] that Uranus was their first King, and that he civilised the people, causing them to dwell in cities and till the soil. He had under his dominion the greater part of the world, especially toward the west and north. Addicted to the study of Astrology, he prophesied many future events, and instituted the solar year and the lunar month as measures of time. The people, struck with admiration for his skill, paid him divine honours after he was dead, and called the starry heavens after his name.

---

[1] Diodorus in this passage seems to speak of the Atlantean State as if it existed in his time. He may, of course, refer to the people of Atlas in Africa, as some parts of his narrative would seem to indicate ; but that his account has, as regards its more ancient application, a reference to Atlantis, the southern continent, and not to the remains of its population in Africa, cannot be doubted.

Uranus had forty-five children by various wives, and eighteen by Titea or Terra, who thus came to be known as Titans, or the Terrene people. His most celebrated daughters were Basilea, and Rhea or Pandora. Basilea, the elder, was so solicitous in her care for her brothers that she came to be known as the Great Mother, and on the demise of Uranus was elected queen by the general suffrages of the people. She espoused her brother Hyperion, and bore him Helio and Selene, later the gods of sun and moon respectively. But her remaining brothers, dreading that Hyperion might usurp the throne, slew him and drowned the infant Helio in the River Eridanus or Po, in Italy. Selene, his sister, who passionately loved her brother, cast herself from the housetop and perished.

Basilea, on learning of the death of her children, became demented, and wandered up and down, with hair dishevelled and bedizened with ornaments, playing wildly on the timbrel and cymbal. When the people endeavoured to restrain her, a dreadful tempest of rain, thunder and lightning suddenly broke forth and she was seen no more. Divine rites were established in honour of her children and herself, and these included the playing of the instruments she had employed in her madness, and the erection of altars on which sacrificial offerings were made.

On the death of Hyperion the children of Uranus divided the Kingdom among themselves. The most renowned among these were Atlas and Saturn. Atlas assumed control of the country bordering upon the ocean, called the people inhabiting it Atlanteans, and its great mountains Atlas, after his own name. Like his father Uranus, he was a wise astrologer, and was the first to discover the knowledge of the sphere, whence arose the legend that he bore the world upon his shoulders. The most celebrated of his sons was Hesperus, who, while observing the motions of the stars upon Mount Atlas, vanished in a tempest. The people, lamenting his fate, called the morning star after his name.

Atlas had also seven daughters, who were called after their father, Atlantides. Their names were Maia, Electra, Taygeta, Asterope, Halcyone and Celæno.[1] Their offspring were the first ancestors of several nations, barbarian as well as Greek. The Atlantides became the constellation of the pleiades, and were adored as goddesses. Nymphs, too, were commonly called Atlantides, "because nymphs is a general term in this country applied to all women."

Saturnus, the brother of Atlas, was profane and covetous. Marrying his sister Rhea, he begat Jupiter, who must not be confounded with Jupiter, the brother of Cœlus, or the sky. This Jupiter either succeeded to his father Saturn, as King of the Atlanteans, or displaced him. Saturn, it is said, made war upon his son with the aid of the Titans, but Jupiter overcame him in a battle, and conquered the whole world. "This is a full account of all the gods mentioned and recorded by the Atlanteans."

In the second chapter of his Fourth Book, Diodorus returns to the subject of Atlas and the origin of the Hesperides. In the country called Hesperis, he says, dwelt two famous brothers, Hesperus and Atlas. They owned a flock of surpassingly beautiful sheep, of a ruddy and golden colour, for which reason poets allude to them as "golden apples."[2]

Hesperis, the daughter of Hesperus, married her brother Atlas, and the pair had seven daughters, the Atlantides, also called after their mother the Hesperides. Busiris, King of Egypt, fell in love with the maidens, and despatched a number of pirates to capture them. But Hercules intercepted the pirates, and rescued the young women, whom he restored to Atlas,

---

[1] Only six names are here given.
[2] *Melon*, in Greek, signifies both a sheep and an apple.

their father.   In gratitude Atlas taught him the art of
Astrology, instructing him in the use of the sphere, from
which circumstance the Greeks invented the fable that
Hercules had for a season relieved Atlas of his burden
in bearing the world upon his own shoulders.

Elsewhere, in the fourth chapter of his Fifth Book, Diodorus confirms in a measure the statement of Plato concerning the submergence of a portion of the Greek peninsula.   He states that the Hellenic coast opposite the island
of Rhodes and Cos was so damaged by the flood of Deucalion, which occurred in the Seventh Generation, that it
lay "under pressing and grievous calamities, for the fruits
of the earth were rotted and spoiled for a long time
together, famine prevailed, and through corruption of the
air, plague and pestilence depopulated and laid the towns
and cities waste."

Diodorus, in his Fifth Book, also states that a certain
Atlantic island was discovered by some Phœnician navigators, who, while sailing along the west coast of Africa, were
driven by violent winds across the Ocean.   They brought
back such an account of the beauty and resources of the
island, that the Tyrrhenians, having obtained the mastery
of the sea, planned an expedition to colonise the new land,
but were hindered by the opposition of the Carthaginians.
Diodorus does not mention the name of the island; and he
differs from Plato by referring to it as still existing.   Pau-
sanius relates that a Carian, Euphemus, had told him of a
voyage during which he had been carried by the force of the
winds into the outer sea, "into which men no longer sail;
where he came to desert islands, inhabited by wild men
with tails, whom the sailors having previously visited the
islands called Satyrs, and the islands Satyrides," whom
some take for monkeys.   Perhaps the whole narrative was
an imposture on the grave traveller.

Strabo (b. 54 B.C.) mentions in his Seventh Book, on the

authority of Theopompus and Apollodorus, the same legend, in which the island was called Meropis, and its people Meropes.   He also remarks in his Second Book that Poseidonius (*fl.* 151–135 B.C.) says that, as the land was known to have changed in elevation, the account of Plato ought not to be regarded as fiction, and that such a continent as Atlantis might well have existed and disappeared. The passage is as follows: "Poseidonius correctly sets down in his work the fact that the earth sometimes rises and undergoes settling processes, and changes that result from earthquakes and other similar agencies, all of which I, too, have enumerated above.   And on this point he does well to cite the statement of Plato that it is possible that the story about the island of Atlantis is not a fiction.   Concerning Atlantis, Plato relates that Solon, after having made inquiry of the Egyptian priests, reported that Atlantis did once exist, but disappeared—an island no smaller in size than a continent; and Poseidonius thinks that it is better to put the matter in that way than to say of Atlantis: 'Its inventor caused it to disappear, just as did the Poet the wall of the Achæans.'"

Pomponius Mela (*b.* A.D. 80) expressly affirmed in his First Book the existence of such an island as Atlantis, but places it in the southern temperate zone.

Theopompus of Chios, a Greek historian of the fourth century B.C., none of whose works has survived, save in the *Varia Historia* of Ælian, a compiler of the third century A.D., alludes to an account of the Atlantic area given by the Satyr Silenus, the attendant of Dionysius, to Midas King of Phrygia, who seized him when intoxicated, and recovered much ancient wisdom from his lips.   "Silenus," says Theopompus, "told Midas of certain islands named Europa, Asia and Libya, which the ocean sea surrounds and encompasses.   Outwith this world there is a continent or mass of dry land, which in greatness was infinite and immeasurable, and it nourishes and maintains by virtue of its green meadows and pastures many great and mighty beasts. The men who inhabit this clime are more than twice the height of human stature, yet the duration of their lives is not equal to ours."

The account of the great continent of Saturnia from the dialogue attributed to Plutarch, "On the Face appearing in the Orb of the Moon," and printed with his *Morals*, tells us that "an isle, Ogygia, lies in Ocean's arms, about five days' sail west from Britain, and before it are three others of about equal distance from one another, and also from that, bearing north–west, where the sun sets in summer. In one of these the barbarians feign that Saturn is detained in prison by Zeus." The neighbouring sea was known as the Saturnian, and the continent by which the great sea was circularly environed was distant from Ogygia about five thousand stadia, but from the other islands not so far. A bay of this continent in the latitude of the Caspian Sea, was inhabited by Greeks, who once in thirty years sent certain of their number to minister to the imprisoned Saturn. One of these paid a visit to the great island, as they called Europe, and from him the narrator learned many strange things, especially regarding the state of the soul after death.

Proclus reports that Marcellus, a writer of whom nothing else is known, in a work entitled *The Ethiopic History*, speaks of ten islands situated in the Atlantic Ocean, close to Europe. He says that the inhabitants of these islands preserved the memory of a much larger Atlantic island, Atlantis, which had for long exercised dominion over the other islands of that ocean. Of the islands, he says seven were consecrated to Proserpina, of the remaining three, one was consecrated to Pluto, another to Ammon, and the third, a thousand stadia long, to Poseidon.

Arnobius, a Christian apologist, of Sicca, in Africa, who

flourished in the fourth century A.D., in his First Book
says: "... ransack the records of history written in
various languages, and you will find that all countries have
often been desolated and deprived of their inhabitants.
Every kind of crop is consumed, and devoured by locusts
and by mice: go through your own annals, and you will be
taught by these plagues how often former ages were visited
by them, and how often they were brought to the
wretchedness of poverty. Cities shaken by powerful
earthquakes totter to their destruction: what! did not by-
gone days witness cities with their populations engulfed
by huge rents of the earth? or did they enjoy a condition
exempt from such disasters?

" When was the human race destroyed by a flood? Was
it not before us? When was the world set on fire, and reduced to coals and ashes? Was it not before us? When
were the greatest cities engulfed in the billows of the sea?
Was it not before us? When were wars waged with wild
beasts, and battles fought with lions? Was it not before
us? When was ruin brought on whole communities by poi-
sonous serpents? Was it not before us? For, inasmuch
as you are wont to lay to our blame the cause of frequent
wars, the devastation of cities, the irruptions of the Ger-
mans and the Scythians, allow me, with your leave, to say
—In your eagerness to calumniate us (the Christians) you
do not perceive the real nature of that which is alleged.

" Did we bring it about, that ten thousand years ago, a
vast number of men burst forth from the island which is
called the Atlantis of Neptune, as Plato tells us, and utterly
ruined and blotted out countless tribes?"

A summary of the remaining classical data concerning
Atlantis must here suffice. Pliny the Elder, in the Second
Book of his *Natural History*, cast doubts upon the tale, but
Philo the Jew, a Platonist, in his *Indestructibility of the
World*, embraced it in its entirety on the word of his great

master. Longinus believed that the Atlantean episode in the *Timæus* was simply a literary ornament without either historic truth or philosophic significance. Syrianus, Proclus's master, regarded the tale as historically accurate, and as a symbol of the dogmatic philosophers. Amelius saw in it the opposition of the fixed stars and the planets, Numenius that of good to evil. Origen, the Christian father, considered the account as an allegory of the constant war between the good and evil genii, and Porphyry saw in it the strife between the flesh and the spirit. Iamblichus was of the opinion that its circumstances bore a striking resemblance to the war between the Greeks and Persians, the strife of the Gods and Titans, and the combat between Osiris and Typhon or Set, or the continual strife between chaos and order, duality against unity.

The notions of the Alexandrian School with reference to Plato's account are to be found in the Eighteenth Book of Ammianus Marcellinus, who mentions the destruction of Atlantis as an historic fact. The Byzantine geographer, Cosmos Indicopleustes, in his *Christian Topography*, included Atlantis in his cosmographical system, but altered its circumstances so as to agree with scriptural authority. He believed that the earth was flat, and that a vast continent environed the ocean. On this continent man had his origin, and for its existence he invokes the authority of the *Timæus*. Plato's account, he thought, was a legacy of the original Mosaic tradition, but Atlantis was to be looked for in the east, and was the land of the ten generations of Noah.

Coming to later times, Serranus, in 1578, declared that he had discovered in the Mosaic writings the sesame to the stone which blocked the entrance to the Atlantean labyrinth. The hint was avidly seized upon by Huet, Bochart and Vossius, an eager trio, who by ingenious misreadings of the Pentateuch, bemused their credulous contemporaries into an acceptance of Plato's island as the theatre of patriarchal history.

But widespread as was agreement with their conclusions, they seemed to Mathew Olivier, a grave advocate of Marseilles, to miss the point and pith of Serranus's main argument. Enlarging upon his master's theory, Olivier placed Atlantis in Palestine itself, assuming, logically enough, that if the Biblical patriarchs were in reality the denizens of Atlantis, and were known historically to have inhabited the Holy Land, that region must indubitably have been Atlantis! About a quarter of a century later, in 1754, Eumenius, a learned Swede, developing the views of Olivier, pushed the theory to its natural conclusion, and explained the entire Atlantean mythology by means of Jewish history. He had, however, been preceded by another Scandinavian of even more portentous erudition, for in 1692 Olaus Rudbeck had published his amazing *Atlantica*, which, in a weird spirit of patriotism, maintained that the Norse Edda rather than the Mosaic writings held the true interpretation of the Atlantean secret. For him Sweden was Atlantis, and Upsala the capital of Plato's shadowy Utopia. In four folio volumes he undertook to prove that the Scandinavian peninsula was not only the centre from which all European civilisation had radiated, but the source of an original world-mythology of which the Edda was a surviving fragment.

The theory of a northern site for Atlantis dies hard. Indeed it still survives, for M. Gattefossé of Lyons has triumphantly asserted it in his *La Verité sur l'Atlantide*, published so lately as 1923. But he had a worthy forerunner in Bailly, a contemporary of Voltaire, who, like Rudbeck, sought to discover the Atlantean region in the frozen north. Not long before Buffon had made popular the idea that the "central fire" which maintained the temperature of the earth had cooled in the course of ages, and Bailly, seizing upon the notion, boldly asserted that the now frozen north had formerly enjoyed almost tropical climatic conditions. Its inhabitants during the torrid period, he maintained, were the Atlanteans of Plato, who upon the gradual cooling of the region, betook themselves to Asia, carrying with them their scientific knowledge and religious beliefs, which they scattered broadcast among the nations. In his *History of Ancient Astronomy* and *Letters on Atlantis* he brought to bear the whole battery of his learning to prove that Spitzbergen was once a fertile and populous country, and was, indeed, the veritable Platonic Atlantis. Strangely enough, his thesis has assumed the quality of legend, and in some parts of Northern Europe the tradition still flourishes that somewhere in the neighbourhood of the North Pole fertile valleys actually exist. In fact the belief has lately received a new lease of life from the statements of recent explorers of the Far North from the American side, who have provided glowing accounts of low-lying valleys in the polar area, fragrant with flowers and swarming with butterflies.

Bailly was a thorough-going disciple of Euhemerus of Thessaly, and believed that all myth had a historical basis. For him Atlas was a king of the once tropical Spitzbergen-Atlantis, an actual human ruler and a distinguished astronomer, the inventor of the sphere. His Hyperborean Atlanteans finally came to rest, after a prolonged migration, on the plains of Tartary. But Bailly's farrago of erudite nonsense was much too gross even for that somewhat credulous Paris which was then on the brink of a human catastrophe even more stupendous then the wreck of Atlantis. In his *Lettre Americain* the Comte de Corli, while neatly disposing of Bailly's absurdities, sprung on a readily accepting public the theory that Atlantis was none other than the American continent itself. Even the imperturbable Voltaire, who had hesitated a humorous doubt regarding the non-

existence of a great Atlantic continent, was somewhat taken
aback by the boldness of the Arctic hypothesis which
Bailly, grasping at straws, had wantonly dedicated to him.

But an even more erudite and determined effort to
locate Atlantis elsewhere, in Asia, to wit, was that made
anonymously in 1779, and by Delisle de Sales, a member
of the Institute, in his *History of the Atlanteans*. De
Sales attempted to prove, by the aid of geology, that the
actual Atlantis had been situated in a vast ancient sea
which formerly occupied the site of Greece and a large
part of the Italian peninsula. The globe, he argued, had
in primitive times been almost completely covered by
water, but in the course of ages this had evaporated,
leaving, however, an immense sea, which united the
Caspian to the Persian Gulf, and the Indian Ocean to the
Mediterranean. From the midst of this ancient oceanic
waste ran the Caucasus range, and this De Sales identified
with the early Atlantis. Thence migrated its cultured
inhabitants, one stream betaking itself to the Atlas range,
then also an insular sub-continent, and another to Central
Asia. The Atlantis of Plato De Sales disposed of by
identifying it with the Ogygia of Homer, the magical
island of the enchantress Calypso, situated "between
Italy and Carthage," and this, he averred, had been
destroyed by an earthquake, the island of Sardinia remaining as a fragment of the wreckage. The Atlanteans he
called "the benefiters of humanity," and described his
system as "the key to ancient history."

A little later Bartoli, in his *Essai sur l'explication*,
tendered a hypothesis seemingly more modest, but in
reality equally bizarre. Solon, he said, had invented
the fable of Atlantis, and had made it the subject of an
allegorical and political poem, in which the Atlanteans
represented the Athenian faction of the Paraliens. Plato,
seizing upon this fiction, had adopted it to later events,

among them the Peloponnesian war. Plato's Atlanteans who besieged Athens, were, according to Bartoli, the Persians, and the whole story a mythic representation of their struggle with Hellas and their final overthrow.

Equally curious are the attempts made to identify the lost Atlantis with America. Treatises on the subject began to appear shortly after the discovery of America, and extraordinary efforts seem to have been made to attach the name of Plato's island to the new continent. In 1553 Gomara in his *Historia de las Indias* unhesitatingly identified America with Atlantis, and eight years later Guillaume de Postel drew attention to the similarity of the native name for Mexico, Aztlan, with that of Atlantis, which he proposed to confer on the New World. Bacon in his *Nova Atlantis* identified America with Plato's isle, although certainly in such a spirit of fantasy as might be employed by Sir J. M. Barrie. In any case he places it in the Pacific. But that Shakespeare had at least some memory of the Atlantis story at the back of his mind when he set the scene of his *Tempest* in a fantastic Atlantic isle, seems not improbable.

But the French geographers, Nicholas and Guillaume Sauson, were by no means designedly fantastic in their methods. In 1689 they published an atlas representing the primitive geographical divisions of America, its partition between the ten royal families who had issued from Poseidon, the father of Atlas, and displaying those portions of the Old World which, according to Plato's story, they had succeeded in colonising. So late as 1762 Robert de Vaugoudy produced a similar atlas in verification of the theories of the Sausons, to the accompaniment of Voltaire's ribald and inextinguishable laughter. Even Stallbaum, the serious critic of Plato's *Timæus* and *Critias*, upheld the identity of America with Atlantis, and thought it probable that the ancient Egyptians had a knowledge of the Western

Continent. Harles in his *Bibliotheca Græca* inclined
against the American theory, and Humboldt in his
Examen Critique regarded it as fabulous, although he
believed that Solon had actually brought back the story
from Egypt. Among other more modern writers Buffon,
Ginguené, Mentelle and Raynal were not unfriendly to
the general theory of the existence of Atlantis, and
Athanasius Kircher and Becman, Genebrard, and Fortia
d'Urban embraced it in its entirety. Baudelot, Tourne-
fort, d'Engel, Cadit, De la Borde and Bori de Saint-
Vincent were its enthusiastic advocates.

Many of these later authors agreed in thinking that
Atlantis had formerly existed, as stated by Plato, but were
at variance regarding the circumstances of the events
which occurred thereon, and the marvels of which he
spoke. Some of them sought to explain the names of
the divinities connected with the tale symbolically, or as
cosmogonical elements personified. The ten Kings of
Atlantis were for some of them representative of the ten
great antediluvian epochs, and they argued that the
history of Atlantis was in reality an allegorical account
of the early history of mankind. Kircher, Ginguené,
Mentelle and others believed that the Atlantic Islands
were the remains of the sunken continent, and Buffon
argued that Ireland, the Azores and America had once
been portions of the great isle of Plato. De la Borde
actually included the Moluccas, New Zealand and other
distant insular masses in the original Atlantean land-
mass, and Engel and the Comte de Corli learnedly insisted
that the Atlantean boundaries had touched Europe and
Africa on one side and America on the other. According
to them, man had passed from the Old World to the New
by way of an Atlantean land-bridge, the submergence of
which had destroyed the ancient communication between
the two continents.

CHAPTER IV

Atlantean Historical Sources Examined

BEFORE proceeding farther it will be necessary to submit the sources of the Atlantean tradition at our disposal to a thorough examination, both as regards their historical integrity and the likelihood of the facts they contain. As regards Plato's account, many of his commentators, from Proclus to Jowett, have given it as their considered opinion that it was merely a fable, "a noble lie," invented by Plato. "It appears to me," says Archer-Hind, "impossible to determine whether Plato has invented the story from beginning to end, or whether it really more or less represents some Egyptian legend brought home by Solon."[1] Elsewhere he remarks upon the improbability of the story. Yet he rebukes Stallbaum for adopting Proclus's misinterpretation of Plato's words that his tale is "not a mere figment of the imagination, but a history of facts which actually occurred." Plato is, indeed, abundantly clear on this point. In the *Timæus* alone he lays stress upon the historicity of his account in several passages. It is, he says, "strange, yet perfectly true." Solon, indeed, intended to make it the subject of an epic, Critias recalled its circumstances vividly, through hearing them as a boy, and they were "indelibly fixed" in his mind "like encaustic pictures" on tiles. Socrates in the *Timæus* is made to say: "The fact that it is no fictitious tale, but a true history, is surely a great point.' In the *Critias* Plato further makes Critias say that his

[1] Timæus, p. 78, note.

39

great-grandfather had possessed an account of Atlantis in writing. Plato, then, took more than usual care to stress the historicity of his account.

The fact of Solon's visit to Egypt also appears as indubitable. Plutarch in his *Life of Solon* (ch. 26) and his *De Iside et Osiride* (ch. 10) states that Solon visited Egypt and spoke with the priest Sonchis at Sais. This, according to Clement of Alexandria, was also the name of the priest who instructed Pythagoras in the science of the Egyptians. Proclus in his dissertation on the *Timæus* says that Plato also visited Egypt and conversed at Sais with the priest Pateneit, at Heliopolis with the priest Ochlapi, and at Sebennytus with the priest Ethimon. He mentions that Pateneit is undoubtedly the priest alluded to in the *Timæus*.

It is stated in the *Critias* that Solon had written a great epic poem on Atlantis, and that his notes on the subject had come down to the younger Critias. These he had received from his grandfather, Critias, the son of Dropidas. Now the second Critias, according to a genealogy preserved by Proclus, was a cousin-german of Plato's mother. Ast and Kleine, in their critiques on Plato's works, give it as their belief that it was he who first brought the Atlantean tradition from Egypt. Plutarch expressly upholds Plato's statement that Solon intended to write a poem on Atlantis, but was compelled to renounce his intention on account of his great age. In the *Timæus* Plato eloquently expresses his regret that he had not carried out his plan. Martin in his *Dissertation sur l'Atlantide* (p. 323) gives it as his considered judgment that Plato, knowing himself to be related to Solon, had piously attempted to carry out the intention of his blood-relation, and for this purpose had employed the traditional material which had come down to him as the basis of his narrative.

Crantor, who died thirty-three years after Plato, and

who was one of his best known commentators, states that in his time the Egyptian priests had shown to the Greeks certain columns or pillars on which they affirmed the history of Atlantis was inscribed. It is, of course, well known that Sais, where Solon heard the story of Atlantis, was a city closely associated with Greece. It was, indeed, a centre of Greek culture. The period of its greatest prosperity was between 697–524 B.C., and one of its monarchs, Psammetichus, maintained himself on the throne by aid of Greek mercenaries. He educated his sons in Greek learning, and encouraged the resort of Greeks to his capital. This intercourse between Sais and Athens was especially promoted by their worshipping the same deity, Neith-Athene, and hence there arose the notion that Cecrops the Saite had led a colony to Athens. The priests of Sais seem, indeed, to have been anxious to curry favour with the Athenians by discovering resemblances between Attic and Egyptian institutions. A separate quarter in Sais was assigned to the Greeks. So strong, indeed, was the Hellenic element in Sais that it was a matter of debate whether the Saites colonized Attica or the Athenians Sais.

This being so, if the priests of Sais related the story of Atlantis to Solon, they must almost certainly have retailed it to the many other Greeks with whom they constantly associated. That no other definite account of their doing so is in existence is not surprising when we take into consideration the commercial character of the Hellenes with whom they must have come into contact. But, if Plato's account had not been inherited from Solon, and had its Egyptian form not been current in Sais, there were thousands of Greeks there who could have contradicted it, and that some negative of the kind would have reached Athens sooner or later seems very clear, when we recall the extraordinary interest which Plato's tale certainly aroused in the ancient world.

With regard to a totally different aspect of Plato's account, it is extraordinary how well the circumstances of his story fit in with those which the science of archæology assures us must have obtained in early Europe.   This point will be treated in detail later on.   It is sufficient to say here that the approximate date of Plato's account of the Atlantean invasion agrees with that at which the Azilian-Tardenoisian peoples, the ancestors of the Iberian race, undoubtedly swarmed into Europe, and those European and African regions which he regarded as tributary to Atlantis. "Libya as far as Egypt, and Europe to the borders of Etruria," are precisely those regions in which the proto-Iberians found their firmest footing.

The *Timæus* states that Athens set Europe free from the Atlantean tyranny.   That there was no Athens existing at that date (9600 B.C.) of which Plato speaks, is certain. The date in question is thousands of years prior to the First Egyptian Dynasty, and all that has been found on the site of Athens of an older date is a small quantity of Neolithic or New Stone Age pottery.   At the same time, as we shall see, Europe and Africa were not then in a state of abject barbarism, and it may be that the memory of the resistance offered by the natives to the increasing hordes of proto-Iberians was dimly remembered by their peoples across the intervening centuries.

"In later times," said Solon's Egyptian informant, "after there had been exceeding great earthquakes and floods, there fell one day and night of destruction; and the warriors in your land all in one body were swallowed up by the earth, and in like manner did Atlantis sink beneath the sea and vanish away."   Here it is noticeable that the Greeks are destroyed by a terrestrial, and the Atlanteans by a marine agency, and I believe that we have in this passage a clue to the true historical character of Plato's account.   Pallas Athene, the patron goddess of

Athens, was the sworn enemy of Poseidon, the god associated with Atlantis as its eponymous deity and founder, and the strife she waged with him for possession of Athens is celebrated in Greek mythology.   Now one of the scholiasts of Plato states that the victory of the Athenians over the Atlanteans was actually represented in a symbolical peplum or woman's garment, dedicated at the Lesser Panathenæa, or festival of Athena.   The inference, then, is that the strife between the Athenians, the people of Athene, and the Atlanteans, the folk of Poseidon or Neptune, god of the sea, came to have for the former a definitely historical character, enshrining a veritable folk-memory.   The Panathenæa, it may be mentioned in passing, was founded at least 125 years before Plato's time, so that, if we can rely on the scholiast's statement, the tradition of the Athenian war with the Atlanteans, whether mythological or historical, must have been well known to the Athenians more than a century before Plato's day, and this would at once dispose of the oft-repeated assumption that he deliberately manufactured the story.   "That it was *entirely* an invention of Plato's," remarks the shrewd Philip Smith, in his article on "Atlantis" in William Smith's *Dictionary of Greek and Roman Geography*, is hardly credible. . . . The legend is found in other forms which do not seem to be entirely copied from Plato."   This reminds us of Strabo's quotation from Poseidonius, that it is more reasonable to believe that Atlantis once existed and then sank, than to say that "its inventor caused it to disappear."

It may be said that if the statement regarding the peplum is true, Plato merely took a local myth for the basis of his tale. Wherefore, then, did he lay stress upon the truth of his account, and derive it from an Egyptian source?   It is manifest that Plato must have known of the Athenian version depicted on the peplum.   He says little of its local sanction, although he must have been well

aware that it had a bearing on the festival of the
Panathenæa, possibly because he regarded Athenian
knowledge of it as notorious and needless to mention.   It
was, as Socrates says in the dialogue of the *Timæus*, specially appropriate to this festival of the goddess, owing to
its connection with her," sure proof that Plato knew of the
Athenian associations of the Panathenæa.   The reason
that he laid stress upon its Egyptian version was, perhaps,
merely because that gave it a more ancient sanction, and
corroborated and strengthened what might seem to the
ignorant a mere local tradition, which had no documentary
evidence behind it, and which might have been mistaken
for a local invention but for its collation with and amplification by the Egyptian account.   Indeed, it is quite possible
that Plato had this intention quite as much in view as the
illustration of his political thesis.

When we recall the strife between Pallas Athenæ and
Poseidon, which appears, as we have already said, to have
a distinct bearing upon the Atlantean legend in Greece, it
is scarcely strange to find a writer in *The Occult Review* for
September, 1923, discovering in the "Odyssey" of Homer
further evidences of the Atlantean implications of this
mythological feud.   Odysseus, on his return from Troy,
lands on the island of the Cyclops, and succeeds in escaping
from that dangerous proximity only after many desperate
adventures.   Indeed, as the writer states : "We have in the
Odyssey, as narrated by Homer, an account of the Homeric
hero, Odysseus, whose wanderings and adventures were in
reality one prolonged struggle with Poseidon, that is with
the Atlantean deity."   In the isle of Ogygia, where he is
made prisoner by the enchantress Calypso, the daughter of
the "magician" Atlas, he is aided by Athene, who has
taken him under her protection.   Once more, then, we
discover the Athenian goddess at odds with the deity of
Atlantis, and this time in a manner which more strikingly

than before, casts light upon the Atlantean associations of
the quarrel. Thus we find Pallas Athenæ, the goddess of
Athens, doubly connected with the personalities of Atlantis. The circumstances that she takes Odysseus' part
against Poseidon the Atlantean god and his granddaughter,
Calypso, the daughter of Atlas, goes to strengthen the
assumption of her connection with the Atlantean myth as
already outlined above.

The truth of the statement that "to this day the ocean
is impassable and unsearchable, being blocked by very
shallow shoals, which the island caused as she settled
down," is abundantly testified to by several writers of
antiquity. Scylax of Caryanda, who wrote prior to the
time of Alexander the Great, and was approximately a contemporary of Plato, states in his *Periplus* that Cerne, an
island on the African Atlantic Coast, "is twelve days coast-
ing beyond the Pillars of Hercules, where the parts are no
longer navigable because of shoals, of mud and of seaweed. . . . The seaweed has the width of a palm, and is
sharp towards the points so as to prick."

When Himilco parted from Hanno in the course of their
voyage from Carthage in quest of lands unknown about
500 B.C., he encountered, according to the poet Festus
Avienus, "weeds, shallows, calms and dangers," in the
Atlantic. Avienus wrote about the fourth century A.D.,
but professes to repeat Himilco's account. He says
"No breeze drives the ship forward, so dead is the sluggish
wind of this idle sea. He (Himilco) also adds that there is
much seaweed among the waves, and that it often holds
the ship back like bushes. Nevertheless he says that the
sea has no great depth, and that the surface of the earth is
barely covered by a little water. The monsters of the sea
move continually hither and thither, and the wild beasts
swim among the sluggish and slowly creeping ships."
Avienus also says elsewhere: "Farther to the west from these

Pillars there is boundless sea." Himilco relates that
. . . " none has sailed ships over these waters, because
propelling winds are lacking. . . . likewise because darkness screens the light of day with a sort of clothing, and
because a fog always conceals the sea."

Aristotle, too, says in his "Meteorologica" that the sea
beyond the Pillars of Hercules was muddy, shallow and almost unstirred by the winds. Aristotle was at one time a
pupil of Plato, and this would seem to afford good proof
that the latter's statement was founded on the best available
information, and was probably acquired from Phœnician
or Greek seamen.

But we have other than classical evidence for the unnavigable character of the Atlantic, evidence dating from a
considerably later period. Edrisi, the Arabic writer, says
that the Magrurin, certain Moorish sailors of Lisbon who
set sail thence in quest of an Atlantic island at some un-
defined period between the eighth and twelfth centuries,
encountered an impassable tract of ocean, and were forced
to alter their course, apparently reaching one of the
Canaries. The Pizigani map of 1367, too, has a rubric
containing a solemn protest against attempting to sail the
unnavigable ocean tract beyond the Azores, in the neighbourhood of which the Sargasso Sea begins.

The details of the *Critias* now command our attention.
The first point that strikes us here is the statement of
Critias that the priests of Sais had already given the names
of the Atlanteans in the account an Egyptian aspect, and
that he (Critias) had been forced to render them "into
Greek." Had the story been fabulous he would scarcely
have taken the trouble to make this clear. But it is difficult to see how, precisely, the names of Poseidon or Atlas
could have been translated into Egyptian. The Egyptians
had no deity corresponding to Poseidon, and none who
could very readily be equated with Atlas, the earth-bearer.

However, the deities mentioned in the account of Diodorus can readily be associated with Egyptian forms, and it may have been that Critias or Plato merely fell back on the names current in the local Athenian version of the Atlantean legend connected with the Panathenæa. This would certainly account for the appearance of Poseidon, who was closely associated in myth with Pallas Athenæ, the patroness of the city, and who was the sole begetter of the Atlantidæ.

The only name of the sons of Poseidon which has been vouchsafed us in its Atlantean form is that of Gadir, "who had for his portion the extremity of this island near the Pillars of Hercules, and that part of it has since borne the name Gadiric." This equates with the classical name for the vicinity of Cadiz in Spain, and assumes a close proximity between the Spanish and Atlantean coasts.

The details concerning the topography and site of Atlantis I propose to discuss in the chapter which deals with its geography. Here it may serve to consider some minor but nevertheless striking points. The climate of Atlantis appears, according to Plato's account, to have corresponded closely to that of the Canary Islands, but two circumstances combine to give it a distinctly African aspect: the statement that large herds of elephants roamed the marshland, and that "a fruit with a hard rind" affording both meat, drink and ointment, flourished there. This can refer only to the coconut. Much has been made of these statements, pro and con. The presence of the elephant as a contemporary of man in southern Europe is usually regarded as "not proven" by archæologists, but there seems no good reason for doubting its relatively late existence in an environment better fitted to it climatically, and probably African in character.

As the government and religion of Atlantis will also be separately considered it will not be necessary in this place

to criticise the passages in Plato's account which allude
to them.   But it may be remarked in passing that Plato's
observations upon them are in consonance with what we
know of the early "Azilian" civilisation of Spain and
Southern France.   In these areas the bull was worshipped
and the ceremony attending its sacrifice, which Plato describes, might well have been illustrative of some dim folk-
memory of a barbaric rite of the Azilian era, which in some
of its aspects continued to survive to "classical" times,
and the last vestiges of which still linger in the sport of
bull-fighting.   Bull-baiting, even in England, continued
to have a semi-religious significance until the beginning
of the eighteenth century, and was associated with a ceremonial undoubtedly of pagan descent.   That it survived
elsewhere in Europe until a relatively late period can also
abundantly be demonstrated.

Plato's account of Atlantean history breaks off short,
and was probably left unfinished because of his death.
He undoubtedly employed it to illustrate his ideas regarding the perfect human political state, but that is not at
all to say that he invented it for this reason.   That its
architectural details have a Greek as well as a Persian
colouring is only natural, but it is not necessary to infer
from the latter circumstance that he intended it as an
allegory of the Persian War, as has so often been stated.
Indeed, many of its details, for example, the insular and
maritime character of Atlantis, render such a theory quite
untenable.   But Plato's account, considered as a whole,
is in itself the best refutation of such an assumption.

The account of Diodorus raises a very different set of
problems.   It at once involves us in a consideration of the
question as to how far the Greek myth of the Hesperides
has a bearing on the question of Atlantis.   In one passage
Diodorus seems to place Atlantis on the West Coast of
Africa, in any case it "borders upon the ocean," and does

not definitely appear as an insular region. Indeed, the
island Hesperia, inhabited by the Amazons, agrees much
more closely with the details of Plato's account, as regards
its site, except that it is described as destitute of corn.
It is volcanic and prone to earthquakes, and is full of
fruit trees and herds of sheep and goats, as the Canaries
still are. But I think I can discern in the description of
the Amazons a close resemblance to the Azilian people
who invaded Europe some 10,000 years ago, as observed
in their cave-paintings still extant. This race, the pro-
genitors of the Iberians, were the first inventors of the
bow, and their effeminate appearance, and their manner of
wearing their hair dressed on the crown of the head, may
have struck their enemies as womanish. The history
of Atlantis, as alluded to by Diodorus, can only be
understood by comparison with the details of Greek
mythology. But the statement of Diodorus that "it is
reported" that an Atlantic tract was swallowed up by the
sea, is valuable as illustrating the fact that nearly four
hundred years after Plato's time the belief in the foundering of an Atlantic region was widely current. We should
also not ignore the statement of a writer so comparatively
early as Poseidonius that the account of Plato ought not
to be regarded as fiction, as the earth was known to have
undergone changes, a statement in which he is backed by
Strabo, and which shows that in the late pre-Christian
era geological opinion in support of the Atlantean theory
was beginning to take shape. Indeed, as Philip Smith
observes in the account already alluded to: "Those who
regard it (the story of Atlantis) as pure fiction, but of an
early origin, view it as arising out of the very ancient
notion, found in Homer and Hesiod, that the abodes of
departed heroes were in the extreme west beyond the river
Oceanus, a locality naturally assigned as beyond the
boundaries of the inhabited earth. That the fabulous

prosperity and happiness of the Atlanteans was in some degree connected with their poetical representations is very probable, just as when islands were actually discovered off the coast of Africa, they were called the Islands of the Blest. But still, important parts of the legend are thus left unaccounted for; its mythological character, its derivation from the Egyptian priests, or other Oriental sources; and what is, in Plato, its most important part, the supposed conflict of the Atlanteans with the people of the Old World."

This shrewd writer has, in these remarks, probed down to the very root of the argument. He says in effect that, if the belief in Atlantis was a mythological one, or in some way connected with the religious or fictional history of the Greeks, the protagonists of that theory cannot leave it at that, but must adduce *proof to account for its mythological origin*. It cannot be too strongly stressed that all tradition has a basis of fact. Races, when semi-civilised or barbarous, do not deliberately manufacture such notions as that which averred that the Fortunate Isles in the west were the places of reward of departed heroes. A hundred myths could be adduced to show that such ideas actually arise out of a memory of a western region from which early migration proceeded. And it is of special interest in connection with the problem before us that some of the skull-burials of the Azilian people already mentioned are so disposed that the faces look towards the west—a certain sign that that region was regarded as of especial sanctity. The myth of the war between the Gods and Titans seems to the writer to supply that proof to account for the mythological origin of the story of Atlantis which Smith demanded.

As regards Plato's chronology, it can be shown that this is by no means based on improbability when all the circumstances of the Azilian invasion of Europe are taken into account. The argument that Plato's date is erroneous has recently been touched upon by M. F. Butavand in his *La Veritable Histoire de L'Atlantide*, where he says (pp. 6–7): "This date is certainly erroneous, for at the period mentioned the Grecian Republic did not exist; the civilisation of Egypt was not in existence; the statements of the priest of Sais are not comprehensible. Mathematical, and above all chronological matter, as touched upon by the writers of antiquity, frequently present errors, and these we are able to rectify in dealing with two well known erroneous computations. The people of the Mediterranean and many others, at a certain fixed epoch, counted by eights before arriving at the use of a decimal system. Those authors who have transmitted ancient accounts have frequently neglected to transform the ancient to the decimal system . . . the figure nine is out of the question, as it does not exist in the octonal system."

For this statement, so far as I can discover, there is no basis of fact whatsoever. An octonal system may well have been employed in early Europe, just as a system equally dissimilar to the decimal was employed in ancient America, but that it has any possible bearing on Plato's chronology, I fail to see. More seemingly reasonable is M. Butavand's statement that Eudoxus of Cnidus, who had studied astronomy in Egypt, and was well qualified to check the account of the priest of Sais, declared that the duration of time indicated by Critias was not nine thousand years, but as many months. This would bring the date of the founding of Atlantis to about 1,400 years before our era, or about the date of the XIX Dynasty in Egypt. But the Egyptian system of chronology, on which Plato's account must manifestly have been based, was certainly decimal in character, and the substitution of months for years in estimating Atlantean chronology is by no means an innovation.

CHAPTER V

THE GEOGRAPHY OF ATLANTIS

WE must now consider the geographical questions connected with the site and topography of Atlantis. With these is inevitably bound up the problem of its actual existence. We are not dealing with a Greece or a Rome, an Egypt or an Assyria, but with a continent submerged, the very existence of which is in some quarters strenuously denied. In the first place, then, before we proceed to draw conclusions with reference to its geographical position and physiographical features from the literary sources at our command, we are compelled to examine such geological proof as we possess that Atlantis existed at all. This must, indeed, be satisfactorily demonstrated before we can reasonably regard the island of Atlantis as a fit subject for anything approaching an historical thesis.

The geological proof for the existence of Atlantis is extensive, and in this place can only be summarized. A full account of it will be found in my former works *The Problem of Atlantis* and *Atlantis in America*. It is here conceded that the only portion of geological time which has a definite bearing on the problem is the Quaternary epoch, which embraces the Pleistocene or Ice Age, and the commencement of which may, for practical purposes, be placed about 500,000 years ago. The Quaternary is subdivided into four glacial epochs and one post-glacial epoch. It is only in this post-glacial

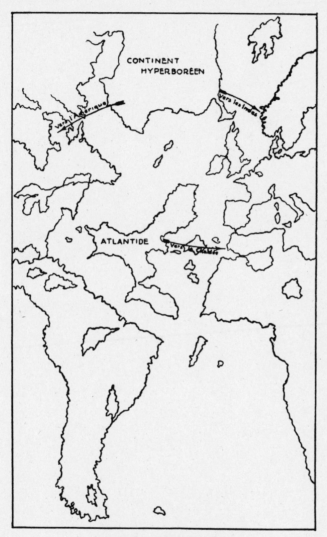

ATLANTIS IN TERTIARY TIMES
(*After* R. M. Gattefossé).

epoch, which probably began about 25,000 years ago, that any human form approaching modern man is to be discovered in Europe. If, then, we are to posit an Atlantis peopled by human types recognizable as modern, the period in which we must do so is confined to the last 25,000 years of European history. Does modern geology uphold the probability of the existence of an Atlantean continent at any time during this period?

M. Pierre Termier, Director of Science of the Geological Chart of France, is one of a growing band of geologists who devoutly believe that a great Atlantean continent existed during the period in question.[1] With the gradual collection of new evidence relative to the geology and the biology of the Atlantic region, the theory concerning the existence of such a land-mass has taken on an entirely new complexion. This evidence does not depend upon the misty surmises of visionaries, or the dogmatic assertions of that type of antiquary who twists tradition and philology into the semblance of testimony, but on considerations the most rational and credible. That an Atlantean continent at one time occupied the present oceanic gulf between Europe and America is a scientific truth now accepted by geologists of all shades of opinion, and the only question of debate which still remains has reference to the precise period in geological history at which this continent flourished.

The bed of the Atlantic is the most unstable part of the earth's surface, says M. Termier. Its eastern region is a great volcanic zone. In its European-African depression sea-volcanoes and insular volcanoes are abundant. Its islands are largely formed of lava, and a similar formation occurs in its American or western region. The bed of

---

[1] See translation of his essay in the annual report of the Smithsonian Institute for 1915.

the Atlantic, this authority assures us, is still in movement, in its extreme eastern zone, for a space of about
1,875 miles in breadth, which embraces Iceland, the
Azores, the Canaries, Madeira and the Cape Verde Islands.
In any part of this area unrecorded submarine cataclysms
may be taking place at any time.

M. Termier believes that a North Atlantic continent
formerly existed, comprising Russia, Scandinavia, Great
Britain, Greenland and Canada, to which was added later
a southern band made up of a large part of Central and
Western Europe and an immense portion of the United
States. "There was also," he says, "a South Atlantic
or African-Brazilian continent, extending northward to
the southern border of the Atlas, eastward to the Persian
Gulf and Mozambique Channel, westward to the eastern
border of the Andes and to the sierras of Colombia and
Venezuela. Between the two continents passed the
Mediterranean depression, that ancient maritime furrow
which has formed an escarp about the earth since the
beginning of geologic time, and which we see so deeply
marked in the present Mediterranean, the Caribbean
Sea, and the Sunda or Flores Sea. A chain of mountains
broader than the chain of the Alps, and perhaps in some
parts as high as the majestic Himalayas, once lifted itself
on the land-enclosed shore of the North Atlantic continent,
embracing the Vosges, the Central Plateau of France,
Brittany, the south of England and of Ireland, and also
Newfoundland, Nova Scotia, and, in the United States,
all the Appalachian region."

The end of this continental era, thinks M. Termier,
came during the Tertiary Period, or that before the
Quaternary, when the mass, bounded on the south by a
chain of mountains, was submerged long before the
collapse of those volcanic lands of which the Azores are
the last vestiges. The South Atlantic Ocean was like-

wise occupied for many thousands of centuries by a great
continent now engulfed beneath the sea. These movements of depression probably occurred at several more or
less distantly removed periods. In the Europe of the
Tertiary era the movement was developing which gave
rise to the Alpine mountain chain. How far did this
chain extend into the Atlantic region? Did some fragments of it rise high enough to lift themselves for some
centuries above the waters? This question M. Termier
answers in the affirmative.

He believes that the geology of the whole Atlantic
region has singularly altered in the course of the later
periods of the earth's history. During the Secondary
period there were numerous depressions, the Tertiary
Period saw the annihilation of the continental areas, and
subsequently there appeared a new design, the general
direction of which was not east and west as formerly,
but north and south. Near the African coast, he holds,
there have certainly been important movements during
Quaternary times, when other changes undoubtedly took
place in the true oceanic region. "Geologically speaking,"
he says, "Plato's theory of Atlantis is highly probable. . . .
It is entirely reasonable to believe that long after the
opening of the Strait of Gibraltar certain of these emerged
lands still existed, and among them a marvellous island,
separated from the African continent by a chain of other
smaller islands. One thing alone remains to be proved—
that the cataclysm which caused this island to disappear
was subsequent to the appearance of man in Western
Europe. The cataclysm is undoubted. Did men then
live who could withstand the reaction and transmit the
memory of it? That is the whole question. I do not
believe it at all insoluble, though it seems to me that
neither geology nor zoology will solve it. These two
sciences appear to have told all they can tell, and it is from

anthropology, from ethnography, and lastly from oceanography that I am now awaiting the final answer."

Criticising this statement, Professor Schuchert writes:[1]
"The Azores are true volcanic and oceanic islands, and
it is almost certain that they never had land connections
with the continents on either side of the Atlantic Ocean.
If there is any truth in Plato's thrilling account, we must
look for Atlantis off the western coast of Africa, and here
we find that five of the Cape Verde Islands and three
of the Canaries have rocks that are unmistakably like those
common to the continents. Taking into consideration
also the living plants and animals of these islands, many
of which are of European-Mediterranean affinities of
late Tertiary time, we see that the evidence appears to
indicate clearly that the Cape Verde and Canary Islands
are fragments of a greater Africa. . . .   What evidence
there may be to show that this fracturing and breaking
down of western Africa took place as suddenly as related
by Plato, or that it occurred about 10,000 years ago, is as
yet unknown to geologists."

Professor R. F. Scharff, of Dublin, who has perhaps
contributed more valuable data to the literature of Atlantean research than any other living scientist, concludes that
Madeira and the Azores were connected with Portugal
in Miocene or later Tertiary times, when man had already
appeared in Europe, and that from Morocco to the Canary
Islands and thence to South America stretched a vast
land which extended southward as far as St. Helena.
This great continent, he believes, began to subside before
the Miocene.   But he holds that its northern portions persisted until the Azores and Madeira became isolated from
Europe.   "I believe," he says, "that they were still connected in early Pleistocene (Ice Age) times with the continents of Europe and Africa, at a time when man had already

[1] In *The Geographical Review, Vol.* 3, 1917, p. 65.

made his appearance in Western Europe, and was able to reach the islands by land." [1]

Among those modern geologists who uphold the Atlantean theory is Professor Edward Hull, whose investigations have led him to conclude that the Azores are the peaks of a submerged continent which flourished in the Pleistocene period. "The flora and fauna of the two hemispheres," says Professor Hull, "support the geological theory that there was a common centre in the Atlantic, where life began, and that during and prior to the glacial epoch great land-bridges north and south spanned the Atlantic Ocean." He adds: "I have made this deduction by a careful study of the soundings as recorded on the Admiralty charts." Dr. Hull also holds the view that at the time this Atlantic continent existed there was also a great Antillean continent or ridge shutting off the Caribbean Sea and the Gulf of Mexico from what is called the Gulf Stream.[2]

These considerations would appear to sustain the contention of modern geologists that the bed of the Atlantic has undergone constant change, and that, indeed, it may have risen and sunk many times since the period of the last Ice Age, as Sir William Dawson once stated.

From such evidence we may be justified in concluding that the hypothesis of a formerly existing land-mass in the Atlantic Ocean is by no means based on mere surmise. The fact that geologists of distinction have risked their reputations by testifying in no uncertain manner to the reality of a former Atlantean continent should surely give pause to those who impatiently refuse even to examine the probabilities of the arguments so ably upheld. But the most significant consideration which emerges

[1] Some remarks on the Atlantis Problem. Proc. Royal Irish Academy. Vol. 24, 1902.

[2] *The Sub-Oceanic Physiography of the North Atlantic.*

is that this modern expert evidence is almost entirely in favour of the existence of a *comparatively recent* land-mass or masses in the Atlantic, and if we take into consideration the whole of the evidence, and the nature of its sources, it does not seem beyond the bounds of human credence that at a period probably no earlier than that mentioned by Plato in his *Critias*, viz. 9600 B.C., this ancient continent was still in partial existence, but in process of disintegration—that an island of considerable size, the remnant, perhaps, of the African 'shelf," still lay opposite the entrance to the Mediterranean, and that lesser islands connected it with Europe, Africa, and, perhaps, with our own shores.

Dealing with the improbability of such an island as Atlantis, ever having existed, Mr. W. H. Babcock objects that: [1] "The advocates of a real Atlantis try to pile up proofs of a great land-mass existing at some time in the Atlantic Ocean, a logical proceeding so far as it goes, but one that falls short of its mark, for the land may have ascended and descended again ages before the reputed Atlantis period. It is of no avail to demonstrate its presence in the Miocene, Pliocene, or Pleistocene epoch, or, indeed, at any time prior to the development of a well organised civilisation among men, or, as Plato apparently reasons, between 11,000 and 12,000 years ago. Also what is wanted is evidence of the great island Atlantis, not of the former seaward extension of some existing continent, nor of any land-bridge spanning the ocean. It is true that such conditions might serve as distant preliminaries for the production of Atlantis Island by the breaking down and submergence of the intervening land, but this only multiplies the cataclysms to be demonstrated and can have no real relevance in the absence of proof of the island itself. The geologic and geographic

---

[1] *Legendary Islands of the Atlantic*, p. 19.

phenomena of pre-human ages are beside the question. The tale to be investigated is of a flourishing insular growth of artificial human society on a large scale, not so very many thousands of years ago, evidently removed from all tradition of engulfment and hence dreading it not at all, but sending forth its conquering armies until the final defeat and annihilating cataclysm."

The reader will observe that I have not "tried to pile up proofs of a great land-mass existing at some time in the Atlantic Ocean," otherwise than to permit him to follow the general argument with clarity, but that I have confined most of the geological evidence to that part of it which deals with the possible existence of Atlantis *at the period indicated in Plato's myth*. As regards the portion of Mr. Babcock's statement which relates to the condition of "human society on a large scale" to be found in Atlantis, I have never subscribed to this notion, but have, in my former works, indicated that I believed such human society as Atlantis boasted to be of a comparatively primitive character.[1] The protagonist of the Atlantis theory need not rely solely upon the evidence of Plato, as Mr. Babcock appears to think. To do so would unduly and unnecessarily limit the sphere of both proof and inquiry.

The soundings taken in the Atlantic by various Admiralty authorities have revealed the existence of a great bank or elevation commencing near the coast of Ireland, traversed by the fifty-third parallel, and extending in a southerly direction embracing the Azores, to the neighbourhood of French Guiana and the mouths of the Amazon and Para Rivers. The level of this great ridge is some 9,000 feet above the bed of the Atlantic. Soundings taken by the various expeditions of the Hydra, Porcupine and Challenger during the nineteenth century especially

---

[1] Although, further on, I adduce sound reasons showing that the civilisation of Atlantis may actually have been of a comparatively high character.

uphold the hypothesis of the former existence of land in the Atlantic region.

Regarding the relationship of the submarine banks of the North Atlantic to the problem, Mr. W. H. Babcock writes: "All of these subaqueous mountain-top lands or hidden elevated plateaus are conspicuously nearer the ocean surface than the real depths of the sea—so much nearer that they inevitably raise the suspicion of having been above that surface within the knowledge and memory of man. It is notorious that coasts rise and fall all over the world in what may be called the normal non-spasmodic action of the strata, and sometimes the movement in one direction—upward or downward—seems to have persisted through many centuries. If we assume that-Gettysburg Bank has been continuously descending at the not extravagant rate of two feet in a century *then it was a considerable island above water about the period dealt with by the priests of Sais*.[1] Apparently the rising of Labrador and Newfoundland since the last recession and dispersion of the great ice-sheet has been even more. Here the elements of exact comparison in time and conditions are lacking; nevertheless, the reported uplift of more than 500 feet in one quarter and nearly 600 in another is impressive as showing what the old earth may do in steady endeavour. *It must be borne in mind, too, that a sudden acceleration of the descent of Gettysburg Bank and its consorts may well have occurred at any stage in so feverishly seismic an area. All considered, it seems far from impossible that some of these banks may have been visible and even habitable at some time when men had attained a moderate degree of civilisation.* But they would not be of any vast extent." [1]

But we have even more valuable evidence from other sources than from geology alone. The evidence afforded

[1] Italics are mine—Author.

from biological research is even more remarkable. Professor Scharff in his paper already quoted from has made it clear that the larger mammalia of the Atlantic islands were not imported, and states that his endeavours to trace "the history of their origin on the islands point rather to some of them, at any rate, having reached the latter in the normal way, which is by a land-connection with Europe."

The presence of large hawks or buzzards, observed by the discoverers of the Azores in 1439, led to the islands receiving the name of Açores, or Hawk Islands. These birds usually live on mice, rats, and young rabbits, and this implies the existence of such mammals on the islands. It appears to be substantiated that the existence of the Azores had already been known to earlier navigators, for in a book published in 1345 by a Spanish friar the Azores are referred to, and the names of the several islands given. On an atlas published at Venice in 1385 some of the islands are mentioned by name, as Capraria, or Isle of Goats, now San Miguel; Columbia, or Isle of Doves, now Pico; Li Congi, Rabbit Island, now Flores; and Corvi Marini, or Isle of Sea Crows, now Corvo. This nomenclature given prior to the discovery—the "official" discovery of the islands, that is—seems to justify the assumption that mammals such as the wild goat and the rabbit flourished there at that period, and had reached the islands from Europe by a land-connection at a remoter era.

Certain zoologists, says Professor Scharff, recognise a distinct division of the marine area of the globe as consisting of the middle portion of the Atlantic, which they call "Mesatlantic." Two genera of mammals are assigned as characteristic of this region—the Monachus or Monk Seal, and the Sirenian Manatus. Neither of these animals frequents the open ocean. Their several species inhabit the Mediterranean, the West Indies, and the coasts and estuaries of the West African and East South American sea-boards. The range of these marine animals seems to many zoologists to imply that their ancestors have spread along some coast-line which formerly united the Old World and the New at no very distant period.

The reptilian fauna of the Atlantic islands is almost entirely European in character. Among the lizards, a North African and a Chilian form are allied. The large family of the burrowing Amphisbænidæ is absolutely confined to America, Africa, and the Mediterranean region. In his monograph on the mollusca of the Atlantic islands [1] Mr. T. V. Wollaston drew attention to the fact that the Mediterranean element is much more traceable in the Canaries than in any other groups of islands. He believes that the Atlantic islands have originated from the breaking-up of a land which was once more or less continuous, and which had been intercolonised along ridges and tracts now lost beneath the ocean.

Professor Simroth, writing on the similarity between the slugs of Spain, Portugal, North Africa, and the Canaries, concluded that there was probably a broad land-connection between these four countries, and that it must have persisted until comparatively recent times. Dr. W. Kobelt, who formerly ridiculed the Atlantean theory, later altered his views. Comparing the European with the West Indian and Central American fauna, he points out that the land shells on the two opposite sides of the Atlantic certainly imply an ancient connection between the Old World and the New, which became ruptured only toward the close of the latter part of the Tertiary period. Dr. von Ihering lays stress on the fact that no malacologist nowadays could explain the presence of these continental molluscs on the Atlantic islands in any other way but by their progresssion on land.

[1] Testacea Atlantica, London, 1878.

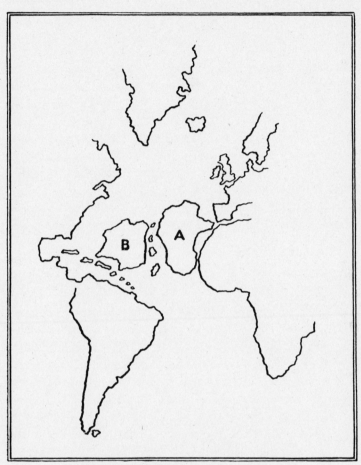

Map showing probable relative position of
Atlantis (a) and Antillia (b)

Sixty per cent. of the butterflies and moths found in the Canaries are of Mediterranean origin, and twenty per cent. of these are to be found in America. Some crustaceans afford proof of the justice of the Atlantean hypothesis. The genus Platyarthus is represented by three species in Western Europe and North Africa, one in the Canaries and one in Venezuela. "There is," says Scharff, "another group of crustacea which yields such decisive indications of the former land-connection between Africa and South America that scarcely anything else is needed to put that theory on a firm basis. The group referred to is that of the fresh-water decapods, the species on both sides of the Atlantic showing a most remarkable affinity."

Experiments have shown that certain snails cannot withstand prolonged immersion in sea-water. Yet these species are found alike in Europe, America, and the Canary Islands. It is therefore manifest that they must have progressed thence by land. Many similar parallels could be drawn from plant life, if space permitted.

At the same time there are biologists who absolutely refute the notion of a land-bridge between the New and the Old World, and who believe the Old World type reached America by way of Behring Strait. This, however, has always appeared to the writer as a hypothesis much more difficult of belief than the Atlantean. The conclusions arrived at in a former work by aid of this evidence were as follows:

That a great continent formerly occupied the whole or major portion of the North Atlantic region, and a considerable portion of its southern basin. Of early geological origin, it must, in the course of successive ages, have experienced many changes in contour and mass, probably undergoing frequent submergence and emergence.

That in Miocene (Late Tertiary) times it still retained its continental character, but towards the end of that period it began to disintegrate, owing to successive volcanic and other causes.

That this disintegration resulted in the formation of greater and lesser insular masses. Two of these, considerably larger in area than any of the others, were situated (*a*) at a relatively short distance from the entrance to the Mediterranean; and (*b*) in the region of the present West India Islands. These may respectively be called Atlantis and Antillia. Communication was possible between them by an insular chain.

That these two island-continents and the connecting chain of islands persisted until late Pleistocene times, at which epoch (about 25,000 years ago, or the beginning of the Post-Glacial epoch) Atlantis seems to have experienced further disintegration. Final disaster appears to have overtaken Atlantis about 10,000 B.C. Antillia, on the other hand, seems to have survived until a much more recent period, and still persists fragmentally in the Antillean group or West India Islands.

If these data be accepted as affording proof, as substantial as in the circumstances can be expected, of the existence of Atlantis at some time within the past twelve thousand years, we may now proceed to a consideration of its exact site.

One of the most popular theories relating to the former site of Atlantis is that which gives it a coincidence of area with the Sargasso Sea. Although the Sargasso Sea is one of the most easily accessible parts of the earth's surface, one of its permanent and conspicuous features, more uncertainty respecting its actual character seems to exist than in the case of the peaks of Everest, or the Desert of Obi. That legend should be so busy concerning a large tract of the Atlantic Ocean, a floating continent of

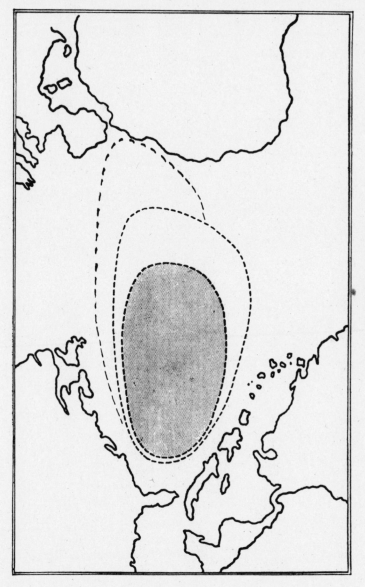

Map of the Sargasso Sea

(The shaded portion indicates where the weed is thickest).

weed, lying no farther from the shores of the United States than does the Bay of Biscay from our own, is chiefly due to the popular ignorance of oceanography which prevails.

During quite recent years the most extraordinary reports have been circulated of the imprisonment in the vast fields of the Sargasso weed of flotillas of sea-going vessels ancient and modern, from the triremes of Tyre to the tramp steamer. These are, of course, gross exaggerations arising out of the persistent traditions of centuries. The Sargasso is, indeed, shunned by vessels for more reasons than one. But it is safe to say that no modern ocean-going liner could possibly become entrapped in its luxuriant masses of vegetation, did it seek to traverse them. But, as we have seen, good evidence exists that in more remote days vessels found much difficulty in navigating the Sargasso, if they were not caught within its toils.

The Sargasso Sea occupies an area of at least 3,000,000 square miles, embracing a tract extending from the 30th parallel of longitude to the Antilles, and from the 40th to the 20th parallel of latitude. This area, indeed, applies only to that portion of the sea which contains at least five per cent. of weed. But the natural region of the Sargasso, estimated not only on the occurrence of Gulf Weed, but also on the prevailing absence of currents and the relatively high temperature of the water in all depths, is at least 5,400,000 square miles, an area somewhat less than half of the continent of Europe.

The weed characteristic of this almost unique oceanic stretch belongs to the brown algæ, and is named *Sargassum bacciferum*, more colloquially Gulf Weed. It is easily recognised by its small berry-like bladders, and is believed to be continually replenished by additional supplies torn from the North American coast by waves, and carried by currents until they accumulate in the great Atlantic whirl which surrounds the Sargasso. It is thought that the older patches gradually lose their power of floating, and perish by sinking in deep water. They become covered with white patches of polyzoa and worms living in twisted calcareous tubes, and small fishes, crabs, prawns and molluscs, inhabit the mass, all exhibiting remarkable adaptative colouring, although none of them naturally belong to the open sea.

The Arcturus expedition, under the direction of Dr. Beebe, of the New York Zoological Society, which is presently investigating these mysterious stretches of weed-encumbered ocean, some time ago dispatched a wireless message to the New York newspapers respecting the discovery of glass, volcanic rock and sponge deposits from the bed of the Sargasso. The chief purpose of the expedition is to determine whether the weed of which the Sargasso is composed is blown out from the land, or propagates itself, and to examine and photograph the strange forms of life which inhabit it.

What is certain is that the Sargasso Sea is the abode of myriads of marine creatures—fishes, crustaceans, molluscs, from the probably gigantic to the infinitely small. It is the feeding-place of many species of birds. Some scientists suppose that as the upper life of this sea zone dies and falls to the bottom it must support a great and wonderful deep-sea life at various levels. These levels, to the very lowest, are now to be explored with the aid of trawls, dredges, hooks, traps and other devices. Living and dead specimens will be collected. Fish from the extreme depths, which explode when brought to the surface, will be taken out in air-pressure apparatus and kept alive in special aquarium tanks.

The present attitude of science towards the problem of the Sargasso may be summed up in the words of Lieut. J. C. Soley of the U.S. Navy, who, in his *Circulation of the*

North Atlantic, says that the South-east branch of the Gulf Stream "runs in the direction of the Azores, where it is deflected by the cold, upwelling stream from the north, and runs into the centre of the Atlantic Basin, where it is lost in the dead waters of the Sargasso Sea." Commenting on this, the U.S. Hydrographic Office observes: "Through the dynamical forces arising from the earth's rotation, which cause moving masses in the northern hemisphere to be deflected toward the right-hand side of their path, the algæ that are borne by the Gulf Stream from the tropical seas find their way towards the inner edge of the circulatory drift which moves in a clockwise direction around the central part of the North Atlantic Ocean. In this central part the flow of the surface waters is not steady in any direction, and hence the floating seaweed tends to accumulate there. This accumulation is perhaps most observable in the triangular region marked out by the Azores, the Canaries and the Cape Verde Islands, but much seaweed is also found to the westward of the middle part of this region in an elongated area extending to the 70th meridian. The abundance of seaweed in the Sargasso Sea fluctuates much with the variation of the agencies which account for its presence, but this office does not possess any authentic records to show that it has ever materially impeded vessels."

It is obvious that this statement is influenced by present-day conditions. If the gigantic rope-like masses of the Sargasso weed could scarcely impede the progress of modern steamers equipped with powerful screws, they may well have hampered the galley oars on which ancient and mediæval navigators had perforce to rely in time of calm. Also it is scarcely credible that small sailing vessels could freely drive through them with an ordinary wind. As we have seen, there is a very large body of testimony that in ancient times the Atlantic was unnavigable, and that the Sargasso Sea formerly occupied a much larger area. If the Gulf Weed was unobstructive, it is difficult to account for the warnings and complaints of the geographical writers of antiquity. In these days, when ocean lanes and sea-ways are so narrowly laid down for steamships, and when the captains of sailing vessels have learned what areas of sea it is best to avoid, formal reports of impediment are scarcely to be expected. But there is assuredly some basis for the age-long evil repute of the Sargasso Sea.

We will recall that Plato in his *Critias*, speaking of the foundering of the continent of Atlantis beneath the waves, remarks that "the sea in these regions has become impassable. Vessels cannot pass there because of the sands which extend over the buried isle." "It must be evident," says Mr. W. H. Babcock, in his *Legendary Islands of the Atlantic*, "that Plato would not have written thus unless he relied on the established general repute of that part of the ocean for difficulty of navigation."

Maury, writing about 1850, describes the Sargasso Sea as being "so thickly matted over with Gulf Weed that the speed of vessels passing through it is often retarded. To the eye, at a little distance, it seems substantial enough to walk upon. Patches of the weed are always to be seen floating along the edge of the Gulf Stream. Now if bits of cork, or chaff or any floating substance be put in a basin and a circular motion be given to the water, all the light substances will be found crowding together near the centre of the pool where there is the least motion. ust such a basin is the Atlantic Ocean to the Gulf Stream; and the Sargasso Sea is the centre of the whirl. Columbus first found this weedy sea in his voyage of discovery; there it has remained to this day, moving up and down, and changing its position, like the calms of Cancer, accord-

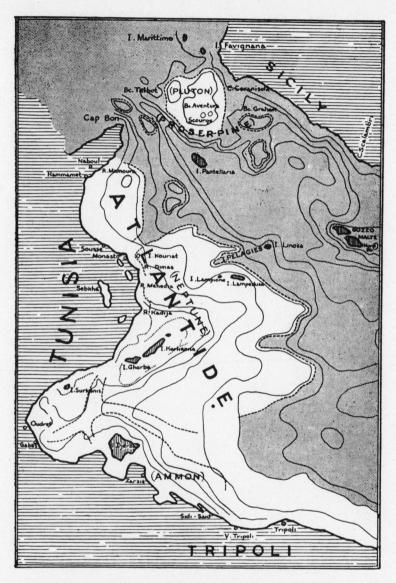

CONJECTURAL SITE OF ATLANTIS OFF THE COAST OF AFRICA
(*After* F. Butavand).

ing to the seasons, the storms and the winds. Exact observations as to its limits and their range, extending back for fifty years, assure us that its mean position has not been altered since that time."

A venerable tradition associated the Sargasso Sea with the sunken continent of Atlantis, and numerous writers have asserted their belief that in its area the former site of Plato's submerged island is to be found. However that may be, the Sargasso weed seems to have persisted for thousands of years. Weed of the same species as is found in the Sargasso occurs in the Pacific Ocean west of California, where it is known land formerly existed. That land once above water is now submerged beneath the Sargasso Sea seems apparent. The great bank mapped out by the several expeditions which undertook the survey of the Atlantic towards the latter part of last century in the Hydra, Porcupine, Challenger and Dolphin, has partial relations with the Sargasso area. This bank commences at a point south of the coast of Ireland, is traversed by the 53rd parallel, and stretches in a direction which embraces the Azores toward the African coast. The general level of this great ridge or plateau is some 9,000 feet above that of the bed of the Atlantic. Other immense banks stretch from Iceland almost to the South American coast, where they adjoin the old sunken land of Antillia. It is precisely above the area where the great sunken plateaux converge, that is between the 40th and 60th parallels of longitude, and the 20th and 40th parallels of latitude, that the Sargasso weed is thickest. There appears, too, to be good evidence that that algæ propagates itself, and does not drift from the North American coasts or the Gulf Stream, as oceanographers formerly believed. But in all probability the matter will be set at rest by the report of the Arcturus expedition, the researches of which can scarcely fail to enlighten us regarding one of the most curious phenomenons of that marine world concerning the deeper mysteries of which we know so little.

It will be admitted that reliable evidence exists for the assumption that the area of the Sargasso Sea coincides with that of sunken Atlantis. A greater amount of proof that the weed of which it is composed is in some manner connected with the detritus of the sunken continent is certainly desirable. Not only does the coincidence of areas between the Sargasso and the traditional site of Atlantis assist such a hypothesis, the antiquity of the classical allusions to the Sargasso accumulation and the obviously wider area it occupied in ancient times appear to strengthen it.

We have here, of course, to consider the site of Atlantis only during that phase of its existence when it was occupied by human life. Practically all geologists are agreed, as we know, that in Miocene or late Tertiary times it still retained its continental character, occupying the whole or major part of the North Atlantic region, but many believe that it disappeared during that era. Others, to whose opinion we adhere, think that towards the end of the period in question, it began to disintegrate, owing to volcanic and seismic causes. This disintegration, as we think, resulted in the formation of the islands of Atlantis and Antillia. We can, for the present, leave the latter out of our considerations. What, exactly, was the geographical position and site of the island known as Atlantis, at the period when its early population, the Crô-Magnon Race, began to leave it for European soil?

The island, says Plato, (1) was situated in front of the Pillars of Hercules, otherwise the Straits of Gibraltar; (2) It was greater than Libya (the Greek name for Mediterranean Africa) and Asia (Asia Minor only in Plato's time) combined. This would give it an area, roughly, of about 2,650,000 square miles, or some 350,000 miles less than Australia. Supposing it to have lain, as Plato says, directly in front of, and at no great distance from, the Hispano-African coasts (as the fact that part of it was called "Gadiric," implies) then we must think of a land-mass which extended westward at least to the 45th parallel of longitude, and from north to south, nearly from the 45th parallel of latitude to about the 22nd parallel of latitude, as shown on the accompanying map. This area embraces not only the Azores and the Canary Islands, but much of the Sargasso Sea as well, though not its thickest part, and lies directly above the great banks surrounding the Azores and the Canaries. If we regard the Canaries as its south–eastern extremity (and it could not have come much farther in this direction without touching the African coast), and the Azores as the northern limit of the Atlantean land-mass proper at the period in question, and prolong it westward towards the 45th parallel of longi-tude, we have not only an area commensurate with that mentioned by Plato, but with those natural features which strikingly demonstrate its former presence. It seems probable, too, that the *original* area of Atlantis may have coincided with that of the whole area of the Sargasso Sea.

This, of course, refers, as I have said, to the "last phase" of Atlantis, from 23,000 B.C. to about 9600 B.C., when it became finally submerged, according to Plato. Naturally it may have undergone some shrinkage during that period, as it certainly had during the period antecedent, but surely Plato must have had at his disposal some information of a very definite character to permit him to make a statement so clearly in accord, as I have shown, with the natural features of the Atlantic basin, submarine and supermarine. It does not seem to me that Mr. W. Scott-Elliot, in his interesting book, *The Story of Atlantis*, or M. Gattefossé in his *La Verite sur L'Atlantide*, have taken these features sufficiently into consideration along with Plato's account in framing the excellent maps which accompany their arguments. The last phase of Atlantis, Poseidonius, as shown by Mr. Scott-Elliot's map, is a world away from the Hispano-African coast, as, allowing for the former existence of the African "shelf" and for Plato's statement, it could not possibly have been, and the same applies to M. Gattefossé's conjectural map of Atlantis in Tertiary times. If the island-continent lay "before the mouth of the strait," as Plato says, and the quicksands left by its submergence hindered navigation at the very mouth of the strait, as Aristotle and Scylax of Caryanda assert, the island which caused the debris must logically have been in close proximity to the Straits of Gibraltar.

The conjectural map of Bory de St. Vincent, which was compiled not only from Plato's account, but from that of Diodorus Siculus, appears more in consonance with the facts as given by these authors, but I think it should certainly have shown Atlantis as extending farther northward, so as to face the straits of Gibraltar, and come more "under Mount Atlas," as Diodorus states it did. Moreover it shows no proximity to the "Gadiric" region of Spain.

The latest theory regarding the site of Atlantis is that of M. F. Butavand, as given in his *La Veritable Histoire de L'Atlantide* (Paris, 1925). He believes that Atlantis was situated *inside* the Straits of Gibraltar, and that it was, indeed, a portion of the ancient coast of what is now Tunis and Tripoli. He thinks that the "sea" alluded to by Plato as having been opposite Atlantis was the Tyrrhenian Sea, and casts doubts on Plato's chronology. The arguments—hydraulic and oceanographic—with which he buttresses his theory are as remarkable as they are ingenious, and he identifies several islands now existing off the sunken coast of Tripoli with those alluded to by Proclus, in his commentary on the *Timæus*, as having

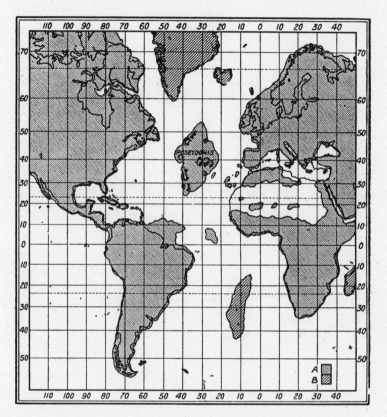

MAP SHOWING POSITION OF ATLANTIS ACCORDING TO SCOTT ELLIOT

been contiguous to Atlantis. He adduces proof that this part of the Mediterranean was particularly difficult of navigation, and argues that it must have been this especial locality which was so alluded to by the Priest of Sais. He further brings philological evidence to his aid, and manages to involve with his thesis the story of the Israelites crossing the Red Sea! Interesting and ingenious as is his essay, however, one must regard it as scarcely designed to contribute to the lucidity of Atlantean study.

And in what circumstances did the Atlantic Ocean come to bear the name of Atlas? Did it not do so because the traditions of Atlantis, the island-continent which had once occupied a considerable portion of it, survived into historic times? Atlantis is the genitive or possessive form of Atlas, meaning "of Atlas," and "Atlantic" is merely the adjective thereof. The handiest dictionary renders it as "pertaining to Atlas." Skeat derives it as "named after Mount Atlas . . . from crude form Atlanti." The name Atlas means "the sustainer, or bearer," from the Sanskrit root Tal, "to bear." But—there is always a "but" in these matters—it seems extraordinary that the island of Atalanta, near Eubœa, the largest island of the Ægean Sea, had a history somewhat resembling that of Atlantis. Strabo in his First Book (3. 20.) says: "And they say, also, of the Atalanta near Eubœa, that its middle portions, because they had been rent asunder, got a ship-canal through the rent, and that some of the plains were overflowed even as far as twenty stadia, and that a trireme was lifted out of the docks and cast over the wall." Diodorus Siculus says that Atalanta was once a peninsula, and that it was broken away from the mainland by an earthquake. Now both writers obviously refer to an earthquake which occurred in 426 B.C., or the year before Plato's birth. Plato must, therefore, have known of the occurrence. There was also a tradition in the neighbouring island of Eubœa that that place had been separated from Bœotia by an earthquake.

"The epithet Atlantic," says Dr. Smith in his *Classical Dictionary*, was applied to it from the mythical position of Atlas being upon its shores." That means it was called after the god or Titan Atlas. But at what date was it first so called? Homer alludes to it as "Oceanus." Plato himself calls it "Atlantic," as if it were a name with which he was well acquainted.

We may then conclude that the island-continent of Atlantis at the time of its submergence extended from a point close to the entrance to the Mediterranean to the 45th parallel of longitude, and from north to south, nearly from the 45th parallel of latitude to about the 22nd parallel of latitude.

BORY DE ST. VINCENT'S MAP OF ATLANTIS

CHAPTER VI

The Races of Atlantis

If we regard the Atlantean continent as a reality and not as a mythical or fictional region, and consider the account of it as given by Plato as enshrining an ancient folk-memory of events which actually occurred, we are faced with the necessity for proving not only by the facts of geology that it formerly existed, but that it was inhabited by men who had reached a fairly advanced type of civilisation. In view of the whole circumstances, and in a case where actual written records are not available, this is a task of no little difficulty and complexity, but I hope to be able to show that Plato's account fits in so accurately with the proven findings of modern archæology and ethnology as to render it a matter of considerable risk altogether to deny it.

Plato tells us that at a date which we may roughly take to be 9,640 years before Christ a host of invaders "marched in wanton insolence upon all Europe and Asia together, issuing yonder from the Atlantic Ocean." Now did any such invasion actually occur about the period mentioned, and does anthropological science cast any light upon such an exodus or folk-movement?

Two well-known German geologists, Penck and Bruckner, find evidence of a series of lesser variations of climate subsequent to the four main glaciations of the great Ice Age, leading gradually to modern conditions. These they call "stadia," and have named them the Buhl,

Gsnitch and Dorn, according to the topographical conditions they appear to have created. The end of the Dorn stadium is roughly dated by Penck at about 7000 B.C., the Buhl, he would place about 20,000, and the Gsnitch between the two, or about 10,000 B.C. This latter is the accepted date for the arrival in Spain and Southern France of a race of men known as the Azilian-Tardenoisian. This people, the Abbé Breuil, the greatest living authority upon the pre-history of France and Spain, believes to have come from "circum-Mediterranean sources" about 10,000 years ago.

The Azilian race derives its name from a cave or tunnel, known as Le Mas d'Azil, in the Pyrenean department of Ariège, where its deposits were discovered by Edouard Piette.[1] He found its remains deposited in nine strata on both banks of the river Arise, which flows through the Mas d'Azil tunnel, and its characteristics, as illustrated by the débris collected, are as follows: The people whose remains he discovered on this site must have been markedly vegetarian and fruitarian, for Piette discovered the stones or husks of oak-acorns, haws, sloes, hazel-nuts, chestnuts, cherries, prunes and walnuts. He also found a handful of barley-seeds, suggesting that they cultivated that cereal.

Harpoons were a feature of the Azilian culture, and this seems to indicate that their users were a people of maritime habits. These weapons were made of stag's horn, and were flat in shape. Over a thousand of these harpoons were found at Mas d'Azil. Along with them were found many necklaces of sea-shells, such as were then to be gathered on the French shores of the Mediterranean and Atlantic, and this would also seem to point to a maritime association in the case of this people.

[1] See his paper *Hiatus et lacune* ; *Bulletin de la Societe d' Anthropologie de Paris*, Series IV, Vol. VI, p. 235.

But the most amazing detail which the Azilian art displayed was a large collection of pebbles having certain marks in red painted upon them with peroxide of iron, mingled with some resinous substance. These marks consist of vertical strokes, circles, crosses, zig-zags and ladder-like patterns. Several characters resembled the letter E, while others seemed to be composed of random lines.

The first assumption of their finder was that these characters were alphabetic, and the suggestion was made that they were the débris of a Palæolithic school. Other authorities believed them to be pieces used in a game of skill. They seemed, too, to bear a close resemblance to the churingas of the Australian aborigines, magical or sacred slabs engraved with fetishtic or totemic symbols. But whereas the Australian churingas were invariably preserved in sacred caverns, the Azilian pebbles appear to have been objects of general use. The Abbé Breuil and Señor Obermeier, the well-known Spanish archæologist, have, however, made it clear by a comparative study that the characters represented on the pebbles bear a close resemblance to those painted on the walls of certain caves in Spain. They are, indeed, human figures highly conventionalised, which, by long usage, have lost all likeness to human shape, just as the letters of our modern alphabet resemble not at all the early forms from which they have been developed. The likelihood is, according to Professor Macalister, that they are representations of the dead, or soul-houses, "abodes for the spirits of deceased members of the community, and were associated with the cult of the dead."[1]

The Azilian culture has been discovered in Spain, especially in the north, at Castello and Valli, and in the Landes of France, the Haute Pyrenees and Ariège. The

[1] Text-book of European Archæology, p. 531.

race penetrated to Britain, and its remains have been found in Yorkshire and Durham, and in Scotland in the famous Oban cave, explored in 1894, when typical Azilian harpoons and other artifacts were found. In the island of Oronsay, too, flat Azilian harpoons were unearthed from a shell-mound, and that Azilian man in this region had some skill in navigation is shown by the presence in the mould of shells of deep-sea varieties of crabs.

Another feature of the Azilian culture are the objects usually described as pygmy or "Tardenoisian" flints, which take their name from Fère-en-Tardenois in the department of the Aisne, in France. These are small splinters of flint, usually less than an inch in length, resembling arrowheads. Most of these have been found in the neighbourhood of the sea, and were probably intended to serve as fish-hooks. These are not necessarily Azilian, though very frequently found associated with that culture, and the name "Tardenoisan" is thus usually applied separately to them. They appear, indeed, to be more specially related to what in now known as the "Capsian" culture (usually attributed to North Africa, and so called from Capsa or Gapsa in Tunis) which flourished in that region long prior to the appearance of the Azilians in Europe, and which itself had invaded the Spanish peninsula. "With the Capsian culture," remarks Macalister, "must undoubtedly be associated the Spanish wall-paintings at Alfera, Cogul and elsewhere. . . . It follows that these are two strong links uniting the Capsian with the Azilian culture. The Capsian Art is the parent from which the painted pebbles of Le Mas d'Azil have been derived, and the Capsian flint industry is the origin of the Azilian-Tardenoisian." The bow, he thinks, was also introduced into Europe by the Capsian people.

Whence came the Azilians and their predecessors the Capsians? "The Azilian bone-harpoon industry," says

Professor Osborn, "like the Tardenoisan microlithic flint industry, was largely pursued by fisher-folk." Breuil believes the Azilians to be of Mediterranean origin, and sees the gradual introduction of Azilian culture in that area slowly mingling with older forms. The Azilian culture in its earliest phase is to be found in North Africa and South-Western Europe.

The question for us here is: did it develop in these regions, or was it introduced? The Azilian people were undoubtedly the forerunners of the Neolithic race, the people of the New Stone Age, and brought with them to Europe an entirely new mode of living, a new art, new religious beliefs. They invaded Europe at a period which, broadly speaking, can be successfully collated with the date given by Plato. They must have poured into Europe in their thousands, dispossessing the older Aurignacian or Crô-Magnon inhabitants and destroying their relatively high culture.

And who were those "earlier inhabitants?" Were they of a character so civilised, did they possess such an art as would in any way identify them with the "Athenians" of Plato's Egyptian priest? They did. "These people," says Professor Osborn, referring to the Aurignacians, "were the Palæolithic Greeks; artistic observation and representation and a true sense of proportion and of beauty were instinctive with them from the beginning. Their stone and bone industry may show vicissitudes and the influence of invasion and of trade and the bringing in of new inventions, but their art shows a continuous evolution and development from the first, animated by a single motive, namely, the appreciation of the beauty of form and the realistic representation of it."[1] Elsewhere he says: "Decorative art has now become a passion (with the Aurignacians), and graving-tools of great variety

[1] Men of the old Stone Age, pp. 315, 316.

and shape, curved, straight, convex or concave—diversified both in size and in style of technique—are very
numerous. We may imagine that the long periods of
cold and inclement weather were employed in these
occupations. . . . Strong and very sharp graving-tools
were also needed for the sculpture out of ivory and soap-
stone of such human figures and figurines as the statuettes
found in the Grottes de Grimaldi, and at Willendorf,
and still more powerful tools for such work as the large
stone bas-reliefs at Laussel. . . . As this industrial
evolution widens, it is apparent that we witness not the
local evolution of a single people, but rather the influence
and collaboration of numerous colonies reacting more
or less one upon the other and spreading their inventions
and discoveries."[1]

This gifted race, the Crô-Magnon, whose art is usually
styled "Aurignacian," from the finds of it discovered in
the grotto of Aurignac in France, was originally traced
by M. E. Lartet near the small village of Crô-Magnon
hard by Les Eyzies on the Vezère.

The discovery of the remains of this race, the forerunners
of the Azilians, at once aroused profound interest in the
scientific world, for the height and brain-capacity remarked
in the skeletal specimens recovered was so extraordinary
as to force anthropologists to the conclusion that at one
time a much higher type of man must have dwelt in
Europe. The average height of Crô-Magnon man was
6 feet 1½ inches, he had relatively short arms, a sign of
high racial development, the brain-case being extraordinarily large in capacity. This race arrived in Europe
at the close of the Ice Age, or roughly about 25,000 years
ago, and seems to have practically wiped out the low
and undeveloped human type, known as the Neanderthal,
which it found in sparse possession.

[1] *Op-cit*, pp. 311, 312.

HEAD OF A HORSE FROM LES ESPÉLUNGUES. (AURIGNACIAN)

(From L'Anthropologie, vol. x).

Crô-Magnon graves present a new aspect in Palæolithic or Old Stone Age archæology. They are amply furnished with flints, pebbles, perforated shells, teeth, and other amulets and charms. Large mantles or gorgets of shells seem to have covered the whole or part of the body, and every sign is present that the race devoutly believed in a future state, and buried his possessions with the individual for use therein. Moreover, some of the burial usages of the Crô-Magnons certainly display the first rude tendencies towards that system of preserving the bodies of the dead which later developed into mummification. The flesh was removed from the bones of Crô-Magnon skeletons and these were painted red, the colour of life. "The dead man was to live again in his own body, of which the bones were the framework," says Macalister. "To paint it with the colour of life was the nearest thing to mummification that the Palæolithic people knew; it was an attempt to make the body again serviceable for its owner's use."

The art and industries of this remarkable people, whose chief seats were on the Biscay Coast and in the Pyrenean region and Dordogne, were greatly more advanced than those of any other Palæolithic civilization, and are still to be observed in the caves which they formerly inhabited in the localities mentioned. Their artistic output is chiefly composed of wonderful drawings, paintings and sculptures of animals, horses, deer, bears, bisons and mammoths, and occasional statuettes of the human figure, which were probably idols or gods. This Aurignacian art flourished over a period of 15,000 years, or during the phase between 25,000 and 10,000 years ago, when the Capsian and the Azilian broke in upon and displaced it. Its greatest period was known as the Magdalenian. A glance at any book which deals with Aurignacian art, say Macalister's *Text book of European*

Archæology, or Osborn's *Men of the Old Stone Age*, will at once convince the reader of its great superiority and "modern" character, and assure him that the race which produced it cannot be classed as merely savage. In fluency and originality, at least, Aurignacian art is, indeed, greatly superior to that either of Egypt or Babylonia, and to achieve a standard of such surpassing excellence it must have persisted elsewhere than in the area where it arrived at fruition for many thousands of years. But where? This highly-developed race of painters and sculptors who designed and carried out works so striking and of such surpassing genius, who possessed a taste so cultivated and a touch so sure, must have had a long history in some other region.

No living archæologist, perhaps, is enabled to pronounce with such authority upon the problem of the upper Palæolithic world as the Abbé Breuil. In his opinion successive invasions of culture occurred either from the Mediterranean region, or from that part of the Biscay coast of France and Spain, which he calls the "Atlantic." "The archæologic testimony," says Osborn, "strongly supports this culture-invasion hypothesis, and it appears to be strengthened in a measure by the study of the human types." "We can hardly contemplate an origin from the east," says Breuil, "because these earlier phases of the Aurignacian industry have not as yet been met with in Central or Eastern Europe." "A southerly origin," says Osborn, "seems more probable, because the Aurignacian colonies appear to surround the entire periphery of the Mediterranean, being found in Northern Africa, Sicily, and the Italian and Iberian peninsulas, from which they extended over the larger part of southern France. In Tunis we find a very primitive Aurignacian, like that of the Abri Audit of Dordogne, with implements undoubtedly similar to those of Chantelperron in France. Even far to the east, in the cave of Antelias, in Syria, as well as in certain stations of Phœnicia, culture-deposits are found which are characteristically Aurignacian"; but "the pure early Aurignacian industry is seen in the regions of the Dordogne and the Pyrenees."

"The Crô-Magnon people," says Macalister, "wherever and however they may have originated, developed and fixed their special characteristics in some extra-European centre, before they invaded our Continent."

We see then that Crô-Magnon man arrived in south-western Europe at a period when great subsidences were taking place both in Europe and the Atlantic area. It is, indeed, significant that these Aurignacian sites which have been discovered in Spain and France are, without exception, situated in the Biscay region, and not on the southern coasts of the peninsula. It is also noteworthy, as I have shown elsewhere,[1] that the culture of the Guanche people of the Canary Islands was undoubtedly Aurignacian. This relationship is upheld by Osborn, René Verneau, and the late Lord Abercromby, and proves that the Crô-Magnon race was indigenous to the Canary Islands, the remnants of Atlantis, and did not drift there from Europe. Like many of the animals and plants of these vestigial islands, Crô-Magnon man was cut off and marooned on them by some great natural cataclysm. At the period in which he lived marine navigation had not even been thought of. He must have invaded Europe at the end of the Ice Age, or about 25,000 years ago, by means of a still existing land-bridge. That he did not proceed from Europe to the Canaries is obvious, as it is as an invader of Europe, a newcomer there, that he is first discovered.

Other evidence is forthcoming that Crô-Magnon man was of extra-European origin. In his *Races of Europe*,

[1] See Problem of Atlantis.

Dr. Ripley advances the theory that the Basques of Northern Spain and Southern France speak a language inherited from the Crô-Magnons. "This hypothesis is well worth considering," says Osborn, "for it is not inconceivable that the ancestors of the Basques conquered the Crô-Magnons and subsequently acquired their language." The lack of affinity between the Basque language and other European tongues is well known, but it has strong resemblances to some American forms of speech. "The fact is indisputable," says Dr. Farrer, in his *Families of Speech* (p. 132), "and is eminently noteworthy, that while the affinities of the Basque roots have never been conclusively elucidated, there has never been any doubt that this isolated language, preserving its identity in a western corner of Europe between two mighty kingdoms, resembles in its grammatical structure the aboriginal languages of the vast opposite continent and those alone." Says Professor J. L. Myres, in the *Cambridge Ancient History* (p. 48): "The similarity between Aurignacian skulls in Europe and the prehistoric skulls in Lagoa Santa in Brazil and other remote localities round the margins of South America suggests that this type had once almost as wide a distribution as that of the older types of implements." The Basque language may thus be the sole remaining remnant of the tongue of Atlantis.

The Crô-Magnons were a race of fishermen, and like the Atlanteans, had a special reverence for the bull, which they frequently depicted on the walls of their caverns.

Now whence came these races of prehistoric antiquity, the Crô-Magnon, the Capsian and the Azilian? If we examine an archæological map, we see that the greater number of Crô-Magnon stations, as is the case with the Azilian, are situated in the Biscay region and in the Dordogne. Here we have an art fully developed and obviously having behind it many centuries of evolution, suddenly appearing in a locality in which there are no signs of its earlier phases. The best and most trustworthy authorities call it "Atlantic" or "circum-Mediterranean," and it certainly does not appear to have come from the East. Nor am I at all satisfied that, as Macalister thinks, it originated in Central Africa. No signs of it have been discovered there, and that is sufficient to put the whole hypothesis (it is really only a tentative hypothesis on Professor Macalister's part, as he admits) out of court.

I believe that Crô-Magnon man was the first of those immigrant waves which surged over Europe at a period when the continent of Atlantis was experiencing cataclysm after cataclysm, partial disruption, or violent volcanic upheaval. Successive outbreaks and the impossibility of remaining in his early habitat forced him across the land-bridge which then existed between Atlantis and Europe into France, Spain and North Africa. The same phenomena occurred in the case of Azilian man. "It seems," says Osborn, speaking of the Aurignacian culture, "like a technical invasion in the history of Western Europe, and not an inherent part of the main line of cultural development." Breuil observes that "it appears as if the fundamental elements of the superior Aurignacian culture had been contributed by some unknown route to constitute the kernel of civilisation." "The only possible explanation," says Macalister, "is that the upper Palæolithic civilisation was introduced into Europe by a new population which entered the continent from without."

The later Azilians appear in precisely the same European region. They probably came by sea, and not by the land-bridge, which, at the period of their coming, had in all likelihood disappeared. We have seen that they were deep-sea fishers, as the finds in the Oban cave demonstrated. Osborn says that their stations are usually to be found on ocean inlets or river-courses, and calls them "a population of fishermen." They must then have possessed sea-going craft of a fairly reliable character. But a closely-knit insular chain between slowly foundering Atlantis and Europe may have assisted their passage.

As a more extended proof of the Atlantean origin of these races has already been given in my book *The Problem of Atlantis*, it is unnecessary to stress it in these pages, and in my *Atlantis in America* I have endeavoured to prove that the Crô-Magnon race also overflowed into America. In the succeeding chapter I shall attempt to give a picture of these races as they appeared in the original Atlantean homeland.

CHAPTER VII

THE STONE AGE IN ATLANTIS

THE most reliable method of comprehending early life in Atlantis can be gained by a consideration of those races of the Old Stone Age who made their way thence to Europe at different periods. In the last chapter we examined these in their European aspect, and we must now attempt some reconstruction of their conditions on Atlantis itself.

We find that the Aurignacians who "appeared suddenly out of the unknown," as Macalister says, and who entered France and Spain, possessed a relatively high stone culture and an advanced art. We must, therefore, regard this race as having dwelt on the Atlantean continent for many centuries. Quite probably it originated there, though on this question, as on many others connected with it, it is impossible to speak with certainty because of the impracticability of applying to the bed of the Atlantic those archæological processes of examination possible elsewhere. Of the rise and development of the Aurignacian race we can posit nothing. We are forced to draw parallels between its conditions in Atlantis and in these regions to which it emigrated.

If we do so, we must think of Atlantis at the remote era of 26,000 years ago as an extensive insular region neither too thickly nor too sparsely populated. If it be granted that it was in area somewhat less than the size of Australia, or say 2,650,000 square miles in extent, we possess data to enable us to make a fair guess at its population. It has been proved that a population which

87

depends upon the chase for its subsistence can support only one family to each forty square miles. The primitive family, for various reasons, can scarcely be estimated at more than six persons on an average, so that this would give us, roughly, a population of some 350,000 for Atlantis in Aurignacian times. But such an estimate fails to take into consideration the fact that the Aurignacians were essentially a people who had attained a fairly high condition of social life. Their art presupposes the association of the people not so much in small tribal groups of families subsisting on the chase, as in fairly large communities of village life. They had their cave-temples and their trades, their rulers and social grades.

Says Osborn: "There can be little doubt that such diversities of temperament, of talent, and of predisposition as obtain to-day also obtained then, and that they tended to differentiate society into chieftains, priests, and medicine-men, hunters of large game and fishermen, fashioners of flints and dressers of hides, makers of clothing and footwear, makers of ornaments, engravers, sculptors in wood, bone, ivory, and stone, and artists with colour and brush. In their artistic work at least these people were animated with a compelling sense of truth, and we cannot deny them a strong appreciation of beauty."[1] Such a people could not have dwelt in small and negligible forest or mountain tribes, but must have grouped themselves into communities of considerable size. Life must have been of a settled character to have given free play to the love of artistic beauty which they so markedly evinced.

It is evident, too, that, as elsewhere, the nature of their religious beliefs assisted the associational character of the people. Spots especially sacred to them were the nuclei of social life. The cave-temple was, in fact, the centre of affairs. Dr. Heinrich Wenkel, speaking of the

[1] Men of the Old Stone Age, p. 358.

Aurignacian cave of Býčískála, in Moravia, described it as "the great cave where once the reindeer man lived whose antechamber was the scene of a cult of the dead, where at a chieftain's grave human sacrifices were offered. . . . It well expresses the feelings which these ancient caverns naturally excite, even in one who lives in the sceptical atmosphere of modern science." Later, Dr. Marett, in his essay on the cave of Niaux, does not hesitate to call it a "sanctuary," and to treat it as such. The existence of fine paintings at the farthest ends of these great and complicated caverns; the presence of the two splendid statuettes of bisons in the remotest recesses of Tuc d'Audoubert, are facts certainly suggestive of animal gods in their "chambers of imagery."

Of the dress and ornaments of these early Atlanteans we can speak with some certainty from the finds in their graves of their descendants in Europe. There are, of course, no remnants of the skins with which they were doubtless clothed. But as we know they bred the horse and cow, and hunted the reindeer, wolf and fox, there can be no doubt that they employed the pelts of those animals for coverings. Indeed microscopic examination of the surroundings of the dead has revealed traces of animal hairs, suggesting that they had been wrapped in hides. As regards their ornaments we are better informed. These consisted of cuirasses and aprons of small sea-shells (Nassa neritea) and fillets or head-bands of the same, necklaces of drilled deer's teeth, fish vertebrae, and ornaments of bone or reindeer horn, shaped like eggs. At Barma Grande was found the skeleton of a boy wearing an elaborate crown of fish vertebrae and a collar of Nassa-shells divided into groups by deer's teeth. These "cuirasses," crowns and collars have been found so frequently in Aurignacian graves that they may be regarded as typical of the ornaments worn by the race.

The tools of the Aurignacians were distinct in shape and had different uses from those of the older European population they displaced, and we must think of these early Atlantean colonists as employing weapons and implements which were probably of their own invention in another sphere. Perhaps the most salient among these is a species of flint knife, of which one edge is trimmed away by chipping, the opposite edge being left untrimmed, to allow it to remain straight and sharp. A scraper for the purpose of preparing skins, and an engraver, with an edge at right angles to the plane of the blade, for working bone, horn and ivory into implements, and sometimes furnished with a beak or cutting-point at the end of the blade, must also have been the primitive chisel with which the Aurignacian sculptor put the finer touches to his images. It is a significant fact that while the races which preceded him used stone or wood, Aurignacian man used bone. He was, indeed, a worker in bone *par excellence*, and this prepares us for the belief that on Atlantis there probably existed large deposits of mammoth ivory. Ivory, says Plato, was one of the principal constituents of the great temple of Poseidon, and he also remarks that elephants abounded on the island-continent.

Smaller engravers or burins were also in use, some of these of the finest character imaginable, and for the first time in European archæology we encounter bone needles with eyes. These were, of course, used to sew skins together. A race which employed the burin and the needle was certainly on the road to civilisation.

The later Solutrean stage of culture, which supposes a second wave of immigrants from slowly disintegrating Atlantis, is somewhat different in its manifestations from Aurignacian proper, but that it emanated from the same region is certain. It appears in Spain and France about 16,000 years ago, and is of a distinctly higher standard

than Aurignacian, so that we must suppose in the intervening thousand years a considerable cultural advance
on Atlantis. Flints were now manufactured *en masse*,
so that it would seem that the Atlanteans had arrived
at the stage of mass production of artifacts, a condition
which implies not only a great social advance, but shows
that labour on Atlantis was in process of becoming
departmentalized. The enormous strata of horse-bones
found in some Solutrean deposits shows clearly that this
people were eaters of horse-flesh, and as a race does not as
a rule suddenly take to a diet to which it has primarily
been unaccustomed, we may well believe that wild horses
inhabited Atlantis in large numbers, galloping about its
prairies or tundras in great herds.

We also encounter numerous hearth-burials in this
stage, from which we are justified in assuming that the
dead were interred in the huts they had occupied during
life. This implies that the people had begun to live in
small stone houses, and that the caves were now utilised
chiefly for religious purposes, or as temples. But the most
striking innovation is the appearance of a much higher
type of flint tool than had before been in use. The
implements of this period, indeed, display a beauty of
line and flaking unsurpassed. They are commonly
described as "willow-leaf" and "laurel-leaf" patterns,
and consist of javelin or spear-heads, scrapers and borers.
Thus a new art in stone had arisen in the course of
centuries in Atlantis. Bone working had to a great extent
been abandoned. This may mean that the deposits of
mammoth ivory had begun to give out, and that the race,
forced back on the use of flint, had addressed itself to
the perfection of a flint technique. We are compelled
to some such conclusion, because in Europe there was no
lack of bone, had the Solutrean workers cared to employ it.

"The Solutreans," says Maçalister, who believes in an

African origin for the Crô-Magnon race, "moved westward, and submerged the Aurignacians temporarily, driving them, perhaps, into Italy; where they were preserved, to reappear, after the Solutrean tyranny was overpast, as the Magdalenians. The Magdalenians seem essentially to have been similar in race to the Aurignacians, but to have lost the tall stature and the excessive cranial capacity—perhaps as a result of the deterioration of climate, and it seems possible to affiliate the Magdalenian culture to the Aurignacian."

With the return of glacial conditions in the Magdalenian stage, we must suppose similar conditions in Atlantis. It is not necessary to assume with Macalister that the Magdalenians were Aurignacians who had long been segregated in Italy. Indeed he remarks elsewhere that no Magdalenian remains are to be encountered there, and it seems much more probable that they represent still another wave of Atlantean immigrants, whose customs had been changed by climatic conditions which were then growing more rigorous on the island-continent as in Europe. One of the outstanding weapons of this period is the harpoon, made from reindeer-horn or bone and used for spearing seals or fish. Another is the *bâton de commandement*, a section of reindeer-horn pierced by a hole, or holes. These were certainly not sceptres, as their rashly assumed name might seem to imply, but have been likened to the rods used by Laplanders which they tie to the reins of the reindeer, to horse-bits, to shaft-straighteners, and to instruments of sorcery. They are frequently ornamented with engravings of animals. I believe them to have been magical implements resembling the "pointing-sticks" of Bornean and Australian savages, which they place in the direction of persons or animals on whom they wish to "put the hoodoo," in West Indian phrase, and the holes with which they are drilled mere conveniences to permit them to be attached to the wizard's belt.

If this theory suffices, we must thus assume the existence of an early form of magic on Atlantis. We also find that a javelin-propellor, the first actual machine invented by man, akin to that used by the ancient Mexicans, and the existing Australians and Eskimos, and the dagger or poignard were introduced.

But above and beyond all, we must regard Atlantis as the home of sculpture and painting. The art of Aurignacian man in Europe, suddenly appearing as if full-blown, leaves no doubt that it must have been perfected in another sphere and after centuries of effort. We must, indeed, assume the rise in Atlantis of a school of art immeasurably superior in its technique to that of Egypt, freer, if not nobler, more realistic, more inspired, more human in every way. There must have existed in the island-continent, we are forced to conclude, some great centre where an art so striking and admirable was developed. Twenty thousand or more years ago Atlantis must have been the scene of mighty artistic impulses of a kind equal to any which have been manifested in the history of mankind, and this presupposes the existence of a former great civilisation on the island, of which, perhaps, the art of the Aurignacians was merely the last degenerate phase.

That a race works in stone or bone, and is ignorant of metals, does not signify that it is destitute of civilisation. For centuries the ancient Egyptians and Babylonians, and the Mexicans and Peruvians of America, possessed no metal tools, yet in the cities inhabited by them a very high standard of civilisation obtained, the equal in every respect of that of China some centuries ago, or of the culture of India, both metal-using countries. Let us suppose that Egyptians and Mexicans, because of some vast cataclysm of nature, had been compelled to abandon their original seats, and colonise Central Africa or South America. Would not their general circumstances of life have undergone a marked degeneration? As a matter of history they *did* throw out colonial branches into both of these areas, with degenerate results. What then is to hinder us in seeing in the Atlantean colonisation of Europe a similar degenerative process at work? For generations America and Australia, after their settlement by Europeans were, for the most part, bear-gardens, inhabited by a rude and almost barbarous people, who bore little resemblance to the cultured classes of the motherland. That Atlantean man succeeded at all in the transplantation of his art to European soil was probably the result of compelling agencies, which enforced the flight of the cultured along with the common people. But that the whole apparatus of Atlantean civilisation was bound to suffer degeneration by the mere circumstances which accompanied its partial removal to Europe, is plain. The civilisation of the "Aurignacians" perished at last, and was totally forgotten and buried in the soil for ten thousand years. Its rediscovery was merely a happy accident.

Such considerations reawaken the old controversy regarding the existence of a civilisation prior to those of Egypt and Babylonia, not a merely barbaric precursor of them, but an ancient culture of superior status, from which they derived. The elder world was full of myths and memories of such a civilisation. The tales of the Antediluvians, of Cyclopean builders, of giant forerunners, the thousand hints and intimations of an older race, embedded not only in Hebrew Biblical literature, but in the chronicles of practically all civilised peoples in Europe, Asia and America, universally point to a fixed belief in the prior existence of a culture of undoubted antiquity and excellence. The Scriptures regard it as historical, and take it for granted. The Babylonian poem of "Gilgamesh" not only refers to, but amplifies, the Biblical chronicles of the Flood. It is alluded to by Hellenic mythographers as the Golden Age. The sacred books of India reflect a whole world of information regarding a great prehistoric past. The Irish and Welsh poems and legends abound in references to it. The Popol Vuh, or legendary chronicles of the Quiches of Central America, contains in its first book numerous stories connected with the prehistoric Titans of Guatemala. Practically all the tribal chronicles of the American Indian "nations" refer to such a period. In the majority of instances this regime of the elder world was regarded as ending in ruin and cataclysm, induced by the wickedness of its rulers, and it is invariably spoken of as having existed at a period so remote that only the broad outlines of its history were, through tradition, available to the writer.

Is it possible that this great mass of traditional material, appearing in the sacred and profane writings of the oldest nations, has behind it nothing of reality? The law, now well recognised, that all tradition of this description rests upon a substratum of fact, is in itself sufficient to dispel such a supposition. The "Diffusionist" School would probably recognise in such a widespread belief merely the passage from tribe to tribe and country to country of a myth originating in some specific nucleus, say in Babylonia, for in Egypt, the favourite centre of the Diffus-ionists, the tradition, so far as I am aware, is not to be encountered, unless we take it that Solon's priest was correct in saying that records of it existed there. But let us remember that whereas the Greeks regarded the gods and Titans as having originated in the West, the American races spoke of them as coming to their shores from the East.[1]

To some extent archæology corroborates these vener-able traditions. It proves the existence of a highly developed art, almost in its decadence indeed, in the Upper

[1] See *The Problem of Atlantis*, Chapter XVIII, The Flood, p. 211, for further information on this head.

Palæolithic levels of France and Spain, and having there neither its roots nor any evolutionary links.   The earliest sites of the race which produced that art are almost exclusively situated on or near the Western coasts of the Franco-Spanish peninsula.   The art itself has been alluded to as "a technical invasion of Europe."   It is obvious that it had its roots elsewhere, and there is not the slightest sign that it came from Asia.   Linking the results of archæology with the traditions which speak of a venerable civilisation cut off in its prime, and of those which insist upon a western *milieu* for this civilisation, it certainly seems as if the Aurignacian remains were the transplanted relics of an ancient culture which had arrived at fruition in a Western oceanic locality, and which, before its removal to Europe, had manifested an even higher ideal than in its new and colonial condition.

The whole of archæology is, indeed, unconsciously straining towards some such explanation of the Aurignacian question.   The Aurignacian race, it admits, was physiologically far superior to any human type presently existing.   That alone calls for explanation, as does the fact of the very exalted position occupied by Aurignacian art.

But, the entire human and cultural conditions of Atlantis must have undergone enormous changes after the emigration of Aurignacian man to Europe.   It seems probable that the bulk of its inhabitants deserted it, and this seems to be borne out by the character of the race it once more cast up on European soil as a fresh human wave in Azilian times, for the Azilian civilisation shows in some ways a marked inferiority to the Aurignacian. Its art-forms are distinctly cruder, and its cultural remains of a more primitive kind generally.

It would seem, indeed, from the human relics of the Azilian period, as if Atlantis must, in the interval between the Aurignacian and Azilian immigrations, have been invaded or colonised itself, and the general osteological character of Azilian remains leads to the surmise that this race may have had an African origin. It might be thought easier to grant a direct migration of the Azilians from Africa to Spain and France, but there seems to be no close connection between the Azilian stages in Africa and Spain and any older form. The relationship between the African and Iberian Azilians is evidently linked up by the Capsian, an African civilisation, which seems to have inherited or absorbed Azilian traits, and there is, indeed, no pure Azilian culture of that period visible in Africa. But that it had a much more remote African origin seems probable, and that it penetrated to Atlantis over the land-bridge which once connected the African "shelf" with the island-continent appears likely.

In any case, North African features obtrude themselves into Azilian osteology and art. This people, the ancestors of the Iberian race, were stamped with the seal of North Africa, and although little or no trace of them is to be found there, for they are by no means the same as the Capsians, that does not militate against their one-time occupancy of the country. We must then imagine Atlantis at some period between 16,000 and 11,000 years ago as having been invaded by a race bearing a strong general resemblance to the Berbers of North Africa, that is, not Negroid or "Arab," but Iberian, a tall, slender high-featured people, dark or brown-haired, grey or blue-eyed, using the bow and arrow, and strongly resembling the Guanches of the Canary Islands, who, were indeed, in part their descendants. These, compelled for some reason to cross the land-bridge connecting Atlantis with the African Continent, must have fallen upon the diminish-ing island in hordes, have vanquished its Aurignacian inhabitants, and have remained there through the centuries until such time as the last cataclysm forced them to return to Europe and to that African soil from which they originally hailed, and where, we will remember, Diodorus expressly states, they had extensive settlements.

This theory not only accounts for the marked change in the character of the immigrants from Atlantis in Azilian times, but suggests an almost radical racial reconstruction in Atlantis itself. We recall that Plato alludes to the admixture of the divine Atlantean race, the original lineage of the gods, with the sons of earth, with ordinary mortals. Who were those "mortals," who impoverished the divine strain? They can only have been the Azilians, whose remnants mingled with those of the Aurignacian or "godlike" stock, and who are still to be found in the Canary Isles, the last vestiges of Atlantis. Many writers speak of the Berber or Iberian relationship of the indigenous population of the Canaries. Of this theory Sergi is, indeed, the chief exponent. He calls the Iberians the "Mediterranean Race," and states that not only did they overflow the Mediterranean area, but penetrated to Britain and Ireland, France and elsewhere.[1]

The Azilian or proto-Iberian age on Atlantis must then have been one and the same with that stage of moral and cultural degeneration which Plato speaks of, and his Atlantean invaders identical with the Azilians or proto-Iberians. These people, like the Aurignacians, were cave-dwellers, or, more properly speaking, employed deep and secluded caverns of great size as temples, and this would seem to show that the Azilian invaders of Atlantis had been converted to the ancient religion of the country. Indeed, so far as it is possible to judge of the religious usages of peoples so remote, there seems to have been little or no difference between the religious ideas of the Aurignacians and the Azilians, save that a grosser species of faith,

[1] See *The Problem of Atlantis*, pp. 76 ff. for extended proof of this statement.

suggesting magic, was practised by the latter. The worship of the bull was, however, maintained, and the ritual was probably similar to that described by Plato.

We must then think of later Atlantis, the Atlantis of the final catastrophe, as having been somewhat degenerate in thought, if not in culture. We say "the final catastrophe," but we have absolutely no evidence to permit us to state with any exactitude precisely when Atlantis was finally submerged. Indeed she was *never totally submerged*, for the Canary Islands and the Azores, her highest peaks, still remain above water as witnesses of her former existence. We know that it is only about three thousand years since the land connection between Great Britain and the Continent of Europe was finally destroyed, and that the English Channel sweeps over the site of forests so recently plunged into ocean's bed. Is there any good reason then, to deny to Atlantis an even longer existence than Plato assumes? With that question we shall concern ourselves later. But at this stage it may be said that such a theory would render Plato's account of Atlantis as a great and flourishing civilised community much more ready of acceptance. If we are to judge her condition from the races she sent to Europe as immigrants, we must in the event assess her culture either as the broken-down remains of a much higher human condition (Aurignacian) or from what we know of the Azilian, as a typical Palæolithic or Upper Old Stone Age culture.

It is impossible for me to believe—and from this belief I am not to be moved by the conclusions of archæologists who are not also students of tradition—that the manifestations of Aurignacian art did not have behind them many centuries of cultural ancestry. To regard these as the spontaneous outcome of savage mentality is, to my way of thinking, an absurdity unsurpassable. No savages to-day practise an art so finished in its technique, indeed recent developments in modern European art appear as greatly more akin to the barbaric than the delicate productions of Aurignacian and Magdalenian man. What truly artistic mind cannot applaud the horse's head from *Les Espélungues*, the clay bisons on the night-bound walls of the *Tuc d'Audoubert*, or the charging bull from Altamira? Compare these for action, motion, with the wooden immobility of ancient Egyptian painting or the crudity of the early Italian Old Masters, and you behold an art brimming with life and obviously proceeding from minds attuned to a veritable realism which at the same time is conscious of the value of inspiration, which has seized upon and pictured-up the real in the spirit of the ideal. Savages! Let us beware how we describe these ancient sculptors and limners, lest posterity, with a more just sense of aesthetic values, accords to them an eminence which it may not accede to ourselves!

And if this ancient art ranks so highly as all enlightened students of aesthetics admit, can we deny to that Atlantis from which it emanated much of the wondrous culture which Plato, obviously the mouthpiece of a much more venerable tradition, claimed for it? What, after all, do we know of the ancient world so far, to permit us to adopt an attitude of negation to the deep-rooted traditional statement so oft-repeated in the most venerable chronicles that at a period almost transcending the imagination a civilisation of a high order, from which all the cultures of this planet proceeded, shone, flickered, and, like a shattered sun, cast its broken lights upon the dark places of our star? If we can discover no material proof of that civilisation, is it not because its remains sleep beneath the Atlantic? But we can surely infer with confidence from its last fragments in Europe, Africa and America, appearing suddenly and having no roots therein, as well as from its well-authenticated tradition, that it assuredly existed.

CHAPTER VIII

THE KINGS OF ATLANTIS

IT is from the writings of Diodorus the Sicilian, as well as from those of Plato, that we are enabled to glean the little we know concerning the royal line of Atlantis. Plato, indeed, assures us that such a succession existed, but he leaves us in the dark concerning the names of any of its members, with the exception of the sons of Poseidon: Atlas, Gadir or Eumolus, Amphisus, Eudemon, Mnesus, Autochthonus, Elassipus, Mestor, Azaes and Diaprepus. Let us examine these first, and see what we can glean from them.

In other myths Atlas is alluded to as the son of Iapetus and Clymene, and brother of Prometheus and Epimetheus, the Titans, along with whom he made war against Zeus. Defeated by the Hellenic Allfather, he was compelled to bear the skies upon his head and shoulders. According to Homer, he is, indeed, the bearer of the long columns which hold the heavens and earth asunder. Indeed, he is what students of Mexican mythology, following the late Professor Eduard Seler, would now call a " sky-supporter," one of these genii who uphold the roof of the world. The idea probably arose from the belief that Mount Atlas, in Africa, like other lofty mountains, actually upheld the skies. Other mythographers, as we have seen, represent Atlas as a wise astrologer, a monarch who first taught men the science of reading the stars. There was, of course, more than one Mount Atlas, and we find mountains similarly named in Mauretania, Arcadia and Caucasus. The Pleides, Hyades and Hesperides were his daughters.

Eumolus, or Eumolpus, otherwise known as Gadir, whose name is associated with Cadiz and the straits of Gibraltar, the ancient Fretum Gaditanum, was regarded as the founder of the Eleusinian mysteries, of which more hereafter. Of Amphisus, Eudemon and Mnesus, we find no mention in classical mythology. The name Autochthonus merely implies "aborigine," but it is to be remarked that it was usually applied by the Greeks to people of the ancient Pelasgian stock, whose story, says Mr. Walters in his *Classical Dictionary*, "may be paralleled from those of the Basques in Spain and the Celts of Wales." They were, indeed, the introducers of all culture to Greece. Elassipus, Mestor and Azaes are all equally unknown to classical tradition, and the same holds good of Diaprepus. We should remember, however, that Plato expressly states that these names had been Egyptianized from the Atlantean language by the priest of Sais, and subsequently Hellenised by Critias, so that there is little hope that they were transmitted in anything like their original form.

So far Plato. Diodorus tells us that Uranus was the first King of the Atlanteans. Uranus was the Greek god of the Sky, and father of Iapetus the Titan, the Biblical Japhet, of Oceanus, the Cyclopes, and many other mythical figures, including the Giants. His most celebrated Atlantean children were Basilea (which simply means "queen") and Rhea or Pandora. Atlas, Saturn and Hesperus are also mentioned as his offspring. The Atlantides became the constellation of the Pleiades. A certain Jupiter—not the god of that name—later became King of the Atlanteans, displacing his father Saturn with the aid of the Titans.

FIGURE OF ATLAS, SUPPORTING THE WORLD
ON HIS SHOULDERS

It becomes clear that the mythical history of Atlantis is in some manner associated with the incidents of the war between the Gods and Titans, which bulks so largely in Greek mythi-history and art. The story of the Titano-machia, or divine war with the Titans, relates that Uranus, the first ruler of the world, cast his sons, Briareus, Cottys and Gyes, the Hecatoncheires, or Hundred-handed, into Tartarus, along with the Cyclopes, "the creatures with round or circular eyes," gigantic shepherds of Sicily. Gæa, his wife, indignant at this, urged the Titans to rise against their father. They deposed him, and raised Cronus to the throne. But Cronus, in turn, hurled the Cyclopes back into Tartarus, and married his sister Rhea. Uranus and Gæa had foretold that he would himself be deposed by his own children, and as these were born he swallowed them, all but Zeus, whom his mother concealed in a cave in Crete. When Zeus came to manhood he gave his father a potion which caused him to disgorge the children he had swallowed, and these turned against Cronus and the ruling Titans. Gæa promised victory to Zeus if he would deliver the Cyclopes and Hecatoncheires from Tartarus. He did so, and the Titans were overcome and themselves cast into the Tartarus.

We find, then, the self-same personages connected with the war of the Gods and Titans as with Atlantis. Indeed it is clear that Diodorus *actually applies the story and personnel of the war of the Gods and Titans to the history of Atlantis.* On what grounds did he do so? He could only have done so because of an existing tradition. He certainly did not invent the tale of the Titanic War, which was in circulation centuries before his time. It seems reasonable to suppose, then, that a tradition actually existed of a great war in the Atlantic Ocean. The Gods, thought the Greeks, had their origin in the West. Thence came the mysteries and all cultures. The Cyclopes and

Titans are likewise connected with the West, the former with Sicily and the Mediterranean isles, the latter with other islands. Pomponius Mela states that Albion, the Titan, son of Poseidon, and the original tutelary god of Britain, was a brother of Atlas, and assisted him with Iberius, god of Ireland, to contest the Western passage of Hercules. Albion is that Alba from which Scotland takes her ancient name of Albany. There was thus a distinct race of Titans connected with the Atlantic, and if Albion and Iberius can be identified with the British Isles it is only reasonable to assume that Atlas was also once the tutelary divinity of a western land in the ocean with which myth persistently connects his name.

The histories of all peoples commence with a dynasty of god-kings, only shading later into "real" history as time proceeds. The Greek and Roman dynasties, the Egyptian, the Babylonian, the Mexican and Central American annals, all began with traditional notions of the lives and deeds of heaven-descended monarchs. Nor is our own Britain any less pious in her royal genealogies. I have seen in a roadside inn a modern illustrated genealogy drawing the descent of King George V from Adam and the early "mythical" Scottish Kings, and have we not our Lears and Arthurs? What is myth in its historical form? Is it not merely traditional history handed down before the age of writing? Mena, the first King of the First Dynasty of Egypt, was regarded as mythical until a reference to him was discovered upon a contemporary tomb. Troy was regarded as a dream of "Homer" before Schliemann discovered it. Chedarlaomer was also considered as legendary before inscriptions bearing his name were found. A hundred instances of great names recovered from myth could be adduced. Is there any good reason, then, for denying that it is quite probable that the names of the

Kings of Atlantis as given by Plato and Diodorus may not at one time have belonged to veritable historical persons?

As I have said, we labour under the disability of having the names of the Kings of Atlantis in a Greek form only. Nor have we the least chronological clue to their period. That they ruled over Atlantis in its Stone Age period is as unlikely as that Lear or Arthur represent the Neolithic Age in Britian. They are called "the first Kings" of Atlantis, and no very extraordinary antiquity is claimed for them prior to the cataclysm.

Everything points to the probability that, just as Atlantis experienced several cataclysmic visitations, so did she experience more than one revolution of cultural and political change. The Aurignacian art which seems to have proceeded from her, exhibits certain signs of cultivation during many centuries long before it reached its European seat, and the Azilian decadence in art, coupled with a progress in things material, indicates another revolution of the wheel of human affairs in Atlantis. The Aurignacian remains, as has been said, seem to point to the prior existence of a very great civilisation upon Atlantis at some time prior to the end of the Pleistocene era.

If this hypothesis be examined without heat or bias, it will be recognised as by no means so wildly improbable as it at first appears.

The Aurignacian colonisation of Europe occurred at the close of the Great Ice Age, or about 25,000 years ago. In Europe, the main ice-cap stretched from Cape North in Norway to the North of France, covering a space coincident with present-day Prussia. Here and there, in the more southerly countries, it manifested itself where greater or less mountain ranges reared their heads, but its phenomena were less imposing in these regions, owing to the smaller size of the mountains, and their situation on a warmer isothermal line. North Africa shows little or no glaciation, and it is, therefore, most unlikely that Atlantis which was much in the same latitude, and which was a maritime country at that, would have experienced any great degree of glaciation, or indeed would during the Ice Age have possessed a climate any more rigorous than that of, say, the North of Scotland to-day.

If this be admitted, and if we also admit the presence upon Atlantis of a race of men—the Crô-Magnon—of undoubted superiority in culture and brain-power (a conclusion at which we are justified in arriving by virtue of the size of the Crô-Magnon brain-case, as well as from the remains of Aurignacian art) there is nothing very outrageous in the assumption that at a period when Europe was either buried beneath the Pleistocene ice, or powerfully affected in its southerly regions by local glaciations, Atlantis, comparatively free from those conditions, and enjoying a climate of reasonably temperate character, should not have nursed a civilisation which at a subsequent epoch was destroyed by a series of cataclysms of a volcanic or seismic nature.

We find that Plato's divine race, the sons of Poseidon, were descended on the female side from an autochthonous or aboriginal strain. These we may regard as the Azilians, for certain considerations seem to render it probable that the great civiliser Poseidon (if we regard him as a human figure), settled in Atlantis some centuries before the coming of the Azilians to Europe, or, roughly, about a thousand years before the submergence of Atlantis. By that time the ancient Aurignacian culture in the island-continent must have been almost totally extinct. That the race itself was not, seems to be implied by the statement in the myth of the war with the Titans regarding the Cyclopes. These Cyclopes were a tall, round-eyed race, clothed in skins, and dwelling in caves. Their description, indeed, answers almost exactly to that of the Crô-Magnons.

who must have been the degenerate aborigines of Atlantis. The Crô-Magnon skull was large, the cheek-bones higher, the eye-orbits immense, and the whole physique powerful. And we know that the Crô-Magnons, like the Cyclopes, dressed in skins and dwelt in caves.

We find then that Poseidon, the culture-bringer, arriving in Atlantis some centuries prior to its final submergence, allied himself with the remnants of the Crô-Magnon aborigines and gave their dying culture a more modern tendency, precisely as did Quetzalcoatl in Mexico. Indeed the myths of Poseidon and Quetzalcoatl are practically identical. In *Atlantis in America* I have adduced proof that the personalities of Atlas and Quetzalcoatl are the same (pp. 199 ff.) and this applies with equal force to Poseidon, the father of Atlas, who possesses the same attributes of the culture-hero. We know that Quetzalcoatl came to Mexico from some locality in the Atlantic. But whence did Poseidon come?

Poseidon, I believe, was the leader of the Azilian or proto-Azilian band of invaders who conquered Atlantis, and colonised it some centuries prior to making their great raid on Europe. He is usually described as a god of "Pelasgian" origin. Now this name Pelasgian, is usually employed to denote a race who colonised Greece at an early period, and who built immense structures of solid stone. They were, indeed, the Mykenean race, the bringers of the mysteries of the Cabiri to Greece, a people of Iberian stock. The Azilians, as we have seen, were proto-Iberians. We, have therefore, good grounds for the statement that Poseidon was the leader or priest-king of the Azilian invaders of Atlantis. That the whole Iberian race is distantly of North African origin scarcely admits of doubt, and it seems probable that Poseidon, "god" of the Mediterranean Sea, must have led his people from the Atlas region of North Africa to Atlantis, whence, some centuries later, they were to invade both Europe and their original home.[1]

If these surely not very dubious conclusions be granted as reasonable, we have the material for a sketch, faint and with many lacunæ, perhaps, of historical events in Atlantis, from the period ante-dating the Crô-Magnon invasion of Europe to the final submergence of the island-continent.

We must, in the first place, imagine Atlantis, an island nearly the size of Australia, as the seat of a great prehistoric civilisation of very considerable pretensions. A race of fine physique—such physique, indeed, as the world has not since beheld—inhabits it. By the aid of flint tools, as well as native genius, it has succeeded under the happy conditions of an environment unhampered by the Pleistocene ice, in developing an admittedly higher type of artistic effort at a period about 23,000 years or more before the Christian era. It celebrates religious ceremonies in large caves decorated with elaborate paintings of its animal and semi-human gods, and further embellishes these with bas-reliefs and statuettes of idols. Its public life circulates and flourishes around these cave-temples, outside of which it probably erects huts and small houses of stone or clay. It develops, as we have seen, social classes, the prototypes of these of the present day.

Then, some 22,000 years ago, its island-home is visited by a severe seismic cataclysm beneath the fury of which portions of the area are hurled into the sea. Terrified, large masses of its inhabitants make for the European continent across the land-bridge. They have previously been averse from settling in the continental area because of the notoriously cold and uncongenial conditions obtaining there, but with the gradual disappearance of

[1] *Herodotus*, Book II, Chapter XL, states that the Greeks received their knowledge of Poseidon from the Libyans (Africans) " by whom he has always been honoured, and were anciently the only people who had a god of that name."

the ice these have been somewhat mitigated, and they now experience little difference between them and those of their native home. Those who remain carry on the ancient culture, which the colonists permit to degenerate somewhat.

About 14,000 B.C. a second cataclysm occurs, and this compels large numbers of the Atlanteans (Magdalenians) to fly to the European area. They carry with them an art which, because it has remained in the ancient home, considerably surpasses in technique and detail the degenerate Crô-Magnon art, but they have later to face a return of the glacial conditions in Europe.

Then, seemingly about 10,500 B.C., "Poseidon" and his Azilian Proto-Iberians invade Atlantis from the North African region.

It is from this point that we obtain a hold upon the realities of Atlantean history. Poseidon must have been an early culture-hero, similar to those whom we find connected with the Polynesian and Mexican migration myths. Indeed, he behaves in Atlantis precisely as these do in their own spheres. Now it is most unlikely that Plato could have personally manufactured a tale which fits in so precisely with the circumstances of other and later culture-hero tales. It is in such cases that Folklore is of assistance to history.

Poseidon takes over the lordship of the island of Atlantis. He marries a native woman. He excavates large canals, and builds a temple upon a hill. He rears a progeny of twins, who subsequently rule the island and the surrounding isles, found a special caste and found a religious system of their own, based on ancestor-worship.

These circumstances are almost paralleled by the legend of Hotu Matua, the culture-hero of Easter Island, in the Pacific, a locality which, like the Canaries, is obviously a remnant of a great sunken oceanic continent.

Marooned on Easter Island with a band of followers, Hotu Motua set himself the task of reconstructing society there. He reared immense structures in stone, walls, rude shrines and statues. By a system of ingenious taboos he secured and perpetuated the religion of his Polynesian fathers.[1]

Other myths exhibit similar circumstances. The Creek Indians say that Esaugetuh Emissee, "the Master of Breath," came to the island Nunne Chaha, which lay in the primeval Waste of Waters, and built a house there. He built a great encircling wall, and directed the waters into channels.[1] What is this but the story of Poseidon in Atlantis?

Manibozho, the great god of the Algonquin Indians, is said to have "carved the land and sea to his liking," just as the Huron deity Tawiscara "guided the waters into smooth channels." The Peruvian god Pariacaca arrived as Poseidon had done, in a hilly country. But the people reviled him, and he sent a great flood upon them, so that their village was destroyed. Meeting a beautiful maiden, Choque Suso, who was weeping bitterly, he inquired the cause of her grief, and she informed him that the maize crop was dying for lack of water. He assured her that he would revive the maize if she would bestow her affections on him, and when she consented to his suit, he irrigated the land by canals. Eventually he turned his wife into a statue.

Another Peruvian myth recounts that the god Thonapa, angered at the people of Yamquisapa in the province of Alla-suyu because they were so bent on pleasure, drowned their city in a great lake. The people of this region worshipped a statue in the form of a woman which stood on the summit of the hill Cachapucara. Thonapa

---

[1] See my *Atlantis in America*, p. 62 ff.
[2] Same work, p. 65.

destroyed both hill and image and disappeared into the sea.

We find in these myths most of the elements which go to make up the story of Poseidon in Atlantis, the sacred hill, the making of zones of land and water, the god marrying the native maiden, the disastrous flood. This is what is known to mythologists as "the test of recurrence." If one part of a myth be found in one part of the world, and another overlapping section of it in another part, it is demonstrably clear that these are floating fragments of a once homogeneous myth, and that the parts of these which do not correspond are supplementary to each other, linked together by those which do correspond.

Now, no such myth, so far as I am aware, was current concerning the Mediterranean islands, or could have been available to Plato. How, then, was it possible for him to make use of material which undoubtedly existed elsewhere, but of which he could not have been aware had not a general tradition of the circumstances of Atlantean history survived, disseminated on one hand to Europe, and Egypt, and on the other to America? Traditions, we know, survive for countless centuries, and there is nothing extravagant in the supposition that that which referred to Atlantis slowly but surely became known to peoples on both continents.

In the account of Diodorus it is clear that Uranus stands for Poseidon as given in that of Plato. Both are described as the father of Atlas, who, for practical purposes, may be called the central or pivotal figure in Atlantean history. Plato provides us with no further details concerning the Kings of Atlantis, after telling us that they reigned there "for generations." Not so Diodorus, who, it would seem, had access to a tradition or traditions of greater scope, so far as this particular part of the Atlantean story is concerned. In fact, he carries on the history of

the Atlantean King until the time of Jupiter, who, he
assures us, was a totally different personage from the deity
of that name.

First, we have Basilea "the great mother," "the queen"
par excellence, who is, of course, no other than she whom
the entire Mediterranean from Carthage to Canaan,
subsequently revered as the Mother Goddess, Astaroth,
Astarte, Diana, Venus, Aphrodite, Isis—that great maternal
figure who had a hundred names, and a hundred breasts,
yet one single personality, and who is also found in
Britain, Ireland and Gaul, and in America, though not
in Germany or among the Slavs. Her "distribution" is
precisely on the lines and currents of Atlantean colonisation and emigration. Wherever her name has gone,
something of Atlantis also has gone. The invading
Atlanteans, Crô-Magnon and Azilian, were the first to
bring her cult to Europe, as their statuettes or idols of
her prove. They portray a woman with the exaggerated
symbols of motherhood, as Macalister remarks. She
was the goddess and along with her, as in the Atlantis of
Plato, went the bull, as will be made clear when we come
to consider Atlantean religion in its proper place. The
myth in Diodorus which speaks of her dementia at the
death of her children is, of course, the madness which, in
many places in classical story, is described as forming
part of her cult—the fury of wild, feral Nature, as displayed
in the story of Isis, and that of the Mother Goddess of
Scotland, the Cailleach Mheur. The madness of Agave
on the death of Pentheus is a distortion of it, the despair
of Kore at the disappearance of Persephone a memory
of it.

Atlas, her brother, who followed her, was, says Diodorus, a wise astrologer, the first to discover the knowledge
of the sphere. Even to this day his name is connected
with the science of Geography. That an entire ocean,

that a mountain range still existing, should be called after him is significant. It is always the eponymous figures from whom localities and races are named, those men who grow in course of time to godhead. Hellas was the father of all the Greeks, the English have Ingwe for their sire, the Scots worshipped Scota or Skatha, whose name still survives in that of the island of Skye, the Romans took their name from Romulus, and hundreds of other races call or called themselves the children of eponymous forebears. There is, therefore, nothing unreasonable in the supposition that the people of Atlantis called themselves after Atlas, the Titan who was once a man, and gave the country his name.

Atlas, says Diodorus, married his sister Hesperis, and the pair had seven daughters, after whom the planets were said to take their names. How long Atlas reigned we have no means of knowing, but it was probably during his tenure of the throne that the city of Atlantis was founded. It could scarcely have been a place of much consideration in the reign of Poseidon the first king, and it seems much more probable that the temple which contained his image and that of Cleito, his wife, was erected subsequent to his death. Against this view, however, may be placed the fact that the statues of his ten sons were also to be found in the sacred building, and that these were very evidently the images of "ancestors," deceased men deified. It may, therefore, be safer to conclude that, although the temple and the statues of Poseidon and Cleito dated from the reign of Atlas, the statues of the deified twins were placed there at a later period.

Atlas, the astronomer, must have employed the palace on the hill above the city as his observatory. But when we speak of "temples," "palaces" and "observatories," the critic may say "let us remember that we are dealing with an epoch more than 10,000 years ago, and that the

Azilian immigrants to Spain did not build such structures. That is as it may be. The fact remains that extensive works of the Azilian period have been discovered at Huelva in south-western Spain by Mrs. Elena Whishaw, of the Anglo-Spanish School of Archæology there. Mrs. Whishaw has succeeded in bringing to light numerous evidences of that Tartessian civilization which flourished in the South of Spain in pre-Roman and even in pre-Carthaginian times. After many discouragements she succeeded in founding the Anglo-Spanish School of Archæology in 1914, first at Seville and later at Niebla, under the patronage of King Alfonso. The museum which she has erected outside the little walled town is a model of its kind, and is filled with the result of her excavations in all their stages from Palæolithic to Arabic times.

The great majority of the Stone Age objects housed in the Museum have been classed in accordance with the views of modern authorities as belonging to the Palæolithic or Old Stone Age. These are of a type apparently unique, for they are not, like the Palæolithic objects of most other regions, of flint, but of various kinds of stone, including quartz, porphyry and slate, mostly recovered from drifts of the last Ice Age. The exhibits also include many Neolithic objects and numerous fragments of pottery, exquisitely polished, some bearing designs in relief. Funeral tiles of pottery have also been encountered near Seville in connection with remains which have been classified as Crô-Magnon, so that the manufacture of earthenware objects by Palæolithic man in this region may at least be suspected.

That a high degree of civilisation flourished in Andalusia for many ages before the occupation of the province by the Romans, is, of course, well known. The ancient kingdom of Tartessus had long been in existence at the period when the Carthaginians entered and exploited Southern Spain. The foundation of this Tartessian culture may, perhaps, be referred to the fusion of the Libyans of the Atlas region of North Africa with the Stone Age people of Spain, but such a theory does not altogether account for the high degree of engineering skill displayed in the formation of great harbours and the erection of Cyclopean walls and strongholds, the remains of which constitute the salient archæological background of the province and exhibit many signs of pre-Tartessian handiwork. At Niebla soundings have been taken to the depths of thirty feet of soil rich in Palæolithic remains without any sign of coming to the end of the deposit. These remains vary from miniature darts of quartz, some less than half an inch long, beautifully chipped porphyry fish-hooks and small arrow-heads, and many other minute objects of the type usually classified as Azilian, the precise use of which remains to be decided. Enormous grain-crushers, too, have been excavated, made from what is known locally as black quartz. None of these objects could have been carried down to Niebla by the river.

For some time Mrs. Whishaw was puzzled to account for the absence of Crô-Magnon dwellings in a neighbourhood so rich in Aurignacian remains. An entire series of caves exists on the banks of the Rio Tinto opposite Niebla, but it was obvious that these had not been inhabited until long after Crô-Magnon man had given place to a later race. But in the neighbourhood of the spot where many of his remains had been unearthed, and well below the foundations of Niebla, there was found the lower courses of a wall chipped in the native limestone. The association of this wall with Palæolithic implements of Aurignacian character would certainly seem to refer its handiwork to the Crô-Magnon race, and when the excellence of Aurignacian sculpture, painting and bone-carving is recalled, the theory seems to do no violence to probability.

Later foundations have also been unearthed which have been referred to the Bronze Age. These are situated outside the walls of Niebla, facing the river on the south side, and occupying a space of about 100 feet in length. They are composed of what is locally known as *hormazo*, a primitive and coarser variety of the later concrete, known as *hormigon*, peculiar to Andalusia. The employment of one or other of these materials affords a criterion by which the approximate period of building-construction in this region can be arrived at, and this determines the early character of a Cyclopean wall of rough-hewn stones of enormous size built along the banks of the Rio Tinto to the east of the town, and held together by *hormazo* mortar.

This structure was revealed in 1923 by the agency of a series of floods. The river has been artificially deepened all along the wall to form a harbour, and if proof were required that such was the design of the primitive builders, it is found in a stairway over thirty feet wide cut in the rock which leads down to the river from one of the five great gate-towers of the town. The wall was doubtless built to prevent the silting-up of the artificial pool, and at the same time strengthen the defence of the city. Mrs. Whishaw has recently received permission under a royal order to excavate freely within the walls of Niebla, and hopes to learn more of the earliest phase of its history when this has been undertaken under expert direction.

Not only then, does it seem to be clear from Mrs. Whishaw's excavations that the Crô-Magnon race actually built in stone, as the Cyclopean wall in question has been found in association with their artifacts, but that the Azilian or Proto-Iberian race constructed the large ancient harbour at Huelva, and the walls and staircases there, some of which reveal work akin to that of the strange polygonal masonry of Incan Peru. Indeed, Mrs. Whishaw, an archæologist of ripe experience, herself attributes the works in question to Atlantean immigrants, and is presently preparing an extended essay on the subject, which she is to entitle *Atlantis in Andalusia*.

There is thus no reason why we should not speak of "palaces" and "observatories" in the Atlantis of the time of Atlas. Probably the latter resembled the inti-huatana of Peru, Incan and pre-Incan, and there seems to be nothing wildly improbable in envisaging the sage Atlas seated in such a building, occupied with the study of the heavenly bodies.

We may infer, from the circumstance that Atlas was engaged in the researches of astronomy, that his reign was a peaceful one. In all probability it was of considerable duration, and witnessed the growth and consolidation of the Atlantean power.

Didorus tells us that Jupiter was a king of the Atlanteans, and as he is careful to assure us that this personage was not the same as the god of that name, we must infer that he was a man named after that god. But there seems to be some dubiety concerning whether Saturnus, the brother of Atlas, or Jupiter, his son, came first to the throne. "This Jupiter," says Diodorus, "either succeeded to his father Saturnus, as King of the Atlantides, or displaced him." It would thus seem either that Saturn reigned first and left the succession to his son in the usual manner, or that Jupiter hurled him from the throne. The latter appears to be the more probable surmise, as Diodorus tells us that: "Saturn, it is said, made war upon his son, with the aid of the Titans, but Jupiter overcame him in a battle, and conquered the whole world." "Saturn," he also remarks, "was profane and covetous." We may thus assume that an irreligious and grasping old king or chieftain, whose avarice and profanity had become a menace to the body politic, was displaced by a more pious and considerate son.   Saturn, we are told, availed himself of the aid of the Titans, that is, probably of the more ancient Aurignacian part of the population, the tall Crô-Magnon people, in his struggle with his son, and it is likely that this use of a people until now quiescent, had not a little to do with later unrest in Atlantis.

We may, then, regard Jupiter as the third King of Atlantis, or at least the third of whom we have any definite knowledge.   It was in his reign that those elements of unrest which were to play so disastrous a part in Atlantean history began to manifest themselves.   But it may be, and indeed it seems much more likely, that the four outstanding figures in Atlantean history, Poseidon, Atlas, Saturn and Jupiter, represent the founders of four separate dynasties as well as individual reigns.   Indeed this may be gleaned from Plato's account, which tells us that, "for many centuries they did not lose sight of their august origin, they obeyed all the laws, and were religious adorers of the gods their ancestors."   Four reigns could not cover such a length of time, and we are driven to the conclusion that the personages named were the first monarchs of new dynastic lines.   This is all the more probable because they have the names of "Classical" gods, bestowed upon them by Plato's informant in default of being able to supply their Atlantean or Egyptian names in a form understandable to Greek hearers.   The founders of new dynasties nearly always go down in history as beings of divine or semi-divine birth.   There are several cases of the kind in Egyptian history, the first King of the Merovingian line of the Franks, Merowig, was supposed to be of supernatural birth, and Roman, Greek and Babylonian examples also exist.

This, too, provides a powerful argument that the only four Kings of Atlantis of whose names we have any record, were not gods, but human men, to whom later divine honours were paid. It would also seem to have been customary in Atlantis to deify kings after their deaths, precisely as it was in Egypt and Rome, and not infrequently among the tribes of ancient Britain and the North-American Indians. This, of course, at once accounts for their being regarded as gods by subsequent generations. They were, in fact, "gods," precisely in the sense that Numa Pompilius or Marcus Aurelius were considered as "gods" after their death.

With what we may then believe to be the dynasty of Jupiter, a revolutionary spirit seems to have manifested itself in the body politic of Atlantis. "In the course of time," says Plato, "the vicissitudes of human affairs corrupted little by little their divine institutions, and they began to comport themselves like the rest of the children of men. They hearkened to the promptings of ambition, and sought to rule by violence. Then Zeus, the King of the gods, beholding this race once so noble, growing depraved, resolved to punish it, and by sad experience to moderate its ambition."

It is here that Plato's account in the *Critias* ends, and I believe it to have remained unfinished because of his death. I also believe that he could have told us much more about Atlantis had he survived to elaborate his account of it. The passage in question applies, in my view, not to the events which prefaced the final catastrophe, but to that part of Atlantean history in which the spirit of revolution first reared its head. Saturn, the miserly and anti-religious occupant of the throne, had evidently aroused popular feeling against his policy, or the lack of it, and had estranged not only his subjects, but his heir. The latter probably headed a public revolt against the aged tyrant, who, unable to obtain the assistance of his subjects, had recourse to the older autochthonous stock of Aurignacians. There was, says Diodorus, a battle, in which he and his allies were defeated, and he was hurled from power.

But the Atlanteans, formerly pacific and law-abiding, had now become inoculated with the fever of party strife. Bad feeling must have been maintained between the opposing factions, even after peace had been nominally secured, and its results were probably to be witnessed in a general state of political unrest and popular disorganisation. It was evidently at this stage that Zeus—through the mouthpiece of his priesthood, of course—issued a general warning to the contending parties. They were probably told by the hierophants that a council of the gods had been convoked by the Allfather, at which their conduct had been condemned. After that all is darkness, so far as Plato is concerned. But there is little doubt that his account would have narrated the terms of the god's strictures and warnings, and have proceeded to acquaint us with its results, which, I believe, would have informed us of the manner in which revolution at home was put an end to by the politic resolve of the governing bodies, royal and spiritual, to divert the public attention to conquest abroad—a policy which ended in the great invasion of Europe recorded by Plato in his *Timæus*, and by archæology as the invasion of the Azilians.

It was probably in the reign of the King of Altantis, known as "Jupiter" that the decision to invade Europe was arrived at for the reason given above. But that the invasion in question was not the first, is made clear by the statement of Plato that the Kings of Atlantis "governed Libya as far as Egypt, and Europe to the borders of Etruria." This, as I have shown, corresponds generally to the spread of the Azilian or proto-Iberian race, but certainly not to that of the Crô-Magnon, from which we may infer that the Azilian people had made good their footing in Europe and Africa some time previously to their mass invasion of those regions.

Now it is strange, but nevertheless true, that for corroboration of the conditions of Atlantis at this particular era we are compelled to turn to a source which might in some ways appear the most unlikely to provide us with the proofs we require, yet which, when once it is carefully considered, we are bound to recognise as affording us precisely the desired measure of confirmation. I speak of the ancient literature of Britain and Ireland, the Welsh Triads and the Irish sagas and folk-romances. In the first especially we receive the fullest and most astonishing clues to the Atlantean history of the period in question. Before pursuing it farther, let us examine this data and glean from it the testimony which it undoubtedly contains regarding the obscure details of Atlantean chronicle.

CHAPTER IX

ATLANTIS IN BRITAIN

IN the ancient books of Wales and Ireland there exist traditions which, if compared with the myth of Atlantis, cannot be accounted for by any other theory than that they were originally derived from it. The traditional material in the ancient books of Wales which deals with the subject of lands submerged by cataclysm is of such extent that to contain it in its entirety an entire volume would be necessary. Before attempting a justification of the theory that the flood-legends of Wales relate to the Atlantean catastrophe, we may, perhaps, examine a few of the better known of these.

In the book of Caradoc, of Nantgarvan, which dates from the twelfth century, and the book of Jevan Brechva, Thomas Jones of Tregarn, in 1601, found certain of the verses known as the Triads of the Isle of Britain. These were printed by the Rev. Edward Davies in his *Celtic Researches* (London 1804). Under the caption of "The Three Awful Events of the Isle of Britain," we read that these consisted of:

"First, the bursting of the lake of waters, and the overwhelming of the face of all lands, so that all mankind were drowned, excepting Dwyvan and Dwyvach, who escaped in a naked vessel (without sails) and from them the Island of Britain was re-peopled.

"The second was the consternation of the tempestuous fire, when the Earth split asunder, to Annwn (the lower region) and the greatest part of all living was consumed.

"The third was the scorching summer, when the woods and plants were set on fire by the intense heat of the Sun, and multitudes of men and beasts and kinds of birds, and reptiles, and trees, and plants were irrecoverably lost."

The deluge alluded to in the first triad was the bursting of the Lake of Llyn Llion. Practically the same story is recounted of Llyn Tegid, near Bala, in Merionethshire, and, as the late Sir John Rhys remarked, "probably all the other lakes of Wales were supposed to have had inhabitants wealthy in herds of cattle, and in our time each mere is supposed to have been formed by the subsidence of a city, whose bells may even now be at times heard merrily pealing."

That the memory of a submerged land should be so universal in Wales surely indicates a tradition most ancient and deep-seated. "The Druids," says Davies[1] "represent the deluge under the figure of a lake, called Llyn Llion, the waters of which burst forth and overwhelmed the face of the whole earth. Hence they regarded a lake as the just symbol of the deluge. But the deluge itself was viewed, not merely as an instrument of punishment to destroy the wicked inhabitants of the globe, but also as a divine lustration, which washed away the bane of corruption and purified the earth for the reception of the just ones, or of the deified patriarch and his family. Consequently, it was deemed peculiarly sacred, and communicated its distinguishing character to those lakes and bays by which it was locally represented."

The Lake of Llion, then, in the minds of the Welsh of the twelfth century, stood for a mythic symbol of deluge and catastrophe by water. Of a somewhat different class is the tradition of the Cantref of Gwaelod, or the "Submerged Hundred," which recounts how the Plain

[1] *Mythology of the British Druids*, p. 142.

of Gwyddneu was drowned. "This," says Professor Lloyd,[1] "first makes its appearance in a poem in the Black Book of Carmarthen (53b, 54a), written in the last part of the book, and, therefore, about 1200. This poem has often been translated; there is, for instance, an English version in Meyrick's 'History of Cardiganshire' (2), 153, and a modern Welsh one in *Cymru Eu* (p. 6). The best is, however, the most recent, that of Sir J. Rhys in the 'Cymmrodorion Transactions' for 1892-3 (pp. 14-16), from which it appears that the Plain of Gwyddneu was overwhelmed by the sea by reason of the wickedness of its inhabitants, who had given themselves up to eating and drinking and insolent pride of heart. The person who let loose this judgment upon the land was a maiden, perhaps called Margaret ('Mererid'), who at a time of feasting suffered the waters of a magical well which was under her charge to escape and overflow the country round. . . . Such was the primitive story; it is supplemented in one point by the compiler of the earliest form of the *Pedigrees of the Saints* (also dating from about 1200), who speaks of five 'Saints' as sons of King Seithennin of the Plain of Gwyddno, whose realm was swallowed up by the sea. For the germ of the modern legend, which is in many ways a very different one, we have to look to the third series of Triads, belonging to the sixteenth century; the third of the Three Arrant Drunkards of Britain (a festive group unknown to the older triadic literature) is there said to be Seithennin, the Drunken, King of Dyfed, who, in his cups, let the sea loose over the Lowland Hundred, a region of fair cities and the patrimony of Gwyddno Garanhir, King of Ceredigion. The well-maiden has now disappeared, Seithennin has become the author of the mischief, and the drowned kingdom is no longer his, but that of his neighbour

[1] *History of Wales*, p. 25, note.

Gwyddno. But the famous embankment has still to be introduced into the story. It was to the antiquary Robert Vaughan of Hengwrt (1592--1667) that the idea first occurred of connecting the story of the Lowland Hundred with the natural causeway near Harlech called by the peasantry, in that age as in this, 'Sarn Badrig' or St. Patrick's Causeway. The popular explanation, no doubt, was that this was the saint's private road home to his beloved Ireland, but for Vaughan it is 'a great stone wall made as a fence against the sea,' which he has no difficulty in supposing to have once been a rampart of the buried realm. Lewis Morris, in the next century, took the same view, and, remembering the poem in the Black Book, added a suggestion of his own, 'that by drunkenness the flood-gates were left open' (*Celtic Remains*, p. 73; cf. p. 390). But one more touch was needed to give the narrative its modern form; the business of the flood gates must be specially laid at the door of Seithennin, who must play the part of the drunken lockman. This is done in Owen's *Cambrian Biography* (1803); under the patronage of so influential a student of Welsh antiquities, the story as thus rounded off won great popularity and furnished an attractive theme for literary treatment. Englishmen were made familiar with it by the fascinating pages of *The Misfortunes of Elphin*; for Welshmen it was vigorously told in the verse of Hiraethog and Ieuan Glan Geirionydd."

Davies quotes the record of the catastrophe as given in the Triads: "'Seithinin, the Drunkard, the son of Seithin Saidi, King of Dyved, in his liquor let in the sea, over Cantre'r Gwaelod, so as to destroy all the houses and lands of the place, where prior to that event, there had been sixteen cities, the best of all the towns and cities of Wales, excepting Caerleon upon Usk. This district was the dominion of Gwyddnaw Garanhir, King of Cardigiawn.

The event happened in the time of Emrys, the sovereign. The men who escaped the inundation came to land in Ardudwy, in the regions of Arvon, and in the mountains of Snowdon, and other places which had hitherto been uninhabited.'

"This is, undoubtedly, the substance of an old Mabinogi, or mythological tale, and ought not to be received as authentic history. For, in the first place, Cardigan Bay did exist in the time of Ptolemy, who marks the promontories by which it is circumscribed, and the mouths of the rivers which it receives, in nearly the same relative situations which they retain at present. But neither Ptolemy, nor any other ancient geographer, takes notice of one of those sixteen cities, which are said to have been lost there in the sixth century.

"In the next place, we know enough of the geography of Wales, both ancient and modern, to form a decisive conclusion, that a single Cantrev or hundred, never did contain sixteen towns, which would bear the slightest comparison with Caerleon, such as it was in the supposed age of Gwyddno.

"Again: the incident is generally represented as having happened, in consequence of someone having neglected to close a sluice; a cause inadequate, surely, to the alleged effect. And the omission is imputed to a son of Seithin Saidi, King of Dyved, a character whom we have already traced into the regions of mythology."

This legend is, of course, nothing more or less than a Welsh version of the legend of Ys, the submerged city of Brittany, the story of which is told in my *Legends of Brittany*;[1] or it would probably be more correct to say that both tales have a common origin, and are deeply embedded in the Celtic tradition of the past. Be it noted moreover that both agree with the Atlantis tradition in the circum-

[1] pp. 184–88.

stance that the land was overwhelmed in consequence of the wickedness of its inhabitants.

A similar story is told of Lake Savadda in Brecknockshire, which is retailed by Davies as follows: [1]

"The site of the present lake was formerly occupied by a large city; but the inhabitants were reported to be very wicked. The king of the country sent his servant to examine into the truth of this rumour, adding a threat, that, in case it should prove to be well founded, he would destroy the place as an example to his other subjects. The minister arrived at the town in the evening. All the inhabitants were engaged in riotous festivity, and wallowing in excess. Not one of them regarded the stranger or offered him the rites of hospitality. At last, he saw the open door of a mean habitation, into which he entered. The family had deserted it to repair to the scene of the tumult, all but one infant, who lay weeping in the cradle. The royal favourite sat down by the side of this cradle, soothed the little innocent, and was grieved at the thought that he must perish in the destruction of his abandoned neighbours. In this situation the stranger passed the night; and whilst he was diverting the child he accidentally dropped his glove into the cradle. The next morning he departed before it was light, to carry his melancholy tidings to the king.

"He had but just left the town when he heard a noise behind him, like a tremendous crack of thunder mixed with dismal shrieks and lamentations. He stopped to listen. Now it sounded like the dashing of waves; and presently all was dead silence. He could not see what had happened, as it was still dark, and he felt no inclination to return into the city: so he pursued his journey till sunrise. The morning was cold. He searched for his gloves, and, finding but one of them, he presently recollected

[1] *Mythology*, pp. 146–47.

where he had left the other. These gloves had been
a present from his sovereign. He determined to return
for that which he had left behind. When he was come
near to the site of the town, he observed, with sur-
prise, that none of the buildings presented themselves
to his view, as on the preceding day. He proceeded a
few steps. The whole plain was covered with a lake.
Whilst he was gazing at this novel and terrific scene, he
remarked a little spot in the middle of the water; the
wind gently wafted it towards the bank where he stood;
as it drew near, he recognized the identical cradle in which
he had left his glove. His joy on receiving this pledge
of royal favour was only heightened by the discovery
that the little object of his compassion had reached the
shore alive and unhurt. He carried the infant to the
king, and told his majesty that this was all which he had
been able to save out of that wretched place.

"This little narrative evidently contains the substance
of one of those tales, which we call *Mabinogion*, that is,
tales for the instruction of youth in the principle of
Bardic mythology. And it seems to have for its object
a local and impressive commemoration of the destruction
of a profligate race by the waters of the deluge.

"Such traditions of the submersion of cities in the
lakes of the country, or of populous districts, by the
intrusion of the sea, are current all over Wales."

These legends are obviously not accounts of actual
historical occurrences, but memories of some far-distant
catastrophe which overtook the Celtic race in another
environment.

In the poem of the bard Taliesin, called "The Spirits
of the Deep,"[1] Arthur, in his mythological character, is
alluded to in connection with a great deluge or similar
catastrophe. The composition in question is obscure in

---

[1] See Davies, *Mythology*, p. 513, ff.

verbiage and import, and evidently, as Turner observes, "involved in mythology." Davies believed the poem to allude "to the mysteries of the British Bacchus and Ceres," which were connected with "diluvian mythology," but admits that "another hand might be more dexterous in moving the rusty wards which guard these mysteries." The poem states that "Thrice the number that would have filled Prydwen (Arthur's ship) we entered into the deep; excepting seven, none have returned to Caer Sidi" (Place of the Circle).

The second stanza of this mysterious song proceeds to praise the lore "which was four times reviewed in the quadrangular enclosure." "We went," it concludes, "with Arthur in his splendid labours."

Farther on, the bard sings: "In the quadrangular enclosure, in the island with the strong door, the twilight and the pitchy darkness were mixed together."

This passage and that which precedes it, appear to me to enshrine a vivid memory of the Altantean tradition. The reader will recollect that, in Plato's account, the city of Atlantis was said to be divided into zones or circles of land and water, and in a previously published work, *The Problem of Atlantis*, I brought a great deal of proof to bear that the circular plan of Atlantis was copied in many subsequent city-sites. The passage which summed up these resemblances is as follows:—

"Starting then from a knowledge of the Atlantean design as described in Plato, we find that is reflected not only in that of Carthage, but in numerous other ancient sites scattered over the length and breadth of those areas where we might expect to find architectural remains approximating to the Atlantean model—on the one hand along the entire stretch of the Mediterranean, and on the other along the sea-coasts of the Western Atlantic to Britain and Ireland. It will not serve to regard them

as arising in historical succession from east to west. The
Iberians, the builders of these venerable monuments,
did not originate in the eastern region of the Mediterranean,
so that it is impossible to regard that sphere as the
starting-point of their architectural history."

The fifth stanza of this weird lay also casts further light
upon its Atlantean significance:—

"I will not redeem the multitudes with trailing shields.
They knew not on what day the stroke would be given,
nor what hour in the serene day Cwy (the agitated person)
would be born, or who prevented his going into the dales
of Devwy (the possession of the water). They know
not the brindled ox with the thick head-band, having
seven score knobs in his collar."

This obviously refers to the populace of a country
unconsciously awaiting the shock of catastrophe by
deluge. As regards the allusion to the ox, "in almost
every British memorial of the deluge" writes Davies,
"the ox is introduced." The ox or bull was, it will be
recalled, the sacred animal worshipped in Atlantis.

The song quoted above evidently refers to the escape from
deluge of a company of persons under the leadership of the
mythological Arthur. These were, it would seem, the leaders
or aristocracy of the island alluded to, who had little or no
anxiety for the populace, and saved themselves by flight. The
circular or quadrangular nature of the city they abandoned
is mentioned, and it is hinted that from it they carried with
them the memory and apparatus of their sacred mysteries.

But do we find in the ancient Welsh traditions any
reminiscences more definite of the lost Atlantis, reminiscences which would justify us in saying that our British
forefathers associated the tradition of a submerged country
with a region in the Atlantic? These appear to be indicated
in the legends relating to Arthur and Lyones or Lyonesse,
and the Isle of Avallon.

In the first place it is clear that the Lake Llion, whose legend we have already discussed, is nothing more or less than a legend of oceanic submergence adapted to a Welsh locality—that indeed the traditions relating to Lake Llion and Lyonesse have a common origin. Nor will it be difficult to prove that Lake Llion, Lyonesse, Avallon and Atlantis are merely names for one and the same oceanic locality.

Let us examine first the traditions associated with the Isle of Avallon. The site of Avallon was regarded by the Celts of Britain as lying in the western ocean. The name has been explained as implying Insula Pomorum, or the Isle of Apples, although the spelling of the word with two "lls" rather seems to signify "Isle of Apple Trees." By Geoffrey of Monmouth it was equated with the dragon-guarded Isle of the Hesperides.[1] A similar account of it is given by an anonymous poet cited in Ian Morti's edition of Geoffrey (pp. 425-6) the verses being ascribed by Usher to the British bard Gildas. From internal evidence in these poems and from William of Malmesbury, it appears that the Insula Avallonia or Ynys Avallach signified the island belonging to a King Avallach, who resided there with his daughter. This Avallach is identified by the Harleian MS as the son of Beli and Annu, and by Rhys with Evalach, the wounded Fisher King of the Grail Legend.

Atlantis, it is needless to say, has been again and again identified with the Island of the Hesperides which contained the sacred apples, so that the association of Avallon with that insular paradise equates the British with the Platonic locality, and Avallon stands revealed as the Atlantis of Plato. If the equation be justified, we must then be prepared to find in Avallach, the King of the island,

---

[1] *Vita Merlina.* (Roxburghe Club edition, London 1830, 11, 908–17 (p. 41).

Atlas in his British form, and in Beli and Annu, his parents, the Greek Poseidon and Cleito of the Platonic tradition.

Seeking for the moment for further associations between the localities of Avallon and Atlantis, before we deal with their respective rulers and inhabitants, we find in the legend of the "Revolving Castle" entered by Peredur, an incident peculiarly Atlantean. This is to be found in the Welsh Seint Greal.[1] The passage runs thus:—

"And they rode through the wild forests, and from one forest to another until they arrived on clear ground outside the forest. And then they beheld a castle coming within their view on level ground in the middle of a meadow; and around the castle flowed a large river, and inside the castle they beheld large spacious halls with windows large and fair. They drew nearer towards the castle, and they perceived the castle turning with greater speed than the fastest wind they had ever known. And above on the castle they saw archers shooting so vigorously that no armour would protect against one of the discharges they made. Besides this, there were men there blowing in horns so vigorously, that one might think one felt the ground tremble. At the gates were lions, in iron chains, roaring and howling so violently that one might fancy the forest and the castle uprooted by them."

This Revolving Castle Rhys unhesitatingly equates with the Castle of the Grail, the abode of the Fisher King. We find this mysterious stronghold mentioned also in one of the poems of Taliesin, in which he says:

"Perfect is my chair in Caer Sidi:
    Plague and age hurt him not who's in it
They know, Manawydan and Pryderi.
    Three organs round a fire sing before it,
And about its points are ocean's streams,
    And the abundant well above it,
    Sweeter than white wine the drink in it."

Ed Williams, p. 325–6 (translation p. 649).

The name "Caer Sidi" signifies "revolving place," and is identified by Rhys with the "Revolving Castle." We will recall that this Caer Sidi was alluded to as the insular locality abandoned by Arthur and his companions on the occurrence of a deluge. This, therefore, identifies the Revolving Castle with an oceanic locality once over-whelmed by deluge. The circumstance of the legend seem to associate it with a locality prone to cataclysm, and on the whole we appear to have an indubitable memory of the Atlantean site. It is situated "on level ground in the middle of a plain or meadow," as was Atlantis, and, like it, is surrounded by a "mighty ditch or fosse." The ground trembles and the castle whirls as if in the throes of an earthquake. The lions which surround it typify the natural forces of destruction. It is, according to the poem, of an insular character. "About it are ocean's streams." "The word used," says Rhys, "is *banneu* or *ban*" (meaning points) and this connects the place with the Benwyk of Arthurian romance, the island kingdom of King Ban. It also implies that it had four corners or angles, which seems to associate it with the "Isle of the Four Precious Walls" in the Irish saga of "The Voyage of Maeldune." These walls met in the centre, and consisted respectively of gold, silver, copper and crystal. This is Atlantis over again, the walls of which were constructed of gold, silver and orichalcum or copper. Let us compare Plato's account with that in the Welsh Seint Greal.

(1) In the Welsh account Peredur rode through wild forests, "from one forest to another." Plato says that the country surrounding Atlantis was deeply afforested.

(2) The Revolving Castle is situated on level ground in the middle of a meadow. Atlantis was built "on a level plain."

(3) Around the Revolving Castle "flowed a large river."
"The plain," says Plato, "was encompassed by a mighty
ditch or fosse, which received the mountain streams and
the outflow of the canals."

(4) Caer Sidi is "The Revolving or Circular Place."
Atlantis was also built in circular form.

(5) "I will not redeem the multitudes with trailing
shields," says the singer in "The Spoils of the Deep" of
the people of Caer Sidi. The landowner in Atlantis, says
Plato, "was bound to furnish the sixth part of a war-
chariot, so as to make up ten thousand chariots, two
horses and riders upon them, a light chariot without a
seat, and an attendant and charioteer, two heavily-armed
infantrymen, two archers, two slingers, three stone-
shooters, three javelin-men, and four sailors, to make up
the complement of twelve hundred ships."

(6) "They" (the multitudes, the plebeians) "know not
the brindled ox with the thick head-band." "Near the
temple of Poseidon in Atlantis," says Plato, "grazed the
sacred bulls, and these the ten kings of the island periodically offered up in sacrifice. . . . They put on azure robes
and judged offenders." They were, in short, an aristocracy of the cult of the bull or ox, unknown to the
multitude.

Perhaps these comparisons render more clear the
Atlantean origins of the Welsh legends of Caer Sidi and
Avallon, and we may now proceed to examine still other
British myths which deal with insular or submerged
localities in the hope of finding further evidence.

In Celtic folklore there stands out, almost pre-emi-
nently, the figure of Morgan le Fay, the fata, fate or fairy
associated with the sea. She is, says Rhys, the same as
that Morgan who, in the Isle of Avallon, had the charge

of healing Arthur of his wounds, and is the Lady of the Lake, the foster-mother of Launcelot, the imprisoner of Merlin. Morgan means "the offspring of the sea," and we may take it that she represents the ocean in its phase of the great abysm of forgetfulness or oblivion. *Mor* is Welsh for "the sea," and perhaps Morgan represents that sea which Pliny in his *Natural History* tells us the dead had to pass to reach the realm of King Cronus, or Time. The sea to the Celts was indeed the pathway to the Other-world, a notion which is to be encountered in many mythologies, and the Celtic Place of the Dead is invariably located in the Western Ocean. Thus it appears probable that the place to which all souls were supposed to depart after death was associated with a locality formerly inhabited by the living, the Place of the Ancestors, the original home. Early man invariably believed that after death he would join his ancestors in an environment of un-terrestrial bliss, and elsewhere I have collected so many myths and legends to show that this idea was connected in some cases with submerged localities that it scarcely appears needful to traverse the ground once more.

In the first place, let us enumerate these localities, other than those already mentioned, which the Celts of Britain believed to have been submerged. Some of them were actually to be found in Wales itself. Thus Llyn Tegid, near Bala, in Merioneth, is of this class. Indeed, Rhys has placed it on record that, "in our time each mere is supposed to have been formed by the subsidence of a city whose bells may even now be at times heard merrily pealing." This proves at least that the idea of submerged lands had taken a strong hold upon the imagination of the Celts of Britain. Wherefore? Myths of this class do not spring up "naturally," but can be shown to have had a long traditional genealogy behind them, and in the event to have originated in some historical fact.

The overflowing of coastal tracts by the sea is also an extension of this tradition of submergence. In some cases, of course, this may actually have occurred, but in others it appears to be nothing but a localisation of a much more ancient tradition of submerged oceanic localities. The legend of the "Bottom Hundred" has already been cited. Akin to it is that of the sunken city of Aberdovey, the bells of which can be heard ringing in Gwydno's realm. Says Rhys: "The Euhemeristic account of the submersion of Gwydno's plain is that it occurred in consequence of the neglect of a certain Seithennyn, whose business it was to take care of the embankments and their flood-gates; he, one day heavy with drink, forgot all about his charge, and the catastrophe took place. The oldest account, however, is contained in a short poem in the *Black Book of Carmarthen;* and it is by no means such a commonplace story: for the author of the poem knows nothing of Seithennyn's drunkenness, as he merely characterises him as a person of weak intellect, while he lays the entire blame on a damsel whom he terms the Well Minister or Fountain Servant. What her duties exactly were we are not told; but she had probably the charge of a magic well, as in the corresponding Irish story of Lough Neagh . . . in which the neglect to keep the lid on the magic spring resulted in an inundation, a catastrophe foretold by the idiot of the family, who occupies there the place of Seithennyn in the Welsh version. Now, the name of the woman who had charge of the well in the Irish story was Liban, which is in Welsh Llion, and occurs in the Welsh account of the deluge resulting from the bursting of Llyn Llion, or Llion's Lake. Further, it is this lady's name probably in some one of its forms, or a derivative from it, that meets us in Malory's *Liones*." The genius of this country is a Dame Liones, the owner of a Castle Perilous hard by the Isle of Avallon. Rhys attaches her country to the West Coast of Cornwall, "lying somewhere *under the sea* between Lundy and the Isles of Scilly. . . . Without dwelling," he says, "on the probable extreme antiquity of the myths underlying these romances, one may venture to point out that we seem to have evidence, dating from the early portion of the Roman occupation of this country, to the equation of some such a hero as Tristram or Lancelot with the Heracles of classical mythology; witness the fact that Ptolemy calls Hartland Point, Herakleous Akron, or the Promontory of Heracles."

The name Liones or Lyonesse, of course, equates with that of the mythical lake, Llyn Llion, which was supposed to have overwhelmed the world in its bursting, and, as has already been mentioned, it can also be associated with the sunken Land of Ys, of Breton legend. But it also seems to me to have an etymological as well as a traditional connection with Atlantis. Indeed, I believe the name Atlantis to be merely a Hellenized version of the Celtic Llyn Llion or Lyonesse, just such, indeed, as the Greeks would give to a Celtic name. Take Llyn Llion, pronounced as most non-Celtic people would pronounce it (Lin Lion) and join to it the Greek ending "is," with the letter "t" added for the sake of euphony. One gets Lin-Lion-tis, Linliontis. It would seem then, that through some such association of the god Atlas with this Western locality, and through the confusion and Hellenisation of the name Llyn Llion, the name Atlantis may have arisen. Or may not the names Llyn Llion and Atlantis proceed from a common root?

Atlas can readily enough be associated with the gods of Britain. He was of the Titan breed, and the brother of Albion, who, like him, was a son of Poseidon. Albion was the original tutelary god of Britain. Both Atlas and Albion contested the western passage of Heracles. According to Pomponius Mela, Albion with his brother

Iberius (the god of Ireland) the sons of Poseidon, challenged and fought the Greek demi-god near Arles. Albion is also that Alba, from which Scotland takes her name of Albany. There was thus a family or gens of Titans connected with the Western Ocean, and if Albion and Iberius can be associated with the British Isles, to which, indeed, their names still powerfully adhere, it is only reasonable to assume that Atlas was also once the tutelary divinity of a Western land in the ocean with which myth persistently connects his name. Albion (Britain), Iberius (Ireland), Atlas (Atlantis). The sequence is precise, and it is hard to believe that if the two former names were attached to islands still extant that the third can be regarded as the deity of a locality which existed only in the mythical imagination, especially as the personages alluded to had the same progenitor, and all belonged to one and the same gens. There is no example in mythical history of a clan of ancestral figures issuing from one eponymous ancestor, some members of which were attached to actual, and the rest to mythical localities. Search the pages of the Old Testament, the Rig-Veda, the Eddas—any body of traditional writings which supply ancestral genealogies—and nowhere in their pages can such an anomaly be encountered.

Let us examine the Greek myth of Geryon, lord of an Atlantic isle, which has Celtic equivalents. Geryon was the ruler of the island of Erytheia, and was furnished with three heads, and a corresponding number of hands and feet. He was the owner of numerous herds of magnificent cattle of a purple-red colour which grazed near the Lands of the Sun, that is in the West, for his isle of Erytheia was situated in the Western Ocean, beyond the Pillars of Heracles, and enjoyed a salubrious climate. Heracles, in the course of his labours, sailed to the island in the golden bowl of the Sun, or the vessel in which the Sun was imagined to float back to the east during the night hours.

On landing in the island Heracles was attacked by Geryon's dog, Orthus, and his herdsman Eurytion, and slew both. Geryon, hearing of this, hastened after Heracles and attacked him, but was likewise slain by the hero, who then drove the cattle to the shore, and, with his horned spoil and Geryon's daughter, safely embarked in the golden bowl.

In almost precisely the same manner, Cuchulainn, the Irish Heracles, carries off the cows and daughter of King Mider of the Inis Fer Falga or Island of the Men of Falga. But more to the point is the circumstance that both Geryon and Mider, who resided in Atlantic islands, were, like the Atlanteans, possessed of a herd of sacred cattle.

We see, then, that the Atlantic island of British Celtic myth is in many of its circumstances the parallel of Atlantis. Not only is it an insular locality, but it boasted a city, Caer Sidi, which was built, like Atlantis, in circular form, surrounded by a great fosse, or canal, garrisoned by heavily-armed infantrymen, and its worship was connected in some manner with sacred cattle. We know, too, that it was thought of as having been overwhelmed by a flood or other cataclysm of nature.

The native myths of Britain contain further references to cataclysmic insular disturbances than those already referred to and associated more with volcanic or seismic upheaval than with flood. Plutarch in his *De Defectu Oraculorum* alludes to one of them as follows: "Demetrius further said, that of the islands around Britain many lie scattered about uninhabited, of which some are named after deities and heroes. He told us also that, being sent by the emperor with the object of reconnoitring and inspecting, he went to the island which lay nearest to those uninhabited, and found it occupied by a few inhabitants, who were, however, sacrosanct and inviolable in the eyes of the Britons. Soon after his arrival a great disturbance of the atmosphere took place, accompanied by many portents, by the winds bursting forth into hurricanes, and by fiery bolts falling. When it was over, the islanders said that some one of the mighty had passed away. For as a lamp on being lit, they said, brings with it no danger, while on being extinguished it is grievous to many, just so with regard to great souls, their beginning to shine forth is pleasant and the reverse of grievous, whereas the extinction and destruction of them frequently disturbs the winds and the surge as at present; oftentimes also do they infect the atmosphere with pestilential diseases. Moreover there is there, they said, an island in which Cronus is imprisoned with Briærus keeping guard over him as he sleeps, for, as they put it, sleep is the bond forged for Cronus. They add that around him are many deities, his henchmen and attendants."

Now this myth is of great importance from more than one point of view. In the first place it refers to "islands around Britain," many of which are called after gods and heroes. Man and Skye, for example are so named. But some were uninhabited. Why? In all probability because at that period such volcanic or seismic disturbances as that described in the above passage were of constant occurrence. The islanders believed these storms and eruptions to be connected in some manner with the dead, that is, with those who dwelt in the West. Further, the allusion to Cronus as being imprisoned in a still more distant island "with Briaerus keeping guard over him as he sleeps," is, as Rhys justly remarks, a parallel with the sleep of Arthur in Avallon, the island which I have already shown to be in all likelihood one and the same with Atlantis. Nennius, too, describes how Benlli, a giant, having resisted St. Germanus, was, together with his entire

court, burnt to ashes by fire from heaven. Now Benlli
is also associated with the island of Ynys Benlli, or Bardsey,
the locality in which Merlin disappeared in his house or
ship of glass, and it too has been equated with Avallon.

Thus we find practically all the broader and more
general circumstances of Plato's account of Atlantis
duplicated in British tradition—the belief in the submergence of a former insular marine locality situated in
the West, its destruction by flood, volcanic or seismic
agency, its possession of a city built in a certain peculiar
manner, and having a religious cult connected with cattle.
The inevitable conclusion is that Atlantean refugees or
emigrants who had come closely in touch with them,
must at some period have settled on British soil, and that
the impression of the great catastrophe which had befallen
their ancestors in the Atlantean continent remained
undisturbed for centuries, acquiring a literary and religious
significance which mere legend could never have achieved.

A study of Irish traditional lore also makes it clear that
numerous Atlantean memories are enshrined therein.
The Formorians of Irish legend were the Domnu, people
of the deep sea, or Fomors, People of the Under Sea, of
the country which had sunk beneath the waves. Like
the Titans, they were a people of gigantic stature, and,
like them, they waged war upon the gods, the Tuatha
De Danann.

The Fenians, another early Irish race, were associated
by tradition with the region about the Pillars of Hercules.
Fenius Forsa, their eponymous ancestor, was the father
of Nial, who married Scota, daughter of the Pharaoh of
Egypt. Fenius and his clan were banished from Egypt
for refusing to join in the persecution of the Children of
Israel and sojourned in Africa for forty-two years. They
travelled through Canaan "near the altars of the Philis-
tines," then passed between Rusicada and the hilly

country of Syria until they came to Mauretania as far as the Pillars of Hercules, when they crossed into Spain.

Mile, leader of the Milesians of Spain, the Tuatha De Danann, was, with his people, exiled to an over-sea paradise in the west, described variously as "The Land of Promise," "The Plain of Happiness," "The Land of the Young," and "Breasal's Island." "Celtic Mythology," says Squire, "is full of the beauties of this mystic country, and the tradition of it has never died out. Hy-Breasail has been set down in old maps as a reality again and again."[1]

The romance of the *Fate of the Children of Turenn* is replete with obvious allusions to the Atlantean tradition. The sons of Turenn were doomed, for the slaying of Kian, to procure certain magical objects, and setting sail in Manannan's Boat, they came first to the Garden of Hisberna (Hesperides) where they took the shape of hawks, and seized upon the golden apples which grew there. After other adventures, they landed in the realm of Asol, King of the Golden Pillars, from whom they received seven magical swine. The pillars in question appear to be the Pillars of Hercules.

The legend of the overflowing of Lough Neagh has already been alluded to as almost precisely the same as the Welsh tale of Seithennyn, but the saga of "The Voyage of Maildun" refers to a number of magical islands in the Atlantic and can scarcely be regarded as anything else than a direct folk-memory of the Atlantean group. One of the first islands which Maildun and his crew encountered was "The Terraced Isle of Birds." It was "a large, high island, with terraces all round it, rising one behind another," and populous with bright-plumaged birds, "a shield-shaped island, with terraces crowned." The Atlantides, the daughters of Atlas became, according to

[1] Squire, *Mythology of the British Islands*, p. 133.

Diodorus, the Pleiades, and according to other classical authorities, birds. The height of the island and its terraced character appear to be reminiscent of the Atlantean legend.

In "a broad, flat island," Maildune and his companions discovered "a broad green race-course," which was used by the sea-folk for the sport of horse-racing. Plato tells us that a great race-course existed in Atlantis. They also came to an Island of Apples, resembling the Hesperides, and to an isle surrounded by a great wall, and on the morning of the third day to another island which was divided into two parts by a wall of brass running across the middle. On either side of the wall was a flock of sheep; and all those on one side were black, and on the other white. A very large man (a Cyclops doubtless) was herding the sheep. The next was a high island, divided into four parts by four walls meeting in the centre. The first was a wall of gold, and the others were of silver, copper and crystal. The "Island of the Big Blacksmiths" is also reminiscent of the Cyclops, and the "Country Beneath the Waves" seems to provide the last proof necessary to the acceptance of the theory that the whole saga is nothing else than a folk-memory of the Atlantean tradition.[1]

The Iberian race, which has probably always been in the majority in Ireland, is, of course, the Azilian in a modern form. They were, indeed, the Fomorians, the "Under Sea" people, the folk skilled in magic and the dark sciences. "Eternal battle between the gods, Children of Danu, and the giants, children of Domnu," says Squire, "would reflect, in the supernatural world, the perpetual warfare between invading Celt and resisting Iberian."[2]

---

[1] See Joyce, *Old Celtic Romances*, p. 112 ff.
[2] *Op. cit.* p. 70.

It is noticeable, too, that the Tuatha De Danann, another Irish race, were regarded as having come from "the southern isles of the World." They had dwelt in four great cities, in which they had learned poetry and magic—Findias, Gorias, Murias and Falias, whence they had brought to Ireland their strange culture and certain relics, among others the Lia Fail, or Stone of Destiny (not that at Westminster, as is generally supposed, but that which still stands at Tara). That these cities were actual places seems most probable. It seems unlikely that a people would deliberately concoct names for regions where they had been settled for centuries.

Many folk-memories of an island-home in the Atlantic are found in Irish lore. The legend of St. Brandan, in the Book of Lismore, tells how Brandan, founder of the monastery of Clonfert, who lived in the seventh century, prayed that a "hidden land" might be revealed to him, and an ancient tradition assures us that he wandered up and down the coast of Kerry "seeking for traditions of the Western Continent." For these he cannot have been encouraged to seek unless he already had some inkling of their presence there. Setting sail, he came to an island "under the lee of Mount Atlas," where he sojourned many years.

The legend of the island of Hy Breasil haunted the Irish imagination for centuries, and has been identified with the Tir-nan-og of Gaelic story.

CHAPTER X

THE TRADITIONS OF ATLANTIS

I HAVE traversed the subject of the traditions relating to Atlantis in Europe, Africa and America so frequently, that a mere summary of them must here suffice. Such a summary, however, is essential to a History of Atlantis, which would be incomplete without some reference to the evidence for the former existence of the island continent in both the Old and New Worlds.

And first of the Atlantean tradition in Europe. We have already seen how living a thing it was in Britain and Ireland, and have reviewed Hellenic and other memories of it. Spain had its legend of Antillia or the Isle of Seven Cities, a rectangular island which appears again and again in the maps of the cartographers of the fourteenth, fifteenth and even the sixteenth century, and which Toscanelli advised Columbus to regard as a halfway house to the Indies.[1] It was thought that Roderick, the last of the Gothic Kings of Spain, had there found a refuge from the conquering Moors, remaining, like Arthur, in his island paradise until Spain needed him once again. Some writers even suggested that Antillia was Atlantis itself, and that its quadrilateral shape resembled that of Atlantis as described by Plato. But Humboldt indicated that Plato had ascribed this form to a particular part of Atlantis only, and not to the whole island.

[1] In *The Problem of Atlantis* and *Atlantis in America.*

The Roman historian Timagenes, who flourished in the first century A.D., preserved traditions of the Gauls which spoke of invaders from a sunken island. The Celts of Brittany, like those of Britain, preserved their own version of the Atlantis story in the legend of the sunken city of Ys, or Ker-is, ruled by a prince named Gradlon, who, warned of the approach of the sea, defended his capital from its incursions by constructing an immense basin to receive the overflow of the water at high tide. This basin had a secret outlet, of which Gradlon alone possessed the key, but his malevolent daughter, the Princess Dahut, feasting with her lover, and proceeding from one frivolity to another, stole the key and opened the sluice gate, and the tide rushing in, submerged the city. Ys, which was wealthy in commerce and the arts, was situated where now the Etang de Laval drifts over the desolate Bay of Trespasses, though some think that it now forms the Bay of Douarnenez, and beneath one or other of these watery plains reposes the palace of Gradlon, its marble pillars, cedarn walls and golden roofs for ever hidden from human eyes.

A strange rite preserved the legend of Gradlon in the town of Quimper. Between the towers of the Cathedral there stands a figure of the King mounted on the charger which saved him from the flood. During the French Revolution, however, it was damaged, but restored. The vine, it is said, was introduced into Brittany by Gradlon, and on every Cecilia's Day hymns were sung in his praise, and a golden cup of wine presented to the statue. This was held to its lips and then drunk by the person who offered it. The cup was then cast into the waiting crowd below, and he who caught it received a prize of two hundred crowns.

Behind these ceremonial acts there would seem to have been a background of ancient religious practice. Gradlon is known as Gradlon Meur or "the Great," an appellation reserved only for gods in Celtic mythology. Indeed, he seems to have been Poseidon. Poseidon was the first breaker-in of horses, who taught men to bestride the steed, and was almost invariably represented, like Gradlon, on horseback, or riding in a chariot. His palace closely resembled that of Atlantis. "A strong dike protected it from the ocean." There were gates which opened and closed on the sea-way, as in Atlantis, and his palace was similarly decorated. The people of his city were similarly punished for their wickedness by the submergence of their land. It seems to me that there is little or no difference between the legend of Ys and that of Atlantis. Indeed the very name Ys or Is, as it is frequently spelled, seems merely an abbreviation of that of Atlant-is.

Did land ever exist off the coast of France to such an extent as to give rise to such legends as that of the city of Ys? In the summer of 1925 the world was astonished to learn of the probable existence of land directly off this coast. I give here the best account I can find of this discovery, which appeared in *The New York Times*:

"France may in a few years find her territory extended considerably, if a report of a tremendous rise in the ocean's bottom made by a French officer commanding the army transport *Loiret* is confirmed by official investigation.

"In his report Lieutenant Cornet says that when the *Loiret* was travelling from Cape Ortegal to Rochefort he noted peculiar waves, such as those washing over sandbars, when a hundred miles off shore in the centre of the Gulf of Gascony.

"Consulting his charts and checking his position by the sextant, the Lieutenant found the depths of this area recorded as between 4,000 and 5,000 metres. He decided to make soundings, and over a length of fifty miles found the depths only thirty-four to seventy metres. The ship's pilot also checked the soundings and specimens of the ocean's bottom brought up revealed sand, pebbles and gravel.

"The naval officers are reported as believing this rise, if a rise there is, occurred at the time of the Japanese earthquake in 1923 and of a tidal wave at Penmarch, Brittany, on May 23 last. M. Fichot, Director of the Hydrographic Service of the French Naval Ministry, is more conservative in his statements, and says the lieutenant's observations are worthy of careful study, even though navigation in the Gulf may not be affected by a depth shallower than had been previously thought. He says a naval commission will be sent to the Gulf of Gascony as soon as possible to check up the data and ascertain the size and location of the submarine plateau.

"He does not believe there will be new land, but a submerged bar, of which the wave effect noted is a customary indication. He says it is difficult to know the exact extent of the modifications which have occurred, as the charts of this area are very old and may have been somewhat incorrect. He finds the existence of such a plateau in the Atlantic as strange, however.

"The location given by Lieutenant Cornet centres about 45 degrees 7 minutes north and 3 degrees 57 minutes west—about the same latitude as Bordeaux and longitude as Brest. This is 160 kilometres from the nearest point of the French coast."

Subsequent inquiry has failed to discover the results of the Commission dispatched to the Gulf of Gascony, if any such body was ever sent there.

The legend of Dardanus, whom the Flood overtook in Samothrace, has a close resemblance in certain of its passages to that of Atlantis. The natives of Samothrace, according to Diodorus Siculus, averred that the sea rose and covered a great part of the level country in their island, and that the survivors fled to the high mountainous land beyond.   As a memorial of their salvation from the Deluge they raised landmarks all round the island and built altars on which they continued to sacrifice to the gods for many succeeding generations.   Centuries later, fishermen drew up in their nets the stone capitals of pillars, the eloquent witnesses of cities deep drowned in the surrounding sea.

The myth of Deucalion and the Flood is interesting to students of Atlantean lore, not only because it is a myth of inundation, but also because it has duplicates in American tradition.   According to Lucian, Deucalion was the Noah of the Greek world.   "I have heard in Greece," says Lucian, "what the Greeks say of Deucalion.   The present race of men, they allege, is not the first, for they totally perished, but a second generation, who, being descended from Deucalion, increased to a great multitude.   Of those former men they thus speak—they were insolent and addicted to unjust actions; they neither regarded oaths, nor were they hospitable to strangers, nor listened to suppliants; and this complicated wickedness was the cause of their destruction.   On a sudden the earth poured forth a vast quantity of water, great rains fell, the rivers overflowed, and the sea rose to a prodigious height.   All things became water, and all men were destroyed.   Only Deucalion was left, for a second race of men, on account of his prudence and piety.   He was saved in this manner.   He went into a large ark or chest, and when he was within, there entered swine, horses, lions, serpents, and all other creatures which live on earth, by pairs.   He received them all, and they did him no hurt, for the gods created a friendship among them, so that they all sailed in one chest while the waters prevailed."

Deucalion was saved in a small boat along with his wife Pyrrha.   Consulting the oracle, they were told to "throw behind you the bones of your mighty mother" (i.e. the stones of the earth). Obeying the behest, they found the stones turned into men and women.

We come now to the evidence from American tradition. This is indeed so rich as to be almost embarassing, and is probably so full because of its considerably later origin.

The Muskhogee Indians preserved a myth to the effect that out of the primeval waste of waters arose a great hill, Nunne Chaha, on which was the dwelling of Esaugetuh Emissee, "Master of Breath," who made men from clay, and built a great wall, on which he set them to dry. He then directed the waters into the proper channels. The hill mentioned in this myth appears to be the same as that on which Poseidon raised his dwelling in Atlantis, and the disposal of the waters bears a suspicious resemblance to the sea-god's disposition of sea and land into zones.

Of Manebozho or Michabo, the great god of the Algonquins, it is related that he "carved the land and sea to his liking," and of Tawiscara, a god of the Hurons, that he "guided the torrents into smooth seas and lakes."

But even more striking are the analogous legends of certain Indian tribes of South America. The Antis Indians of Bolivia and North-west Brazil say that the world was visited by a great flood, in which men were forced to take refuge in caves. Volcanic upheavals followed, and humanity was ultimately destroyed. The Macusi tribe of Arawaks tell how the only people who survived the deluge repeopled the earth by changing stones into human beings, as did Deucalion and Pyrrha in the Greek myth. The Tamañacs have a similar myth, in which the survivors were said to have thrown over their heads the fruits of the Mauritius palm, from the kernels of which sprang men and women.

Perhaps one of the most "Atlantean" of American myths is that of the Mundruku, who record that the god

Raimi created the world by placing it in the shape of a flat stone on the head of another deity. This is, of course, merely another form of the Greek myth in which Atlas attempted to relieve himself of the eternal burden of bearing the globe on his shoulders by asking Hercules to hold it for a space. The Caribs believe that their supernatural ancestor sowed the soil with stones, which grew up into men and women, another variant of the Deucalion myth. A legend of the Okanguas states that a great medicine woman ruled over a "lost island," and the Delaware Indians have legends telling of a mighty inundation and a hasty folk-migration in consequence.

The Aztecs of Mexico possessed many traditions which seem to preserve the memory of early cataclysmic events. According to different authorities these had been either four or five in number. The *Codex Vaticanus* states that "in the first age or sun, water reigned until it destroyed the world." This age lasted 4,008 years, and men were changed into fishes. The second age lasted 4,010 years, and terminated with the destruction of the world by violent winds, and the transformation of men into apes. The third ended with fire and the fourth with famine.

The Peruvian god, Pariacaca arrived, as Poseidon had done, in a hilly country. But the people reviled him, and he sent a great flood upon them, so that their village was destroyed. Meeting a beautiful maiden, Choque Suso, who was weeping bitterly, he inquired the cause of her grief, and she informed him that the maize crop was dying for lack of water. He assured her that he would revive the maize if she would bestow her affections on him, and when she consented to his suit he irrigated the land by canals. Eventually he turned his wife into a statue.

Another Peruvian myth recounts that the god Thonapa, angered at the people of Yamquisapa, in the province of Alla-suyu, because they were so bent on pleasure, drowned

their city in a great lake.   The people of this region worshipped a statue in the form of a woman, which stood on
the summit of the hill, Cachapucara.   Thonapa destroyed
both hill and image and disappeared into the sea.

These Peruvian myths bear a close resemblance in detail
to that part of Plato's account which deals with the wooing
of Cleito, the enclosure of the hill, and the making of an
irrigation zone.   The statue of the wife of the god is also
alluded to, and the god himself is described as disappearing
into the sea, as Poseidon might well have done.   The
flood, too, we see, was brought about by the wickedness
or love of pleasure of the human race.

The legends of the Tupi-Guarani of Brazil preserve a
similar tradition to that of Plato, so far as its catastrophic
part is concerned:

"Monan, the Maker, the Begetter, without beginning
or end, author of all that is, seeing the ingratitude of men,
and their contempt for him that had made them thus
joyous, withdrew from them, and sent upon them *tata*, the
divine fire, which burned all that was on the surface of the
earth.   He swept about the fire in such a way that in
places he raised mountains and in others deep valleys.
Of all men, one alone, Irin Magé (the One who Sees),
was saved, whom Monan carried into heaven.   He, seeing
all things destroyed, spoke thus to Monan: 'Wilt thou
also destroy all the heavens and their garniture?   Alas!
henceforth where will be our home?   Why should I live
since there is none other of my kind?'   Then Monan was
so filled with pity that he poured a deluging rain on the
earth, which quenched the fire, and, flowing from all sides,
formed the ocean which we call *partana*, the great waters."

Says Brinton in his *Myths of the New World*, regarding
the American tradition of a deluge:

"How familiar such speculations were to the aborigines
of America there is abundant evidence to show.   The early

Algonkin legends do not speak of an antediluvian race, nor any family who escaped the waters. . . . Nor did their neighbours, the Dakotas, though firm in the belief that the globe had once been destroyed by the waters, suppose that any had escaped. The same view was entertained by the Nicaraguas and the Botocudos of Brazil. . . . The Aschochimi of California told of the drowning of the world so that no man escaped. . . . Much the most general opinion, however, was that some few escaped the desolating element. . . . by ascending some mountain, on a raft or canoe, in a cave, or even by climbing a tree. No doubt some of these legends have been modified by Christian teachings, but many of them are so connected with local peculiarities and ancient religious ceremonies that no unbiassed student can assign them wholly to that source. . . . There are no more common heirlooms in the traditional lore of the red race. Nearly every old author quotes one or more of them. They present great uniformity of outline, and rather than engage in repetitions of little interest they can more profitably be studied in the aggregate than in detail. By far the greater number represent the last destruction of the world to have been by water. A few, however . . . attribute it to a general conflagration which swept over the earth, consuming every living thing except a few who took refuge in a deep cave. . . . There are, indeed, some points of striking similarity between the deluge myths of Asia and America. It has been called a peculiarity of the latter that in them the person saved is always the first man. This, though not without exception, is certainly the general rule. But these first men were usually the highest deities known to their nations, the only creators of the world, and the guardians of the race."

A myth of the Mixtecs, a highly civilised race of Southwestern Mexico, also appears to have a strong Atlantean connection. It says that: "In the days of obscurity and darkness, when there were as yet no days nor years, the world was a chaos sunk in darkness, while the earth was covered with water, on which slime and scum floated. One day the deer-god and goddess appeared. They had human form, and out of their magic they raised a great mountain out of the water and built on it beautiful palaces for their dwelling. These buildings stood in Upper Mixteca, close to the place Apoala (Accumulation of Water) and the mountain which was called "Place Where the Heavens Stood." These deities had twin sons, and all four were skilled in magic. "The deer gods had more sons and daughters, but there came a flood in which many of these perished. After the catastrophe was over, the god who is called the creator of all things formed the heavens and earth and restored the human race."

Here once again we encounter the mountain, the twins, the "accumulation of water" or canals, and the male and female deity dwelling in an enclosed place in undisturbed peace, as did Poseidon and Cleito.

Another Mexican myth relates how the god Tlaloc, the deity of water, raised the earth out of the waters of the deluge. At the festival of the Quaitleloa children were sacrificed to him by drowning. His wife Chalchihuitlicue is represented in a picture in the Aubin M.S. as standing in a torrent down which are borne a man, a woman, and a treasure-chest, intended to portray *otocoa*, or "loss of property," the verbal significance of the symbol being "all will be carried away by water." The picture may be taken as implying a cataclysmic flood occurring in a civilised region. In the Codex Telleriano-Remensis she is alluded to as "the woman who saved herself in the deluge," "the woman who remained after the deluge." Professor Seler sees in her the goddess of change in human affairs, of speedy ruin. Tlaloc and Chalchihuitlicue seem comparable with Poseidon and his Atlantean spouse

Cleito. Tlaloc, like Poseidon, is God of the Sea, and his face, armed with huge tusks, appears to be that of a walrus or similar marine animal. His tunic is the "cloud-garment," and his sandals symbolise the foam of the water. To his paradise after death the drowned and dropsical folk repaired, all, in fact, who perished by the agency of water.

The Mexican myths relating to the god Quetzalcoatl and his people the Toltecs are eloquent of Atlantean reminiscence. Torquemada, in his *Monarquia Indiana* describes the Toltecs as a race clad in robes of black linen, who entered Mexico by way of Panuco, and who settled at Tollan and Cholula. Their chief was one Quetzalcoatl, a man with a long beard and ruddy complexion. They were able handicraftsmen, architects and agriculturists.

A native Mexican historian, Ixtlilxochitl, gives an account of the Toltecs which bears a surprising resemblance to the Platonic story of Atlantis. He tells us that the city of Tollan was a place of magnificent palaces and temples, the kings of which were at first wise and politic, but later gave way to licentious and profligate habits. The provinces rose in revolt, and the gods grew wroth with both King and people because of their selfishness and love of pleasure. Alternate frosts and heats of great severity visited the city, so that the crops perished and the rocks melted, and plagues completed the ruin. It is obvious that no such visitations could have occurred on Mexican soil, where frost is seldom experienced, and it seems probable that the story is a reminiscence of cataclysm in another and more distant sphere, and that the melting rocks are significant of seismic or volcanic outbreaks. This ancient tale, revived from the folk-memory of the Mexicans, appears to have been adapted to explain the political break-up of the Toltec power.

Other myths which have collected round the personality of the god or culture-hero Quetzalcoatl have also an

Atlantean bearing. This personage was regarded both as chief of the immigrant Toltecs of Mexico and the Maya of Central America. The most complete account of Quetzalcoatl is that of Sahagun, who describes the prosperity of Tollan in his day. He was a great culture-bringer, his palaces were magnificent, and in his time the maize-crop was immense. But native sorcerers gave him a draught which awoke in him a strong desire to return to the home in the Atlantic whence he had come. The magicians informed him that he must return to Tollan-Tlapallan across the sea, and this he did in a raft of serpents.

The Codex Telleriano-Remensis says of Quetzalcoatl: "Quetzalcoatl, they say, was he who created the world. And they bestowed upon him the appelation of Lord of the Wind, because they say that Tonacatecutli, when it appeared good to him, breathed and begat Quetzalcoatl, . . . They celebrated a festival on the sign of the four earthquakes to the destroyer with reference to the fate which again waited the world: for they said that it had undergone four destructions and would again be destroyed. He alone had a human body like that of other men. The other gods were of an incorporeal nature. After the deluge the custom of sacrificing commenced. . . . They name him 'One Cane,' which is the star Venus, of which they tell the fable accredited among them. Tlauizcalpan Tecutli is the star Venus, the first created light before the deluge. This star is Quetzalcoatl."

The interpreter of the *Codex Vaticanus A.*, a similar document, says: "He it was, as they say, who caused hurricanes, and in my opinion, was the god who was called Citaladuali, and it was he who destroyed the world by winds. . . . The son of the virgin, Quetzalcoatl, knowing that the vices of men were necessarily the cause of the troubles of the world, determined on asking the goddess Chalchihuitlicue, who is she who remained after the deluge with the man in the tree (ark) and is the mother of the god Tlaloc, whom they have made goddess of water, that they might obtain rain when they stood in need of it. . . . Of Quetzalcoatl they relate that, proceeding on his journey, he arrived at the Red Sea, which is here painted, and which they named Tlapallan, and that on entering into it they saw no more of him nor knew what became of him. . . . They say it was he who effected the reformation of the world by penance, since as, according to his account his father had created the world and men had given themselves up to vice, on which account it had frequently been destroyed, Citinatonali sent his son into the world to reform it. . . . They celebrated a great festival on this sign, as we shall see on the sign of four earthquakes, because they feared that the world would be destroyed in that sign (or date) as he had foretold them when he disappeared in the Red Sea, which event occurred on the same sign."

Now these passages are eloquent of Quetzalcoatl's connection with the tradition of Atlantis. He is connected with an oceanic region east of Mexico, with cataclysm or earthquake, with the story of the Flood, and with the archaic legend that the world had been destroyed because of the wickedness of mankind. The Maya legends present even more striking associations with the Atlantean tradition.

An ancient book in the Maya tongue, destroyed by Nuñez de la Vega, but quoted by him, tells how Votan (the Quiche name of Quetzalcoatl) was commanded to proceed to Mexico to civilise the country. With this intention he left the land of Valum Chivim, and, coming to Central America, founded the city of Palenque. He made several visits to his ancestral home, and left a record of his travels in a temple near the Huehuetan River, known as "The House of Darkness," which Nuñez de la Vega professed to have discovered when he visited Huehuetan in 1691.[1]

That such a civilised race as these legends speak of actually did arrive in Central America is certain. The Maya appeared in that region about 200 B.C. in possession of a fully-developed civilisation, which it must have taken centuries to evolve. There are no signs of its growth on American soil, so we must assume that it came to fruition elsewhere. This alone gives probability to the tradition of Quetzalcoatl's settlement in Central America. Moreover, the Atlantean significance of Quetzalcoatl's myth is clear, as has been indicated. The architecture of Tollan, as described by Ixtlilxochitl and others, bears a striking resemblance to that of Atlantis as described by Plato, the seismic or cataclysmic circumstances are present in both accounts, and the sinfulness of the denizens of both regions is a significant circumstance.

Quetzalcoatl's father was Citallatonali, to whom his son dedicated a special cult. He is represented by the sign *cipactli*, the dragon or whale from which the earth was made, and which rose out of the sea. In Maya myth he is alluded to as "the Old Serpent covered with green feathers, who lies in the ocean." Quetzalcoatl's mother was Citlallinicue or Coatlicue, a name which seems to bear a suspicious resemblance to that of Cleito, the maiden whom Poseidon espoused, and who bore him Atlas and other sons.

Quetzalcoatl can readily be compared with Atlas. In several places in Mexican art he is represented as the earth-bearer, especially in a statuette found in Mexico City, at Chichen-Itzâ and elsewhere. In these he is depicted as bearing the world or the sky upon his head, and Dr. J. H. Spinden, a leading authority on Maya

[1] A full critical account of the Mexican ideas relating to Quetzalcoatl will be found in my *Atlantis in America*, Chapter III, and an exhausted study of him in my " Gods of Mexico."

archæology, has described these figures as "Atlantean," because of their resemblance to the Greek caryatids of Atlas. Like Atlas, too, Quetzalcoatl was a twin, the expression *coatl*, signifying both "snake" and "twin."

The fact that Quetzalcoatl periodically returned to his original home seems to imply that it had not yet been wholly submerged, but that occasional cataclysms had rendered it so unstable that its ruling classes had considered the possibility of settlement elsewhere. A similar condition of things has been recorded by Professor J. Macmillan Brown in his *Riddle of the Pacific*, in which he alludes to the settlement of Hotu Matua, a culture-hero from a sunken region in the Pacific, upon Easter Island. It seems probable, then, that Quetzalcoatl and his people were immigrants from Antillia, the westward portion of the Atlantean continent, which, I believe, long survived the eastern or Atlantean portion proper. I have, as already mentioned, dealt fully with this aspect of Quetzalcoatl's myth elsewhere.

We find, then, that Plato's account of Atlantis by no means stands alone, but has many equivalents in European and American tradition; and that these traditions were drawn from actual colonial settlement in more than one of the regions where they flourished will be seen when we come to deal with the subject of the Atlantean colonies.

CHAPTER XI

LIFE IN ATLANTIS

FROM what has gone before, we should now be able to draw such conclusions as will afford us a reasonably trustworthy picture of life in Atlantis at the period of its last phase—that preceding its final submergence. We have already gleaned some information regarding its conditions during the earlier period, and must now approach its "reconstruction" as a community probably much on the same level of civilisation as was Mexico at the arrival of Cortez, or China before the era of European intervention, with, of course, the exception that its people were unacquainted with metals of any kind.

In the course of centuries the face of the island-continent must have undergone great changes under the civilising agency of a race eminently well fitted for the tasks of advancement. Plato's account speaks of canals more than a thousand miles long and roads which evidently stretched far inland. The circumstance that the country was divided into cantons and that each land-owner was bound by law to furnish his quota of men for the Army and Navy, leads to the assumption that a very considerable part of it was cultivated and that it had also a fairly large sea-faring population. But it can scarcely be doubted that very large tracts of wild and desert region existed, and that, indeed, the greater part of the island was still under those tundra conditions which prevailed in Europe at the era in question. The presence of a great mountain-range must have affected both agriculture and the general climatic conditions, and it is possible that Atlantis must have been densely afforested in parts.

We hear of no other towns or cities excepting the capital, but we cannot doubt that others existed. It is possible to gather a general idea of the style of architecture in vogue, both from the account of Plato, and the researches of the Anglo-Spanish School of Archæology at Huelva in Spain, already alluded to. Plato states that the style of architecture affected by the Atlanteans was "barbaric," and this to a Greek certainly meant "Oriental." He tells us that the exterior of the great temple of Cleito and Poseidon was garnished with silver, that its pinnacles glittered with gold, and that the interior was roofed with ivory, gold, silver and orichalcum, or copper. But in view of a complete ignorance of all metals on the part of the Azilians, such a description is certainly misleading. It is much safer to rely upon the results of the recent Spanish excavations at Huelva, and regard Atlantean architecture as of the "Cyclopean" type, such as is encountered at Mycenæ and elsewhere.

Such buildings are constructed of large blocks of stone accurately squared, with well-fitting beds and joints, but unequal in size. Enormous monoliths were usually employed for gateways. But the term "Cyclopean" is also given to walls constructed of polygonal blocks, which in many cases are fitted together with great skill and care. Examples of this species of masonry exist not only in Greece, but also in many sites in Etruria and America, and there can be no doubt of the extreme antiquity of the method employed.

Examples of this particular kind of architecture are to be encountered in many parts of Europe and Asia, and, indeed, it seems clear that it is nothing more or less than a form of the ancient Atlantean mode of building construction. The people who introduced it to Europe, whence it probably spread eastward, were undoubtedly the proto-Iberians, the "Mediterranean Race" of Sergi, and the earliest sites on which it has been discovered seem to justify the assumption of its introduction from a Western area. It certainly did not progress in historical succession from East to West, as the Iberians, the builders of these venerable monuments, did not originate in the eastern region of the Mediterranean. As much may be said of the rough stone monuments usually associated with Iberian handiwork, the stone circles, menhirs and dolmens of Britain, France and the Iberian Peninsula, the brochs of Scotland, the great stone forts of Ireland, the nuraghi of Sardinia, and the similar talayats of the Balearic Isles. It has also been shown that the rough stone monuments of Portugal are practically all to be found near the Atlantic sea-coast, and very few inland.

I have also shown elsewhere[1] that the general architectural plan of the city of Atlantis, as described by Plato, appears to have been copied far and wide. It is well known that the plan and outline of the great cities of antiquity were frequently carried out in their colonial settlements, and many sites, both in Europe and Africa, appear to have been copied from the Atlantean model. Of these the most outstanding is Carthage, the plan of which is almost identical with that of Atlantis. Indeed, both Atlantis and Carthage had a citadel hill encircled by zones of land and water, a canal to the sea, and bridges over the zones, fortified by towers. In both cases the docks were roofed in, the cities were encircled by three walls, both had great cisterns for the supply of drinking water and baths, and both were guarded by a great sea-wall, masking the entrance to the harbour.

This circular design, "an island within an island," was formerly fairly common in West Africa. Hanno, the

[1] *Problem of Atlantis*, Chaps. II. and XVI.

Carthaginian voyager, discovered such a plan in that region, and it is indubitably found also in America, especially in the ancient plan of the Aztec city of Mexico-Tenochtitlan and elsewhere.

The question of the presence of pyramids in Atlantis also arises. It seems unlikely that they were actually to be found there, but it is probable that the pyramid in Egypt and America is merely a later reminiscence of the sacred hill of Atlantis. In early Egypt, Mexico and Peru certain hills were regarded as especially sacred, as the homes of powerful supernatural beings. In Mexico the mountain was regarded as the home of the Goddess of Fertility, and in some parts of that country it was faced with stone, like the Egyptian pyramid, although in the region inhabited by the Mound Builders of the Mississippi, it was constructed from earth alone. The link between the Mexican pyramid constructed from masonry and the simple earthern hill is provided by the earthern mound sacred to the goddess Coatlicue close to the teocalli or pyramid of her son, Uitzilopochtli, at Mexico. Personages of importance were buried in these American pyramids just as they were in those of Egypt, which were also obviously developed from the idea of the sacred mountain. Indeed several of the Egyptian pyramids were called by such names as "Mountain of Ra," and similar titles.

Egyptian and American pyramids have thus a common evolutionary history. The idea must have sprung from a common centre. Both would appear to trace their descent from the sacred hill of Atlantis. Moreover, pyramids were to be found in the Canaries and the Antilles, the insular links in the chain between Europe and America, of which Atlantis is the missing link.

The food supply of the Atlanteans has been outlined by Plato. He states that the island produced a wealth of roots, fruits, vines and corn, but in this latter statement he is, perhaps, corrected by Diodorus, who, writing of the island Hesperia, which in this case is to be identified with Atlantis, says that corn was unknown to its inhabitants. Corn, the grain of Kore or Demeter, the agricultural goddess of Crete, is generally supposed to have been first cultivated in that country, or in Egypt, from a comparatively wild "grass," believed to be native to the Fayyoum or to Southern Palestine. But its origin is wrapped in impenetrable mystery, and the fact that it was so closely associated with the Eleusinian mysteries and with those of Osiris, both of which had a Western origin, might, perhaps, be taken as good evidence that it originated in Atlantis, although it would not be wise to dogmatize on the point. The fruit with the hard rind grown in Atlantis which afforded both meat, drink and ointment has already been alluded to, and was obviously the coconut, or some species thereof.

Animal food was supplied by cattle, large flocks of sheep and goats, and fish. The great plains would supply plenty of pasture to the ruminant animals, but it is unlikely that the horse was regarded as a food animal, as in the early ages, once it had become a beast of burden. The same applies to the elephant. That this animal was used in war is most probable. It will be recalled that the Carthaginians, who had many Atlantean memories, employed it for this purpose against the Romans and the Iberian tribes of Spain.

A notion of the costume and dress of the Atlanteans can only be gathered from the drawings which the Azilians have left us of themselves. These seem, to the writer, to resemble somewhat the costume of the Cretans of the Minoan period. In most of the upper Palæolithic engravings of Europe the men are naked, but the man of Laussel wears a narrow girdle. The women, in the

Spanish paintings, however, are usually clothed in a skirt which reaches from just above the waist to a little below the knees, leaving the upper part of the body bare. But it would not be reasonable to infer from these pictures that almost complete male nudity was universal, or even customary. Ceremonial costumes were certainly worn by the priests, as seen in the dancing figures from *l'abri Megè*, who wear skins and animal masks, and the circumstance that many of the dead were wrapped in skins and leather jerkins on which shells had been sewn, justifies the assumption that in life they wore similar garments. The head-dresses of the statuettes found at Willendorf and Brassempouy closely resemble Egyptian head-coverings, and a number of the men in the Alpine paintings are represented as wearing plumed headdresses very like those still in use among Red Indian tribes. Others wear hats of high triangular shape, not unlike a Scots bonnet, and some of the women conical caps, made, perhaps, of bark or fur. Some of the men wear plumed bands beneath the knee and round the ankles like the Masai of south-eastern Africa; and probably both sexes wore ornaments of shells and teeth, painted or plain. Indeed, the general costume of the Azilians seems to have resembled that of the Aztecs of Mexico in some of its aspects, as well as that of the early Mediterranean peoples.

Did the Atlanteans possess a literature, and, if so, was it expressed in written documents, or merely handed down orally? From the general tendency of their civilisation, as well as from other circumstances, one is tempted to believe that both a written and an oral literature flourished among them. We have already seen that the so-called alphabetic pebbles found among Azilian remains are more probably representations of the human form expressed conventionally and symbolically, but that is not to say that the more civilized Azilians of

Atlantis did not possess some system of writing, hiero-glyphic or pictorial. The mere fact that the Azilians of Europe possessed something in the nature of a symbology is pretty good proof that their contemporaries in Atlantis had at least advanced as far as the use of a pictorial writing similar to that by which the Aztecs of Mexico expressed themselves, keeping accounts of tributes, fixing the date of religious festivals, and even chronicling the facts of history as well as the fancies of fiction. Plato, in stating that the laws of Atlantis were engraved on a column of orichalcum implies that they possessed some system of writing.

On this subject we may, perhaps, quote the opinion of Dr. T. Rice Holmes[1]: "Many people have heard vaguely of the painted pebbles and the frescoes of Mas d'Azil and the other caverns in the Western Pyrenees which the veteran archæologist, Edouard Piette, has for many years diligently searched. On one of the objects found in the cavern of Lorthet—a spirited engraving on reindeer-horn representing reindeer and salmon—are to be seen two small lozenges, each enclosing a central line: 'Justly proud of his work,' says Monsieur Piette, 'the artist has appended his signature.' Be this as it may, other explorers have exhumed from the Placard cave at Rochebertier and the caves of La Madelaine and Mas d'Azil antlers incised with signs which exactly resemble various Greek and Phœnician letters, and may be compared with signs that have been found in an island of the Pacific. These signs are not letters but symbols; they are not combined in such a way as to form words or inscriptions. 'But,' says Monsieur Piette, 'being symbols, they do constitute a kind of primitive writing.' True writing is, however, evident on a potsherd taken from a neolithic settlement at Los Murcielagos in Portugal.

[1] *Ancient Britain*, pp. 99–100.

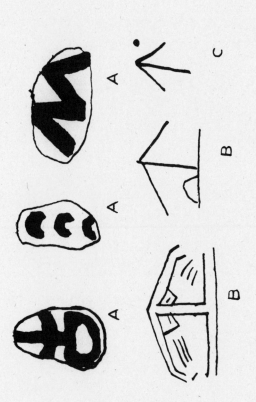

Aurignacian Writing and Symbols

A—A. Inscribed pebbles from Mas d'Azil.
B—B. Tectiform signs from Aurignacian caves.
C. Tectiform sign, American Indian.
D. Aurignacian inscription from Rochebertier, France.

If this fragment could itself be proved to be of neolithic age, it would follow that in that remote time the art of writing was already known to at least one branch of the Mediterranean stock."

If we examine the history of writing and symbolism in Europe and America, certain facts emerge which might, after all due caution was employed, point to an Atlantean origin for certain elements in both European and American symbols and glyphs. It is not claimed for a moment that the European alphabetic system which we presently employ is other than Phœnician in origin, with a possible Egyptian background. But the known origin of all systems of writing in symbolism, the identity of many European, Egyptian and American symbols which were used for the purposes of communication, and the obvious necessity for presupposing for these a link situated in an Atlantean locality, are circumstances which plead for careful consideration.

The late Augustus Le Plongeon professed to find complete identity between the Egyptian and Central American forms of hieroglyphic writing. But as a student of the latter, who has also more than a passing acquaintance with the script of Egypt, the present writer is quite unable to discern any superficial resemblances between Egyptian and Maya or Mexican writing, and cannot subscribe to Dr. Le Plongeon's "translations" of Maya inscriptions and manuscripts. That affinities do exist is certain, but, when revealed, they will be found to lie much deeper than Dr. Le Plongeon believed, and to have been communicated by channels very different from those he considered as having borne them.

The fact that certain symbols, described as "tectiform" or "roof-formed" by some anthropologists, occur on the painted representations of buffaloes, both in Aurignacian caves and in the drawings of the Plains Indians of

America is a good central point to start from in such a discussion, and serves to prove almost at once a symbolical connection between Europe and America. That these have no mere fortuitous resemblance is obvious, and this is rendered more clear by the circumstance that they occupy the same position on the body of the animal.

Says Macalister[1]: "Some of these marks or groups of marks have been claimed as proving the astonishing theory that Magdalenian man had evolved a form of writing by symbolic signs." Yet if the paintings from Alpera and elsewhere reveal anything to the student familiar with the origins of picture-writing, it is that those who created them were on the verge of discovering some such system. They are every whit as much of the nature of picture-writing as the similar drawings of the American Indians, Australians and Eskimos, or as the well-known Aztec story-book usually called the Codex Nuttall, in which the life-story of a hero is told by pictures along with which only a few symbols of names appear as "text." In places in the great Alpera wall-painting appear symbols precisely the same as those found on the painted Azilian pebbles, which proves conclusively that they were used as symbols, and probably name-symbols at that, and above these in more than one place are strokes evidently referring to numbers, and associated with the name-symbols in question. Moreover, in this especial instance, the "tectiform" device is apparent in association with these names and numerals, and the numerals are precisely similar to those in use among the Maya to express the figure "five." The entire scene, I believe, is not only the record of a great hunt, but of the names of some of the heroes who took part in it, and of the number of beasts accounted for. Now, practically the self-same symbols as appear in Azilian art are to be found in the

[1] *Op. cit.*, p. 479.

picture-writings of the North American Indian tribes as the appended illustrations show. The American Indian symbols are assuredly connected with the more highly conventionalised writing systems of the Mexicans and Maya, just as the Azilian are, on the other hand, with those of Egypt and Babylonia. No other conclusion can be reached, then, save that the early pictorial symbols of the Old World and the New must have originated from one common source probably in the Atlantic area. If we deny this, we must assume either that the symbols of the Old World and the New are of separate and spontaneous origin, or that these Azilian symbols reached America via Asia.

The first assumption is one now generally rejected by students of symbology for the very obvious reasons that man is by no means an original "animal," and that symbological resemblances are usually much too precise to be fortuitous. The second is equally frail, because we find all the advanced systems of picture-writing in America strongly established on the Eastern side of the continent, and only their modern, broken-down or degenerate remains on the Western Coasts.

Arguing from such data, then, it seems reasonably clear that the symbolic system of painting anciently in use in both Europe and America must have had its inception in some area whence it could easily have been communicated to both. Such an area could only have existed in the Atlantic Ocean. Indeed, as I have already shown elsewhere [1] a considerable proportion of the symbols in use among the Maya had a definite bearing upon a tradition of cataclysm. Moreover, these symbols are now known to students as "calculiform" or pebble-shaped, and seem to have been developed from painted pebbles, like the Azilian writing.

[1] *The Problem of Atlantis*, pp. 135-139.

There is thus no good reason for denying to the Atlanteans the art of picture-writing, in an elementary form at least, and probably as highly developed as that which subserved the purposes of the great and far-flung Aztec Empire. Doubtless they had their civil and religious books, carved on stone or painted on cavern walls. As we have seen, the Canary Islands abound in caverns, "Where," says Osborn,[1] "the ceilings were covered with a uniform coat of red ochre, while the walls were decorated with various geometric designs in red, black, grey and white." Réné Verneau, a French anthropologist of experience, writes of them: "All these walls (in the Grotto of Goldar) are decorated with paintings."[2] Thus, in the last remaining portion of Atlantis, proof is forthcoming that its ancient inhabitants possessed a symbolism of their own. All symbolism is merely a stage on the way to written expression, and pictures are as much thoughts brought to sight as words or printed pages. Nor is it likely that the dwellers in these caverns, shepherds or hunters, would have been on an equal cultural level with the inhabitants of the cities of Atlantis, any more than the shepherds of the Vosges are the cultural equals of the *literati* of Paris, or the cowboys of the far West the intellectual peers of the scholars of Boston or New York.

Regarding the manners and morality of the people of Atlantis, we are enabled to speak with greater freedom. All authorities are at one in arguing that the latter were by no means praiseworthy. Plato, indeed, paints rather a black picture of the morals of the Children of Poseidon. But we must remember that he is in some respects biased, as he was obviously endeavouring to make the Atlantean power a foil to his own native state of Athens, to play the one off against the other, to show that the Poseidonians,

---

[1] *Men of the Old Stone Age*, pp. 454–455.
[2] *Cinq annes de sejour aux iles Canaries*, p. 47.

the progeny of the rather obnoxious sea-god, were by no means the equals either in morality or courage, of the People of Pallas Athene. There are, however, other good reasons why we may regard the later Atlanteans at least as a people who were by no means without blame. As I have said before, it seems perfectly possible that Atlantis may have survived until a considerably later date than Plato fixed for its submergence, and if this be so, we have a period of time in which its people may have advanced from the comparative state of barbarism which undoubtedly distinguished them in Azilian times to a condition of much greater mental complexity than was possible in that era.

If this be so, their invasion of the soil of their neighbours speaks badly for their general state of mind. Nor does the cruel sport of bull-baiting, which they appear to have indulged in, afford other than a picture of brutality which chimes ill with their alleged culture.

May it not be that the vices usually attributed to the "Antediluvians" in the sacred writings of many peoples are nothing but a memory of the flagrant behaviour of the Atlanteans, who similarly perished by flood? The Scriptures assure us that the divine or heavenly race had become corrupted through intermarriage with the earthly denizens of the world. "The sons of God (or civilised race) saw the daughters of men (aborigines) that they were fair; and they took them wives of all which they chose." This was precisely what Poseidon and his sons did. There were also, we are told, "giants (Titans) in the earth in those days." So evil did men become that the Creator resolved to destroy them.

In the seventy-first chapter of the Koran Noah is made to recite a prayer which shows clearly that, according to the traditions of the Mussulmans the Antediluvian race perished because of its sins. "Lord, leave not any families of the unbelievers on the earth, for if thou leavest them they will seduce thy servants, and will beget none but a wicked and unbelieving offspring," but this prayer, we are told was not actually uttered by Noah until he had found the Antediluvians to be reprobate and incorrigible during the 950 years he is said to have tried them. Noah also exclaimed: "Lord, forgive me and my parents, and every one who shall enter my house, and add unto the unjust doers nothing but destruction." On this subject the Oriental commentators on the Koran are divided, some maintaining that Noah here referred to his own dwelling-house, and others to the temple he had built for the worship of God, or to the Ark then in progress.

The Koran affirmed that Noah, while he was building the Ark, often replied to the scoffings of the unbelievers in this manner: "Though you scoff at us now, we will scoff at you hereafter, as ye scoff at us; and ye shall surely know on whom a punishment shall be inflicted, which will cover you with shame, and on whom a lasting punishment shall fall."

In the Babylonian epic of Gilgamesh the god Ea grows angry at the sinfulness of the people of Suruppak, and precipitates such a disastrous flood that "no continent appeared on the waste of waters." The Greek myth of Deucalion states that the Antediluvians "were insolent, and addicted to unjust actions; they neither regarded oaths nor were they hospitable to strangers nor listened to suppliants; and this complicated wickedness was the cause of their destruction. Of a sudden the earth poured forth a vast quantity of water . . . and all men were destroyed." Ovid, in his Latin account of the Deluge makes Jupiter say: "It were endless to repeat the aggravated guilt which everywhere appeared." Egyptian legend relates that the god Tem let loose the waters of the primeval abyss over the earth to destroy mankind because of its wickedness.

Vishnu, in Hindu myth, sends a flood upon the earth because "all creatures had offended him." In Breton legend the city of Ys is overwhelmed by the waters because of the profligacy of its princess, "who had made a crown of her vices, and taken for her pages the seven capital sins." In a myth of the Arawak Indians the god Aimon Kondi scourges the world with fire, followed by a flood, because of the shortcomings of man, and countless other myths speak of the drowning of the human race for its wickedness. That a myth so widespread could have arisen without some most definite cause seems highly improbable. It is much more likely that evidence so overwhelmingly united must have behind it an actual historical condition.

Not the least valuable evidence from America is the myth of the destruction of the wicked as given by Mr. Jeremiah Curtin in his *Creation Myths of Primitive America*, and as described by an American Indian:

"There was a world before this one in which we are living at present. That was the world of the first people, who were different from us altogether. Those people were very numerous, so numerous that if a count could be made of all the stars in the sky, all the feathers on birds, all the hair and fur on animals they would not be so numerous as the first people.

"These people lived very long in peace, in concord, in harmony, in happiness. No man knows, no man can tell, how long they lived in that way. At last the minds of all except a very small number were changed. They fell into conflict—one offended another, consciously or unconsciously, one injured another with or without intention, one wanted some special thing, another wanted that very thing also. Conflict set in, and because of this came a time of activity and struggle, to which there was no end or stop till the great majority of the first people—

that is all except a small number—were turned into the various kinds of living creatures that are on earth now or have ever been on earth except man—that is, all kinds of beasts, birds, reptiles, fish, worms and insects, as well as trees, plants, grasses, rocks and some mountains. They were turned into everything that we see on the earth or in the sky.

"The small number of the former people who did not quarrel, those great first people of the old time who remained of one mind and harmonious, left the earth, sailed away westward, passed that line where the sky comes down to the earth and touches it, sailed to places beyond; stayed there or withdrew to upper regions and lived in them happily, lived in agreement, live so to-day, and will live in the same way hereafter."

Surely such a world-wide memory of the profligacy of the Atlanteans cannot possibly have sprung from chance invention. We see that it deals with a world submerged for its vices, as Atlantis was. It is, then, possible to speak, as we shall see later, of pre-Platonic evidence for Atlantean history.

CHAPTER XII

THE ATLANTEAN STATE AND POLITY

FROM the account of Plato we receive a very full description of the type of government which obtained in Atlantis. We are told in the first place that each of the twelve kings of Atlantis was absolute in his own island, but that so far as their government was concerned they were almost completely tied down to the mere carrying out of the ordinances of the ancient Atlantean rulers engraven on the column of orichalcum in the temple of Poseidon. This is reminiscent of the laws of the Medes and Persians, which, we will remember from the Book of Kings, were unchangeable and unalterably fixed, but it is not at all uncommon to discover in an early state of society that the legal institutions of a people are rendered incapable of alteration, and this indicates of course that, as they were held to proceed from the gods, it was considered impious to tamper with them.

Anything resembling a fixed condition of the law renders it impossible for a state to advance politically or economically to any great extent, and such must have been the case with Atlantis. But it would seem probable that in the course of time anything like uniformity between the twelve provincial islands and the mainland as regards the legal code could scarcely obtain. Doubtless they were all close enough to make anything like a strong dissimilarity improbable, but it seems possible that the very reason for their kings assembling in the temple of Poseidon once in six years was to refresh their memories with the

code on the pillar of orichalcum. The main reason for
this conference, however, must have been the consideration
of the affairs of the Atlantean Empire at large, and the
very fact that it was held at such long intervals is conclusive
as showing that the distance between the several islands
of which the nucleus of that empire was composed could
not have been very great. Although on the other hand
it might be argued that such a lapse of time between
conferences presupposes a very considerable distance
between the several groups of the archipelago.

We observe, too, from Plato's account that the government of Atlantis was closely connected with its religion,
that it must have been of a sacerdotal character, and that
the kings also acted as priests or hierophants. Their Par-
liament, however, was practically the temple of Poseidon,
and as their laws were ready-made for them, they were
in the happy position of not requiring to debate them
on the occasions on which they assembled. Their constitution seems in one particular to have adumbrated that
of the United States of America, for we are told that
the several states were not permitted to take up arms
against one another.

Military leadership, like sacerdotal pre-eminence, was
vested in the children of Atlas. The government of the
country seems to have been on a feudal basis, and indeed
it is noticeable that it was in these very countries which
were first colonised by Atlantis that later the feudal idea
of government arose. The country was divided into
cantons or provinces, each about twelve miles square, and
each of these furnished an armed contingent. The
agricultural portion of the land furnished altogether about
sixty thousand men-at-arms, but the mountainous country
of the hinterland, we are told, supplied an innumerable
host of warriors. As we have seen, the ratio of fighting
men which each canton must furnish included charioteers,

cavalrymen, foot-soldiers, archers, stone-shooters, and sailors, and it is especially observed that this array was drawn only from the central island, the other parts of the empire having a separate military economy.

The governance of this host would seem, from the evidence in our possession, to have been not unmingled with anxiety for the rulers of Atlantis, especially when the period of unrest began to manifest itself. The reader will remember the passage in the Welsh Triads which almost indubitably refers to a memorial of rebellion in Atlantis. "I will not redeem the multitudes with trailing shields. They know not on what day the stroke would be given . . . they know not the brindled ox with the thick head-band." This, as has been said, is obviously the plaint of a leader who had taken strong umbrage at the irreligious attitude of the plebeian men-at-arms towards the sacred ox or bull. It seems to refer to that period in Atlantean history when the people had grown tired of hearkening to the priesthood, and were possibly manifesting their impatience with an oppressive ritual and an equally oppressive military service. It is possible that at this time the ruling caste in Atlantis, as ruling castes have done elsewhere, sought to distract the attention of the people from internecine troubles by proposing to them a great scheme of foreign conquest, a campaign by which they might overrun the adjacent European region and achieve possessions even for the humblest.

No doubt they were also menaced by neighbouring communities. The Amazons, for example, may have been a numerous tribe, not of women, but of people under female rule or employing female soldiers. Diodorus has put it on record that they attacked the Atlantean communities with a large army and even subdued them, and that the Gorgons, another neighbouring people, similarly oppressed the Atlanteans. Doubtless because they were surrounded by barbarous enemies, the Atlanteans were compelled to dwell in a constant state of armed vigilance, and this, more than any other condition, would contribute to popular unrest and the disintegration of the State.

What we read in Plato and other authors regarding the state and polity of Atlantis has little or no reflection in any Mediterranean form of government as described by the classical writers of antiquity. We must recall that we draw our classical knowledge of things Atlantean from an Egyptian source, and in the account of the priest of Sais, as furnished in Plato, it cannot be said that we discover much that would lead us to think that it had been modelled on Egyptian ideas. True, the various provinces of Atlantis might reflect the nomes of ancient Egypt, and the military economy of Atlantis certainly bears some slight resemblance to that of the Nile country, but on the other hand the Pharaoh was supreme in Egypt and such a conference of kings as is mentioned in Plato's account would never have been possible in a state whose monarch was regarded as a deity, and whose provincial governors, even though vested with a great degree of power, would never have presumed to place themselves on anything like equality with the reigning monarch. And this, it seems to me, is perhaps one of the strongest justifications of the reality of the Atlantean account, of its basic probability, that we find in it such conditions as by no means obtained in any of the states, African, Asiatic or European, as were contemporary with Plato, if perhaps a few minor resemblances be excepted.

We find, however, that in those countries where the Atlantean power planted its first possessions, a condition of things very much more resembling those reflected on Plato's account. In early Britain and Ireland, for example, we encounter such a state of government as we read of in the Platonic statement. In both of the British islands and in Gaul, if we refer to the earliest historical accounts which deal with them, we find the great mass of the people under the stern rule of an aristocracy which regarded them practically as serfs, we find the country broken up into similar cantons ruled by petty kings, and a system of military service obtaining under which foot-soldiers, charioteers and slingers were recruited precisely as in Atlantis. We know, too, that the laws of these peoples were regarded as proceeding from divine influence, that they were unalterable, and that every consideration of state was dictated through divination by the priesthood. Cæsar in his sixth book says: "There are only two degrees of men in Gaul who have any power in the administration of public affairs—the Druids and the nobility—for the commons are esteemed no more than servants and are never admitted to their debates." The Druids, he proceeds to say, have the entire care of divine things, of private and public sacrifices, with the interpretation of their religion. The manner in which the Druids convened, also, is reminiscent of the conference in the temple of Poseidon, for once a year they had a general rendezvous at a consecrated place in the midst of Gaul, where all such as had controversies to decide flocked to submit to their judgment. A similar condition of things obtained in Spain. Indeed the entire tract from the Iberian peninsula to Orkney was in the earliest historical period governed by a dispensation resembling that reflected in Plato's account so closely that it might well have stood for its exemplar. The free republics of Greece, on the other hand, reflect no such condition of affairs, and if Egypt does so to some extent it is probably because it also had imbibed much of the Atlantean culture.

CHAPTER XIII

THE RELIGION OF ATLANTIS

As regards the type of religion which flourished in Atlantis, the Platonic account affords us some very precise details. For example, we are informed that a particular rite attended the deliberations of the kings which took place once in every six years. Before the assize of justice which was held on that occasion ten bulls were brought into the sacred zone, and each one of the Atlantean kings made a vow to offer up one of these bulls to Poseidon without employing the agency of iron. The animals were then led to the graven copper column and immolated, after which the kings passed the members of each bull through the fire, making a libation of the blood and drenching the column with it, after which the sacrifices were totally consumed by fire. The remainder of the blood was placed in small vases of gold and splashed on to the fire, a little of it being drunk.

Now this ceremony very closely resembles several of those practised by the Aztec peoples. The Mexican priests were in the habit of leading their human victims to a similar graven column, of making libations of their blood from vases of gold, and even of drinking some of it. That they employed human rather than animal sacrifice is simply to be accounted for by the fact that no large animals were known in Mexico, but further north the Indian tribes, from whom the Aztecs were derived, sacrificed the buffalo almost in the self-same manner in which the Atlanteans immolated the bull.

We know also that the bull was the sacred animal of the Aurignacians, as its presence in many of their cave-temples proves, and that they actually sacrificed it there can be little doubt. The cult of the bull was perhaps the first and certainly one of the most widespread religions in Western Europe, and that it penetrated to Egypt is of course well known. Let us examine the bull-worship of Egypt briefly and see if it is capable of throwing any light upon the circumstances of the Atlantean cult.

That bull-worship in Egypt was certainly of very early origin is proved by the statement of Manetho, an Egyptian priest, who traces the cult of Apis to a King of the Second Dynasty, about 3000 B.C. Ælian, indeed, goes further back and assigns the origin of the practice to Mena, the first king of the First Egyptian Dynasty. This, of course, implies that the cult was probably very much more ancient, as practically everything pristine in Egypt was regarded as having been introduced by Mena, the great culture-hero, or introducer of civilisation into the Nile region. Herodotus describes the Apis bull as black in colour, but having a square spot of white on the forehead, and on the back the figure of an eagle, with double hairs in the tail and the mark of a beetle on the tongue. The Egyptians believed that the soul of Osiris had passed after death into a bull, and that when this bull died it was necessary to find a bull calf which had the self-same markings, in order that the soul of the god might live on.

Now it has been already observed that the cult of Osiris with its concomitant practice of mummification, was of western origin, that indeed it was nothing more nor less than an Egyptian adoption and amplification of the ancient Aurignacian belief that the soul resided in the bones, and that, if the spirit were to survive, the bones must be carefully preserved. It is obvious that this particular cult must have become amalgamated with the other

Aurignacian worship of the bull, therefore it is not surprising to find the religion of Osiris associated with the bull and Osiris himself identified with it.

We find the bull in Egypt primarily regarded as an oracle, its every movement being interpreted as having some special significance. We also find that oxen were sacrificed to it, which clearly indicates that it was regarded as being among that class of animal which is thought of by barbarous people as being the chief or "king" of his "people." The Indian tribes of America, for example, were wont to pray to the Great Deer to send his "people" as prey to them, and he was placated whenever a deer was killed. In like manner certain barbarous fishing populations entreated the Great Fish to send shoals of his subjects into their nets. In ancient Peru a Great Potato Mother was worshipped as the prototype of all potatoes, a Maize Mother as the progenitor of the maize plant, and so forth. It seems probable then that the Aurignacians had been in the habit of worshipping a Great Bull who kept them supplied with meat, and that this notion gradually passed into Egypt, whose people probably did not understand or had forgotten its original significance.

We find the Osirian worship linked up with that of the bull by the practice of embalming and mummifying the dead Apis bull, the remains of numerous Apis animals having been discovered in the famous Serapeum.

This worship of Serapis or Osiris-Apis spread from Egypt throughout Europe, was adopted by Rome, and finally reached Britain, where a great temple to the dual god was built at York. But it must have met on British soil with a similar faith, with which, perhaps, it amalgamated, for bull-worship and sacrifice had undoubtedly been practised in Britain for centuries. The bull was worshipped by the Celts and its immolation was part of the Druidic ceremonial, as the old Welsh Triads show.

In Scotland its figure is graven on many of the ancient Pictish stones, and these are associated with religious symbols. So late as the beginning of the seventeenth century more than one Highland Presbytery issued a denunciation of the practice of bull-sacrifice by the peasantry. Indeed, there is plenty of evidence that the cult of the bull had a most ancient and enduring influence in Britain, as is attested not only by the foregoing circumstances, but by the popular sport of bull-baiting, which appears to be nothing more or less than the original rite of bull sacrifice in a state of attrition.

It seems clear, then, that the Atlantean system of bull-worship penetrated into all the countries to which the sunken island had once been contiguous. Students of comparative religion are now beginning to see that any theory which does not allow for the origin of any custom, religious or otherwise, in one especial sphere is scarcely worth credit, and if this be admitted, it is obvious that the origin of bull-worship must be looked for in one especial area. This would imply that bull-worship from Britain to India had an Atlantean genesis. But when it is found that in Spain it was associated with the beginnings of the embalmer's craft, and that in Egypt it was identified with mummification, it will scarcely be doubted that the Egyptian and Aurignacian cults must have had a common beginning. If we believe that the Aurignacians came from Atlantis, we can scarcely doubt that they brought the cult of the bull along with them, and surely we find corroboration of the fact in the Platonic account of Atlantis. Indeed the whole circumstances of the bull-cult, as drawn from the comparative study of its phenomena in Spain France, Britain, Crete and Egypt, are eloquent of its origin in sunken Atlantis, where, according to Plato's details, themselves drawn from an Egyptian source, we also find the worship of the bull in full celebration.

How far Plato's account of bull-sacrifice in Atlantis was sophisticated by a similar sacrifice in the Hellenic worship of Bacchus may be gauged from a brief study of the Bacchic ceremony. In one of his phases—an early phase —Bacchus appears as a bull. Even in the time of Euripides Bacchus was adored in his bull-form in Macedonia, if not in more cultured Athens, and in the Orphic mysteries the worshipper, before he was made one with Bacchus, devoured the raw flesh of a bull. "That a feast of raw flesh of some sort was traditionally held to be a part of Bacchic ceremonial," says Miss Jane Harrison in her *Prolegomena to the study of Greek Religion* "is clear." Firminius Maternus, the Christian father, says of the Cretans: "They tear in pieces a live bull with their teeth, and by howling with discordant shouts through the secret places of the woods, they simulate the madness of an enraged animal." If the bull-eater did not inhabit Athens in the days of Plato, he must have been known there at least, and it seems not improbable that Plato coloured his account of the bull-sacrifices of the Atlanteans by the light of what actually happened in the Orphic mysteries.

The connection of the bull with Poseidon brings us to the question of the personnel of the gods of Atlantis. The bull was the especial symbol of this deity, bulls were sacrificed to him, and when we recall that he was the god of the earthquake as well as of the raging sea, the allegorical connection of the bull with this god seems clear enough. It was undoubtedly regarded from very early times as the embodiment of wrath, the bellowing beast which stamped the earth—the earth-shaker, so to speak, affording an excellent animal picture of earthquake and tempest. Perhaps Poseidon was himself originally regarded as a bull, precisely as other gods had originally an animal form, and his massive torso in classical art certainly lends some colour to such an assumption. However that may be, the bull was the beast of Poseidon *par excellence*.

The gods of Atlantis, though dim enough in all conscience, may yet be gathered into a species of provisional pantheon. Poseidon himself was believed by the Greeks to be a Pelasgian or Asiatic deity somewhat resembling the Assyrian Ea or Dagon, whose fish's tail is so prominent in Assyrian and Babylonian sculpture. This god was also worshipped by the Phœnician people of Carthage, but it seems quite probable that, just as Osiris was of western origin, so was Poseidon. In the first place, he, like all the other Titans, hailed originally from the west, and the greater number of the legends connected with him associate him with western localities. Moreover, we find him in Plato's account most definitely associated with Atlantis, where we are told his temple was the chief seat of worship in the island.

The association of Atlas in a definite group with other gods whose names still cling to existing countries makes it very plain that his own name was not associated with Atlantis by a mere figment of the Platonic imagination. We find him in Greek mythology grouped along with his brother Titans, Albion and Iberius, the giant gods of Britain and Ireland, in a most definite manner. These, it may be assumed, formed a species of archipelagic pantheon. All three were Titans, and, as we know, the Titans were merely western gods. The myth of the Titans in itself is significant for our study. Indeed, it seems to me that this ancient story of giant gods coming from the west and invading Olympus is almost certainly an allegory of the invasion of Europe, or rather of the Mediterranean area, by the gods of an alien religion, and that some such idea not only originated the myth, but that it lingered long in popular consciousness, is plain from the fact that it was one of the most popular subjects in classical art. We find these gods indissolubly connected with the Atlantic area, and the names of at least two of them still connected with the British islands. It is absurd to suppose that the Greeks invented the names of certain gods or Titans and imposed them as protective deities upon Britain and Ireland. In fact it is known that the names Albion and Iberius are of Celtic origin and have reference to tutelary gods. This being so, how are we to account for Atlas? His island has disappeared, yet his name and that of Atlantis remain. Were Britain, which we are told "arose above the azure main," to sink back to its original place in the bed of the Atlantic, men ten thousand years hence might well doubt her former existence, and the name of her god Albion might be regarded as merely an effort of classical ingenuity to render more probable what all "sensible" people would look upon as a mere myth.

Surely it seems most likely, then, that these very definite notices of a Titanic pantheon which had its origin in the Atlantic area, and the names of which are still attached to certain of the islands over which they presided, arose out of the memory of an ancient and powerful religion which had a widespread influence not only in the then existing Atlantic archipelago, but which overflowed into the Mediterranean area.

Nor is this theory at all weakened when we come to observe the very great sanctity in which the peoples of the Mediterranean held the western oceanic area, for there they placed the locality of the Fortunate Islands and the Gardens of the Hesperides. The earliest Greek poetry situates the abode of the happy departed spirits far beyond the entrance to the Mediterranean, on islands in the midst of the River Oceanus. Pindar, under Orphic influence probably, alludes to them as the destination not only of divine favourites, but of all righteous persons.

ENGLISH MAP OF AMERICA, SHOWING ATLANTIS, DRAWN IN THE YEAR 1500
(From Fletcher and Kipling's "*School History of England*" by kind permission of the Oxford University Press).

There, he says, the gales of Ocean breathe over the Island of the Fortunate, the earth laughs with golden flowers, and the good appear to occupy themselves chiefly in horsemanship and music. The former avocation, it will be remembered, was in high favour among the Atlanteans. In Greek myth the Fortunate Islands are frequently confounded with the Hesperides, or Islands of the Golden Apples, situated on the River Oceanus, or, according to later notions, off the North and West coasts of Africa. Many details added by popular superstition to the state of happiness which the poets taught as existing in the Fortunate Isles, may be found in the second Book of Lucian, and in his *Necyomantia*.

The notion that the dead betook themselves to the west, may indeed be added to the number of ideas which in another chapter will be found as composing what the writer calls the Atlantean complex, but it is included in this place not only because we are now dealing with the religious part of our subject, but because it is perhaps rather more dubious than the remainder of the proof which seems to justify the former existence of such a complex.   There are, however, good grounds for believing that the whole idea of the continued existence of souls after death in the West arose out of the memory of Atlantis. Indeed, we find it believed in by all those races who must have in some degree acquired the Atlantean civilisation. The Celts, whose long association with the Iberians in Spain must have imbued them with the idea, devoutly believed that the abode of the dead was situated in the Atlantic, and we find the Greeks, Romans and Cretans holding the same belief. The very fact that the whole of Western and Mediterranean Europe looked to the west as the location of the great Island of the Dead, is surely sufficient proof that they regarded it as the ancient home from which their religion and culture had been drawn. Man's paradise, his sacred soil, is always regarded as that spot whence he originally came. We find both the peoples of Palestine and those of Central America taking the utmost pains and undergoing the utmost dangers in order to bury their dead in ancestral soil. We find the Peruvians passionately attached to their *Paccarisca* or mythical place of origin—often a cave or mountain-side—and desiring burial within its precincts. The western half of Crete, in Minoan times, was left almost unoccupied because it was regarded as the home of the departed, just as the western islands of Britain were thought of as being haunted by disembodied spirits, just as Britain itself was regarded by a primeval Europe as an island of ghosts. The Egyptians also looked towards the west as the place of the dead. It will not do to attempt to explain this idea by saying that it is natural for Man to regard the west as the place of sleep after life simply because the sun sets there, for we find many races looking towards other parts of the compass as the region of mortality. The Aztecs, for example, regarded the north as the place of souls. The Chinese looked to the east, and we have seen that Hotu Matua, the culture-hero of Easter Island, although he looked to the west when he called to the spirits who hovered over his submerged home, is still associated with the myth which tells how a large archipelago existed three hundred miles east of the island. Quetzalcoatl, too, the culture-hero of Central America, looked eastwards, and many other myths of an Oriental paradise could be supplied.

We find then that not only was there a well-founded memory of the former existence of a great religion in the Atlantic region, but that the locality in which it had flourished had been erected into a paradise by the peoples who had accepted that religion in part. In part, because they regarded its Titanic pantheon as in a measure

inimical to their own, and this especially applies to the
Hellenic peoples of the eastern Mediterranean, who,
less than any others, perhaps, had come under the influence
of the Atlantean culture and religion. Our fragmentary
knowledge of Carthaginian religion scarcely permits us
to say how far this Asiatic people, settled in North-West
Africa, had accepted local beliefs regarding Atlantis,
but there can be little doubt that, as many classical
authors admit, many of the fundamental ideas connected with the religious mysteries of the Mediterranean
races, such, for example, as those of the Cabiri,
passed through a Carthaginian crucible before they
reached Greece, and that they had no connection with
that Palestine, whence the Carthaginians came, is clear
enough.

We must regard the Atlantean pantheon as being composed not only of Atlas himself, but of his nine brothers,
his mother Cleito, and his brother Saturn. These are all
more or less connected with the constellations. Atlas
himself is alluded to as a great astronomer, which may
simply mean that his pantheon was closely associated
with the heavenly constellations. Just as the ancient
Christian superstition believed that the stars were the
fallen angels, and just as the Babylonians associated their
gods with certain planets, so possibly the Atlanteans identified their deities with this or that luminary. Hesperus,
the son of Atlas, says Diodorus, became the morning
star, and his daughters, the Atlantides, became the
constellation of the Pleiades, and Saturn, his brother, the
planet of that name. Once the idea of personality, of
godhead, had been connected with the planets, they were
regarded as powerful enchanters or deities, who were
constantly striving to direct the actions of man in such
a manner as to bring them into harmony with some
vaster plan of their own. The idea of a cosmic symphony

had been established. Man must work in harmony with
the higher powers.   This notion, of course, if it is brought
out anywhere in the writings of antiquity, appears in those
of Plato. A score of commentaries were written by his
successors regarding his beliefs in this respect. In the
very works in which he tells the story of Atlantis he
outlines these beliefs.

This leads to the assumption that the religion of Atlantis
was closely associated with astrology. It has become a
truism almost that the ancient science of astrology had
its beginnings in the plains of Babylonia, and indeed it
is almost a popular belief nowadays that the ziggurats
or temple-towers of Chaldea were the world's first observatories.   But the study of star-lore must greatly ante-
date the civilisation of the Euphrates. The immovable
brilliance of the fixed stars must have imprinted itself
upon the eye and the imagination of Man almost from
the first, must have intrigued and puzzled him, or have
been accepted by him without emotion as a phenomenon
duly to be explained away in terms of myth.

Anything like direct proof that astrology was of western
origin is almost entirely lacking. Indeed all the proof
seems to lie in the other direction. We know, however,
that the Druids of Britain and Ireland were familiar with
it, and one as yet almost unexamined system of astrology
provides material for thought on the lines that it may
have proceeded from Atlantis. The allusion is to the
astrology of the Aztecs of Mexico, which has little or
no resemblance to that of the Orient, and which, it is not
at all improbable, emanated more or less directly from
Atlantis. Regarding the manner in which it reached
the American continent, along with other manifestations
of the Atlantean culture, the reader must be referred to
my *Atlantis in America*. But when we find that the entire
Aztec religion was practically built up out of what is known

as the Tonalamatl or Calendar, and that many of its gods were practically mere chronological dates, and when we find that this strange religion had no cultural connections whatsoever with the west, but regarded its beginnings as having originated in the east, the importance of its consideration is borne in upon us.[1]

The word tonalamatl means "Book of the Good and Bad Days," and it is primarily a Book of Fate from which the destiny of children born on such and such a day, or the result of any course to be taken or any venture made on any given day, was forecasted by divinatory methods similar to those which have been employed by astrologers in many parts of the world and in all times. It was indeed a book of augury and over its days certain gods presided. These days thus became significant for good or evil, according to the nature of the gods who presided over them or over the precise hour in which a person was born, or any act performed. As in Eastern astrology, a kind of balance was held between good and evil, so that if the god presiding over the day was inauspicious, his influence might in some measure be counteracted by that of the deity who presided over the hour in which a child first saw the light, or an event occurred.

Now the twenty gods who presided over its twenty day-signs are all capable of being identified with certain stars or planets. Quetzalcoatl, for example, can be identified as the planet Venus, and it is notable that several of the gods in this calendar can be equated with certain members of the Atlantean pantheon, Quetzalcoatl, for instance, with Atlas, as has already been demonstrated, and Coatlicue with Cleito, whilst Tlaloc, Tezcatlipoca and Xochiquetzal have all an Atlantean significance, so far as their myths and symbols are concerned, as has been proved in other parts of this work.

[1] See the writer's *Gods of Mexico* passion.

We find, too, that the method in which the Aztecs and the Maya of Central America computed the synodic revolutions of the planet Venus has a distinct Atlantean connection, as that planet was particularly identified with the god Quetzalcoatl, who was said to have come from some locality in the Atlantic Ocean, and who, like Atlas, bore the world upon his shoulders. He was also regarded as the inventor of the tonalamatl, which was thus looked upon as the sacred divinitory book or table of a culture-hero who had come from some region in the Atlantic Ocean. This in itself is surely sufficient proof that the astrological system of Mexico either emanated from Atlantis or had Atlantean associations. Its methods are wholly unlike those of the East, and that it had been introduced into America seems plain enough. Greek myth assures us that the Atlantean deities were closely associated with the stars and that Atlas was a great astrologer. When we find him in another form in America, but with the self-same attributes as those of Atlas, and regarded as the creator of the astrological system of Central America (which he carried to its shores) in an Atlantic locality, a good deal of adverse proof will be required to discredit the theory that Central American astrology did not draw its origins from Atlantean sources.

We can imagine the Atlantean religion, then, as associated with a pantheon of Titanic beings and as having a powerful astrological connection. These are no mere surmises, but basic facts. That the early Hellenic, Mediterranean and British religions were also founded on a similar basis is obvious, and it was only in later historical times that notions similar to those which must have obtained in Atlantis began to be overlaid by departmental deities, gods of the virtues and vices, gods of trades and agriculture. The older gods of Europe, like those of Atlantis, were Titanic and eponymous, having a relation to the regions over which they ruled. The Celtic gods of Britain, for example, and of Scotland and Ireland in especial, are known to have been gigantic forms, whose names and legends still haunt many a locality. Practically every mountain in Scotland has its familiar giant. Cornwall overflowed with them, and such names as Scarborough and the Giants' Causeway are eloquent of their former presence. The Scottish mountains harboured Titans, who were great stone-throwers, like the Titans of Central America, and the Fomorians of Ireland were of monstrous height. A careful examination of the giant-lore of Europe undoubtedly brings to light the existence of a former great Titanic pantheon, and it is remarkable that the majority of the legends connected with these gigantic beings speak of them as having come out of the western seas. The Fomorians, as their name implies, are merely "the People out of the Sea," the Greek Titans had the same origin, the giants of Spanish lore almost invariably dwell on islands, and those of Cornwall seem to be associated with sunken Lyonesse. The Anglo-Saxon word, Etin, still found in Scottish legend, is merely the same as Jotunn, the Scandinavian form, and both can be philologically equated with Titan. All these allied words refer back to the Sanskrit root, "tith," "to burn," which shows that the idea of these beings was connected with that of conflagration. or earthquake, and we know from the terms of myth that the Titans were further associated with the forgings of thunder-bolts and terrestrial disturbances. It is not in Greece alone that we find the story of the battle between the gods and Titans. It is substantially outlined in Irish myth in the wars of the Fomorians with the Tuatha de Danaan, and in Britain by the exploits of Arthur and his knights (each of whom can be referred to a place in the Celtic pantheon) with the British giants. In the story of Atlantis there can be no doubt we have the origin of these

numerous legends. The Atlanteans, the tall Aurignacians, were almost certainly those "giants," and the
Azilians, their successors, the giant-worshippers, who invaded Europe at widely different periods, and left behind
them so many stories of tall, skin-clad, club-wielding men,
who for generations put up a stern fight against newer
races until they were killed out or absorbed.

A more exhaustive study of the giant-lore of Europe,
and especially of its western portions, would in all probability throw a great flood of light upon the whole circumstances of the Atlantean legend, especially if the central
story of the battle between the Titans and the gods and
the Atlantean origin thereof were carefully kept in view.
It might also have good results as bringing out more
specific information regarding the general characteristics
of the Titan deities, and thus enlightening us upon the
pantheon of Atlantis, whence probably the idea of all
had sprung. The giant of European traditon is either a
cave-dweller, or has his home in an island or in a castle
perched on some craggy height, and the nature of these
abodes indicates in some measure the Atlantean origin of
the stories connected with them. The British Islands
alone are capable of supplying a wealth of illustration to
such a thesis, and if these records were carefully examined
there is little doubt that the research would be justified by
results. The very fact that the eponymous deities of our
twin islands, Albion and Iberius, are grouped in classical
myth along with the figure of Atlas, the god of Atlantis,
should be sufficient to give pause to those who might be
dubious regarding the utility of such an examination.

The rites connected with this ancient Titanic religion
are by no means well-known, for the very good reason
that when it is first recorded in history it is as a dying
religion, but one circumstance connected with it ob-
trudes itself. The great Titanic gods are one and all the

possessors of a gigantic appetite. Saturn devours his
children. The Dagda, one of the ancient Irish gods, has
an appetite which is never satiated, although his porridge
pot is ever full. Crom Cruach, another Irish deity, whose
statue was overthrown by St. Patrick, can only be appeased
by the sacrifice of large numbers of children. The appetite of Gargantua, the Breton giant, who is one of the
Gorics of the French peninsula, has become classical
through the lively pen of Rabelais, and the giants of Britain
and the Jotunn of Scandinavia alike were famous for
devouring sheep and oxen whole. It is remarkable, too,
that Moloch, a god especially favoured by the Carthaginians—a people with many Atlantean memories—was a
great devourer of children. From the collective idea of
these sprang the idea of the ogre—that is the Orcus or
creature of the lower world, the submerged world. In
America we find a similar state of things a belief in
an older panthem of giants, indeed a nation of ogres,
among the Aztecs, a people especially prone to cannibalism and human sacrifice. Wherever the Atlantean
tradition is to be found, indeed, the idea of the immolation of human beings is likewise to be encountered, and
although we discover in Plato's account nothing at all
which would justify us in saying that the Atlanteans as a
race were prone to human sacrifice, it is not too much, in
view of what is said regarding their exceeding wickedness,
to suppose that they may have been addicted to practices
of the kind, especially when we find the rites of the holo-
caust, and especially of infant sacrifice, associated with the
religious beliefs of the people who seem to have emanated
from the sunken continent. This idea is in no way
incompatible with a very considerable advance in civilisation, as is obvious from all we know of the Aztec religion,
and there are certainly many circumstances connected
with the Aurignacian culture which might lead us to infer

that cannibalism and infant sacrifice were not unknown to its creators.

One religious system which survived into the historical period has certain traits which would seem to connect it with the Atlantean religion, such as it is assumed to have been in the the foregoing pages. The reference is to Druidism. Now it is well known that Druidism was not a religion of Celtic provenance, but of Iberian origin. Cæsar, in a well-known passage, remarks that it was thought to have arisen in Britain, and to have been brought thence into Gaul. The Iberians, who seem to have instituted it, were, as has been said before, the direct descendants of the Azilians, one of the waves of Atlantean immigrants, so that it seems more than probable that Druidism was the last phase of an imported Atlantean religion. We know that it was also practised in Spain and in the Canary Islands, the last terrestrial vestiges of Atlantis.

Rice Holmes, writing of Druidism (*Ancient Britain*, p. 289), says: "It is not unreasonable to believe that the Celts learned it from some non-Aryan people, for there is nothing to show that the Gauls whom the Romans first encountered had ever heard of it."

The Druidic religion, from what we know of it, appears to have had a strong resemblance to the Atlantean. The first notices of it make it clear that in Cæsar's time it had become Celticised, but behind the Celtic pantheon there loomed great figures like Merlin and Crom Cruach, the Dagda and Balor, which obviously show that at one time the Druidical religion had boasted of a Titanic pantheon. Moreover the Druids sacrificed human beings, imprisoning them in monstrous idols of wickerwork and burning them alive as an offering to the gods. They also immolated captives for the purpose of divination. One of their chief doctrines was the transmigration of souls, which is

often erroneously believed to be a purely Oriental idea.
It is thought that the Druids owed their conception of
immortality to the influence of Pythagoras, as Diodorus
Siculus and Timagenes imply, and Pythagorean symbols,
or, properly speaking, one example of them, have been
found on a British uninscribed gold coin found at Re-
culver. But it is strange that if the Druids held the
Pythagorean doctrine that it should not be more fully
represented in their surviving literature, as found, for
example, in the Welsh Triads. The Druidic doctrine of
Abred, which alludes to the innermost of three concentric
circles representing the totality of being in the Druidic
cosmogony, has been taken by some authorities as having
reference to the Pythagorean doctrine, but is in reality
quite different from that doctrine. The Druids believed
that there was an Elysium in the west, which again points
to an Atlantean origin for their faith rather than to a Greek
one. Rice Holmes says wisely: "If the Druids, as Cæsar
said, taught that souls passed 'from one person to another,'
they meant, perhaps, that after death the soul entered a
new body—the ethereal counterpart of that which it had
left behind."

We find, too, that the Druids had a pillar of "orichalcum" or bronze, such as stood in the temple of Poseidon
in Atlantis. This pillar was discovered at the end of last
century at Coligny, in the department of the Ain. It is
a calendar engraved with lucky and unlucky days according
to the revolutions of the moon, and the language in which
it is couched is the subject of dispute, some authorities
holding that it is Celtic, while others believe it to be Ligu-
rian. The Ligurians were a people utterly different from
the Celts, having affiliations with the older populations
of France. Moreover we find that the Druids, according
to Pliny, sacrificed white bulls before cutting the mysterious
mistletoe from the oak. It is in the remains of Druid

poetry, too, as found in the Welsh Triads, that we discover those recurring notices which manifestly apply to certain phases of Atlantean history.   It seems then most probable as has been said, that Druidism was the last phase of the ancient religion of Atlantis.

It has often seemed strange to the writer that European Theosophists should seek to draw and infer the origin of the system they support from Oriental sources, when it must be manifest, as the founder of modern Theosophy upheld, that the very beginnings of the system emanated from Atlantis.   It has always seemed to the writer a work of supererogation to seek to prove that the ancient world-religion originated in the East, when in the very lands in which those persons reside who stress its Oriental origin numerous evidences of its past abound.   Let Theosophists and mystics generally pay more considera-tion not only to the evidences of the Atlantean origin of world-religion and philosophy, but make a deeper study of the remains of the Atlantean system as observed in Druidism, the ancient religion of our own island.   To nothing, perhaps, more than mysticism does the old proverb, "Far fowls have fair feathers," seem to apply strikingly to-day, when we find students of the mysterious making deep excursions into the tenets of Vedic, Buddhistic and Egyptian religion and almost entirely neglecting that which is nearer to their hand, at their very doors, so to speak, and the fragments of which can be gleaned from British folklore.   It may be argued that no such body of literature as is to be found in the Vedic writings, for instance, or in the Egyptian Book of the Dead, is available to the student.   That is a wretched plea, for a literature, if not so extensive, at least equally mystical, is available to him in the Welsh Triads, the Irish legends and the vast epic of the Grail, which con-tains an extraordinary amount of Druidic reminiscence overlaid by early Christian ideas. Let the Theosophist and the student of world-religion betake himself to the source rather than to the affluents. This is not to say that he should neglect the Indian and Egyptian phases of the subject, but that he should prefer the later Eastern above the earlier Western mysticism has always seemed to the writer as being a curiously perverted choice. We find the germs of a mysticism in Europe among the Aurignacians 25,000 years ago. From that germ sprang the whole process of Egyptian religion, with the associated rites of the embalmer's art. The proof is irrefragable, and should not Mysticism commence the study of its alphabet with the A of Atlantis?

CHAPTER XIV

ANIMAL LIFE IN ATLANTIS

WE are on rather surer ground in dealing with the subject of the animals and plants of Atlantis than in touching upon the history of its kings, for we have certain excellent data upon which to build sound hypotheses. In the first place, certain fragments of the sunken Atlantis, the Azores and the Canary Islands, still remain above water, and their fauna and flora provide us with a certain amount of comparative material from which we can argue regarding the general conditions of plant and animal life in Atlantis. In the second place we can compare the biological conditions of western Europe with those of eastern America, and if we find similarities between them it is open to us to assume that a biological link formerly existed in the Atlantic region, and that conditions upon it must have borne a strong resemblance to those obtaining in the two areas with which it was formerly connected.

It must, however, be borne in mind that the conditions of animal and plant life on Atlantis were not the same in the various phases of its history any more than they were during the long and changing periods and phases of climatic change in Europe and America. At the same time it may be taken for granted that the recurring periods of the Ice Age, whatever their duration, can scarcely have had any great effect on the climate of Atlantis, although there is equally no doubt that they must have exercised a certain influence upon the meteorological conditions prevailing in the island-continent. But as

we are dealing with the history of Atlantis subsequent
to the Ice Age, it will be sufficient for our purpose if we
regard conditions there from that point of view alone.

A very considerable literature has gathered round the
question of animal and plant life on Atlantis. If we
confine ourselves first to the fauna of the Continent we
find that the question of animal life on the Azores opens
up some considerations of very great interest. The very
name of the Azores means the "hawk islands," and if
hawks abounded in the archipelago when it was discoveied
it is safe to say that they did so in that part of Atlantis to
which it formerly belonged. This implies that the
animals on which they are wont to live, chiefly rodents,
rabbits, rats and mice, must also have been present in
large numbers. It would seem, too, that this group of
islands was known to geographers before its official
discovery in 1439, for in a book published in 1345 by a
Spanish friar the Azores are certainly referred to and the
names of the several islands given. On an atlas, too,
which was produced some forty years later at Venice,
several of the islands are indicated by name as Columbia,
or the Isle of Doves, now Pico, Capraria or the Isle of
Goats, now San Miguel, Li Congi or Rabbit Island, now
Flores, and Corvi Marini, or Isle of Sea Crows, now
Corvo. These names go to show that the islands in
question, although long isolated from Europe, abounded
in animals and birds of the species through which they
came to be known, and that these species must have
flourished there for countless centuries prior to their
official discovery.

It has indeed been argued that the rabbit may have
reached the Azores and Europe from America by way
of the ancient land-bridge. Professor Osborn, Dr.
Major, and Lyddekker have indicated the connection
between the rabbit forms of Africa and America and

have drawn the conclusion therefrom that the species must have migrated from one of these continents to the other. Professor Scharff, however, believes that the land-bridge which joined Africa and South America must have been situated farther to the south than the Atlantic islands, but that from North Africa there was intercourse with southern Europe with which the Atlantic islands were connected, and that by this rather round-about route South American species would have been able to reach Madeira and the Azores. But may not the rabbit and other leptorrhine species have originated upon Atlantis itself and have spread eastwards and westwards to America and Africa? If, as Professor Scharff states, the land-bridge connecting these two continents lay considerably south of the Atlantic islands, it seems a little difficult to account for the fact that the rabbit prevails in much greater numbers in the more temperate northern latitudes. We find the rodent species invading and re-invading European soil in the more severe phases of the recurring Ice Ages, in fact Macalister has laid it down that as the glaciations drew near, and the forests began to give place to steppe conditions, the small rodents invariably returned to European soil, and it is their presence, indeed, which delimits the later interglaciations. At the same time it is notorious that the rabbit flourishes exceedingly in such a mild climate as that of Australia, to which the climate of Atlantis must have borne a certain general resemblance, so that it seems a little difficult to account for the species pressing from a genial climate into an area where tundra conditions prevailed. It seems probable, however, that the rabbit may actually have originated upon Atlantean soil—a habitat most suitable for its development and speedy propagation, and that later the struggle for existence through overcrowding forced it into less congenial regions.

It has frequently been pointed out, too, that the carnivorous animals of Tertiary times in Europe are closely connected with those of America. The European Atlantic islands are somewhat destitute of animals of this species, but it is quite possible that in the course of the many centuries which separated the Tertiary era from the final submergence of Atlantis that they may have been utterly rooted out by a civilised people, precisely as the wolf was rooted out in Britain.

It has occasionally been stated with some authority that Atlantis may have been the cradle of all animal life. Such a statement, in view of our lack of knowledge on the subject, should be regarded cautiously. Certain circumstances exist, however, which seem to render it not improbable that some species may have had their beginnings on the island-continent. The data connected with the migrations of the eel, for example, lend colour to this assumption. Dr. Johannes Schmidt, the Danish biologist, who has paid great attention to the migrations of the eel, is inclined to think that it may have originated in the ocean fastnesses surrounding the site of Atlantis. The parent eels annually leave our shores and deposit their eggs deep down in the Atlantic Ocean between the Bahama Isles and Europe, after which all trace of them disappears, but their young make their way back more than four thousand miles to our rivers. For nearly three years they swim on, steering a steadfast course for the shores of Britain, while the American eels, which are distinguished by a shorter back-bone, unerringly make their way back to their own country. This would seem to indicate that their instinct carries them to the primeval breeding-place from which both the eels of Europe and America originally migrated.

A similar phenomenon is to be witnessed in connection with the lemmings of Scandinavia. The lemming, a small rodent, periodically seems to feel a migratory impulse of a southerly tendency, during which countless numbers of these animals leave the Norwegian coast and swim far out into the Atlantic. When they reach the spot to which the migratory impulse has called them they swim round for some considerable time as if searching for land which instinct tells them should be there, but at last, growing exhausted, sink into the depths. Large flocks of birds, too, follow their example and tumble exhausted into the sea, and the beautiful saffron-winged catopsilia of British Guiana, which has been described by Dr. William Beebe, the American naturalist, obeys a similar oceanic call. Annually the males of this species take part in the fatal flight. In great coloured clouds they fly into the sea. If these migrations are not eloquent of an animal impulse to return to the lost Atlantis, it would indeed be difficult to say what was.

Two well-known biologists, the Messrs. Slater, in their work *The Geography of Mammals*, regard the mid-Atlantic area as a separate division of the biological area of the globe which they call the "Mesatlantic." To this region they assign two species of marine animals, the Monk Seal and the Siren. Neither of these animals frequents the open ocean, but is invariably to be found in the vicinity of land. One species of the Monk Seal inhabits the Mediterranean and another the West Indies, while the Siren is to be found in the estuaries of West Africa, along the South American coast and among the West Indian islands, and the inference drawn is that their ancestors must have spread along some coastline which "united the Old World and the New at no very distant period."

Plato assures us that the elephant was a denizen of Atlantis. It has always seemed to me probable that the passage relating to the elephant is one of those which serves to reveal the historical value of Plato's account. The elephant disappeared from Europe at a comparatively early era, Elephas antiquus being discernible in the Late Lower Palæolithic Age, and Elephas primigeneus in the Middle Palæolithic or Crô-Magnon Age. The Marques de Cerralbo discovered the bones of Elephas antiquus along with human artifacts at Torralba in the province of Soria, Spain. If then, this animal existed in Spain in the period in question, a period which witnessed human immigration from Atlantis, it is not improbable that it was still wandering to and fro between the European mainland and the island-continent over a still-existing land-bridge, and that, after this land-bridge disappeared, it became extinct in Europe, but continued to flourish in Atlantis, where it was marooned. I cannot, however, find any trace of its former existence in the Canaries or Azores, but excavation in these groups had been of so perfunctory a character that when it is undertaken on a larger scale surprising developments may be expected. In any case, there is nothing extravagant in the supposition that elephants actually existed in Atlantis. If they did not, it is most unlikely that the Egyptian tradition, as handed down by Plato, would have alluded to them at all. The elephant was an animal by no means familiar in Egypt, although known to the Egyptians to exist in Central Africa. It is, therefore, unlikely that it would have been dragged in by the priest of Sais merely to render his tale still more highly coloured.

From the humbler forms of life on the Azores and the Canaries we can glean a good idea of how similar life in Atlantis appeared. For example, we find many of the butterflies and moths of the Canaries represented in both Europe and America. Sixty per cent of them are to be found in Europe, and twenty per cent in America, sure proof of their former presence in a submerged continent once lying between these regions.

Referring to the continental origin of the Fauna of the Atlantic islands, M. Termier remarks: "Two facts remain relative to the marine animals, and both seem impossible of explanation, except by the persistence, up to very nearly the present times, of a maritime shore extending from the West Indies to Senegal, and even binding together Florida, the Bermudas, and the bottom of the Gulf of Guinea. Fifteen species of marine mollusca lived at the same time, both in the West Indies and on the coast of Senegal, and nowhere else, unless this co-existence can be explained by the transportation of the embryos. On the other hand, the Madreporaria fauna of the island of St. Thomas, studied by M. Gravier, includes six species—one does not live outside of St. Thomas, except in the Florida reefs, and four others are known only from the Bermudas. As the duration of the pelagic life of the Madreporaria is only a few days, it is impossible to attribute this surprising reappearance to the action of marine currents. In taking all this into account, M. Germain is led to admit the existence of an Atlantic continent connected with the Iberian peninsula, and with Mauritania, and prolonging itself far towards the south, so as to include some regions of desert climate. During the Miocene period, again, this continent extends as far as the West Indies. It is then portioned off, at first in the direction of the West Indies, then in the south, by the establishment of a marine shore, which extends as far as Senegal and to the depths of the Gulf of Guinea, then at length in the east, probably during the Pliocene epoch, along the coast of Africa. The last great fragment, finally engulfed, and no longer having left any other vestiges than the four archipelagoes, would be the Atlantis of Plato."

CHAPTER XV

THE COLONIES OF ATLANTIS

AT least a score of writers have insisted that Atlantis, at the era of her fall, sent out numerous colonies to all parts of the world. The colonial expansion of Atlantis has especially been stressed in more recent times by Donelly, Brasseur de Bourbourg and Augustus Le Plongeon, all of whom seek to establish an Egyptian connection. The general attitude of the majority of those writers who believe in the Atlantean penetration of America or European countries may, perhaps, be summed up in a passage from an article "Some Notes on the Lost Atlantis," which appeared in *Papyrus*, the official organ of the Theosophical Society in Egypt, for March, 1921. "Atlantis sent her children over the entire world," says the writer of this article. "Many of them are to this day living as Red Indians in Canada and the United States of America. They colonised Egypt, and built up one of the mighty Egyptian Empires. They spread over the North of Asia as the Turanians and Mongols—a tremendous and prolific race, still constituting a majority of the population of the earth."

Of course the obvious retort of the "official" anthropologist to such a statement as this, if he troubled to retort at all, would probably be: "What tangible evidence have you of the presence of Atlanteans in any American or European country? Can you point to any documents relating to their presence there, to any existing monuments raised by their hands?"

The answer is that tradition, if carefully employed, is a document of equal sanction with anything in black letter, a view which is being slowly but none the less certainly adopted by experienced students of Folklore, if not by all archæologists; and that it is impossible to point to anything in the nature of existing Atlantean monuments, because we cannot compare them with originals. It is, however, possible to say almost definitely that the architectural remains of the Maya of Central America are of less remote Atlantean origin, coming as they did from Antillia, the western and more lately submerged portion of the Atlantean continent.

But the question of Atlantean colonisations cannot so easily be settled as its protagonists and antagonists seem to think. Sufficient evidence, traditional and ethnological, has been adduced to show that it is one which demands reasonable consideration. Surely such a mass of corroborative tradition could not exist without some basis of actual fact, nor can it be disproved that the races which entered Spain and France at the conclusion of the great Ice Age came from an Atlantic area. Plato's account seems to enshrine a very clear memory of the Azilian or proto-Iberian invasion of Europe from an Atlantic country. He writes about it, taking his facts from Egyptian sources, in much the same manner as a mediæval historiographer might have written—basing what he says entirely upon a still older authority. He tells us that the Atlanteans already had possessions in Europe before the invasion and the catastrophe, and the facts of archæology seem to bear out his testimony.

Sufficient has been said regarding the Atlantean colonisation of France, Spain and Britain. The reference by Diodorus to settlement in Africa by the Atlanteans is plain enough, and the fact that the inhabitants of North West Africa in Roman times were known as Atlanteans is significant. "These Atlanteans," says Dr. Badichon, who resided in Algeria for many years, "among the ancients passed for the favourite children of Neptune. They made known the worship of this god to other nations—to the Egyptians, for example. In other words, the Atlanteans were the first known navigators."[1]

It must be clear that if Atlantis actually sunk about 9600 B.C., as Plato's account would give us to understand, all Atlantean colonial settlement on European soil must have ceased with that period, and if that be conceded, we must regard all Atlantean expansion in the Mediterranean and other European areas as identified with Azilian or Iberian expansion. No anthropologist of experience will for a moment seek to gainsay the Iberian penetration of the entire Mediterranean area from Spain to Egypt, even though he may not support the nation of its Atlantean provenance. But Sergi, the great originator of the theory that the Iberian race had made widespread settlements in all parts of Europe, laid stress on the circumstance that it emanated from Western Africa—that is, from the very region which is still known as the Atlas region, and from that part of the dark continent whose people in Roman times were still known as "Atlanteans," and were so called by Diodorus. "The idea," he says, "has arisen that Western rather than Eastern Africa was the original home of these people, "the ancient and modern Egyptians, Nubians, Abyssinians, Gallas, Somalis, Berbers, and Fulahs." He "will not deny to the Sahara the possibility of being the cradle" of his Mediterranean race. His conclusions regarding the North African genesis of the Iberians nowadays find tacit agreement among anthropologists.

[1] I recently received a letter from a lady who knows North-West Africa well, in which she states that many traditions of Atlantis are still to be found among the native population. An Arab Emir of her acquaintance is quite an authority on the subject, and has even written a book on Atlantis in Morocco. The names of the author and of the book she does not mention.

If we agree that these Iberians and their forerunners, the Azilians, were of Atlantean stock, this settles the matter at once—for us at least. This race cherished the memory of its Atlantean origin during countless generations, and spreading along both shores of the Mediterranean, at length reached Greece and Asia Minor in the North, and Egypt to the South. It is much more reasonable to infer such a process of steady racial progression than to assume the arrival in, say, Egypt, of a great Atlantean fleet in pre-dynastic times as Le Plongeon does.

But did Atlantis finally sink in 9600 B.C. or thereabouts? Did not a considerable portion of her territory survive for many centuries subsequent to this date, and contrive to send out colonial and cultural influences to Europe, as Antillia seems to have done to barbarous America? I confess the notion has long haunted me. I refer to it as a "notion," simply because I cannot find sufficient proof to exalt it into a definite hypothesis. I have already dealt with the question of the existence of a great Atlantean prehistoric civilization of which the Aurignacian may have been the "broken-down" remains. Let us see what can be said for the existence of an Atlantean civilisation of considerably later date than that given by Plato for the final submergence of the island-continent, a culture which had either recaptured the ancient spirit of the pre-Aurignacian times, or which had developed from the Azilian type, and continued to exist into the "historical" period of European archæology.

The period possible for the existence of such a civilisation must naturally fall many centuries later than Plato's date of 9,600 B.C., to permit of the development of a civilization more advanced than the Azilian, and, judging from the analogy of the growth of Egyptian culture, it will not be exceeding probability to place it somewhere about 5000 years B.C. And it is obvious in any case that

CANOPIC JAR FROM A TOMB AT ZAACHILLA, MEXICO

Atlantis itself must have finally disappeared before the
period in which vessels were regularly engaged in Mediterranean commerce, say about 2,000 B.C. Have we any
record of cultural influences entering Europe during the
period in question? We seem to have one at least in the
tradition of the origin of the Cabiri, the deities of a strange
mystery cult of western origin.

From the great mass of antique writings concerning
the Cabiri the following material may be extracted. The
Cabiri were twin deified brothers, later identified with
the Dioscuri, Castor and Pollux. They are described
by Dionysius of Halicarnassus as "two youths armed
with spears." Sanchoniathon, the Carthaginian writer,
states that they were of Carthaginian or African origin.
The cult of the Cabiri, indeed, seems to have been brought
from North-west Africa to Egypt and Greece, and it is
definitely stated that it was "delivered to the Egyptian
Osiris." The Cabiri are said by Sanchoniathon to have
been the inventors of boats, of the arts of hunting and
fishing, of building and agriculture. They also invented
the arts of writing and of medicine. In fact it seems
that the ancient myth of the Cabiri enshrines a tradition
of the invasion of the Mediterranean area by a civilised
race at a period when that region was as yet in a condition
of barbarism. It certainly originated in North-west
Africa. At first I was under the impression that the
myth referred to the entrance of the Azilian peoples to
the Mediterranean, but chronological reasons seem to
militate against such a presumption, and it appears much
more probable that it is connected with a cultural invasion
from the west at a much later period, say some 3000 years
B.C.

This cult could scarcely have originated in North-West
Africa. In that region we find no record of the former
existence of a civilisation pre-eminent in the arts of

architecture, agriculture and writing. That the cult
of the Cabiri is in some manner connected with that of
Osiris seems reasonably clear. A temple at Memphis
was consecrated to them, and they seem to have shared
the eastward march of the Osirian religion from North-
West Africa to Egypt.[1] May it not be that the secret
cult connected with the Cabiri emanated from an Atlantis
still existing about 3000 B.C., and that it spread eastward
from North-West Africa through later Carthaginian
influence to Greece and Asia Minor? There seems to
be no other way of accounting for the appearance of a cult
which could not have originated on African soil.

It would seem, too, that Crete was penetrated by
Atlantean civilization, that, indeed, the Atlantean culture
was responsible for the beginnings of Minoan progress.
The theory has been put forward that Plato's account of
Atlantis was, indeed, a mere reminiscence of the fall of
the Minoan civilization of Crete. A writer in *The Times*
of February 14, 1909, stated that: "The disappearance
of the island corresponds to what archæology tells us of
the utter collapse of the empire of Knossos, followed by
the replacement even of Cretan sailors by Phœnicians at
Egyptian ports."

It is, however, unlikely that a cultural collapse, which
took place about 1,200 B.C., should have been magnified
only 600 years later by Egyptian priests into a cataclysm
which had occurred 9,000 years before! It is as if we
were to place the fall of Constantinople away back in the
Neolithic Age! The ancients, even without the aid of
documentary evidence, knew their history better than
that, and had a better conception of chronology than
some modern historians seem to think. It is too frequently forgotten that written history, as we know it, is
merely a thing of the last two or three centuries. Tradition

[1] See *The Problem of Atlantis*, pp. 150 ff.

aided by meagre written records, took its place formerly, and became as much an art as written history is to-day.

It is much more likely that the Minoan civilisation of Crete was modelled upon that of an Atlantis which had possibly survived to a much later date than has been thought possible until now. Civilization in Crete was undoubtedly of very ancient introduction. Early Minoan civilisation dates, roughly, from about 3,400 B.C., and certain of its phases bear a strong resemblance to Plato's picture of life in Atlantis. The bull was its sacred animal, as in Atlantis, and the great arena at Knossos was certainly used for bull-fights or sacrifices. The Cretans were largely of Iberian race, and had labyrinthine cave-temples like those of the Aurignacians of Spain and France. Our prime authority for the myth of the labyrinth is Plutarch, whose account, more or less sophisticated, ran through a maze of romantic legend quite as intricate as the extraordinary site which inspired it. It was for generations identified with the winding cavern of Gortyna, which penetrated a little hill at the foot of Mount Ida, the endless ramifications of which seemed to mark it as the veritable lair of Theseus' monster. But when Sir Arthur Evans in 1900 first undertook his memorable excavations on the site of Knossos, he felt inclined to identify the palace of Minos itself as the true Labyrinth, basing his theory on the intricate and truly labyrinthine character of its winding passages and staircases.

As we have seen, the caverns which, according to good authorities, served the Palæolithic Aurignacians as temples or places of worship are rich in painted and sculptured representations of the bull, which seems to have been the chief deity of this race, or at least an object of veneration or placation by a hunting population. Doubtless the legend that a Great Bull actually haunted the recesses of those almost impenetrable caverns—that at Niaux in the

Ariège is more than a mile in depth—would become an honoured tradition in the course of generations.

The Minoan civilisation of Crete had almost certainly a cultural descent from the Aurignacian, as illustrated in its wall-paintings, its Tanagran statuettes, which link up with those of Spain by way of the Balearic Islands, and its cult of the bull, the representation of which in its palaces strikingly resembles the art of the early Aurignacian painters. It was, then, probably, some venerable myth of a tauric deity dwelling in a labyrinthine cave, and anciently derived from Spain or from the common source of Atlantis, which gave rise to the Cretan tradition of the Labyrinth. This presupposes that the cave of Gortyna was the true Cretan labyrinth connected with the myth of Theseus and the Minotaur.

The idea that Egypt was a colony of Atlantis has not met with great acceptance from many writers on the subject. It is a little difficult at first sight to recognise the justice of the claim. A work which insists upon the theory is the late Dr. Augustus Le Plongeon's *Queen Mòo and the Egyptian Sphinx*, which tells us how Mòo, a princess of the Maya of Central America, fled to Egypt after the catastrophe which ended in the submergence of Atlantis, and founded the Egyptian civilisation. But we cannot surmise such a condition of things as would allow of the settlement of Egypt by a princess who was also responsible for Maya civilisation. Chronological and other considerations simply will not permit of a hypothesis of the kind.

It is much more probable that any Atlantean influence which reached Egypt did so by way of North–West Africa.

In the first place, the most unexceptionable kind of evidence exists that Egypt was populated at an early date by people of Iberian stock. Authorities agree that the Iberian race was a large factor among those ethnological constituents which helped to make up the composite stock known as the ancient Egyptians, and that they must have entered Egypt from the West. That the Iberians were Atlanteans I have already tried to prove, and, if that is accepted, it must also be granted that they introduced Atlantean culture into the valley of the Nile.

The evidence which appears most strongly in favour of the introduction of Atlantean influence into Egypt is connected with the cult of Osiris. That this worship was not indigenous to Egypt is obvious, but it is difficult to say at what era it was introduced into the Nile country. It is certainly found at Abydos during the First Dynasty, but certain Pyramid Texts prove that it had an even more archaic history in the land.

Budge believes the Osirian worship to be "Libyan" or North African. But it is the *Book of the Dead* which gives us perhaps most insight into the character and provenance of the Osirian religion. Four thousand years at least before the Christian era certain parts of it were in use in Egypt, and that these were even then associated with the cult and art of mummification is clear. As the ritual of mummification grew more intricate, the *Book of the Dead* grew in importance, and it was believed that without a knowledge of its texts no deceased person would be preserved to enter the abodes of bliss.

There is little doubt, however, that many of the texts in the *Book of the Dead* are of a more archaic character than the First Dynasty. They were edited and re-edited many, many times, and even at a date so early as 3,300 B.C. the scribes who copied them were so misled by many passages which they contained as scarcely to be able to follow their general meaning. Dr. Budge remarks: "We are in any case justified in estimating the earliest form of the work to be contemporaneous with the foundation of the civilisation which we call 'Egyptian' in the Valley of the Nile."

One of these texts was indeed "discovered" in the First Dynasty, and was then referred to a date which equates with 4,266 B.C. When, then, was it first reduced to writing, or to literary shape?

The *Book of the Dead* was almost certainly a survival of a Neolithic ritual for the preservation of the body in order that it might live again. We know that the Aurignacian people had such a conception of immortality residing in the bones of the body. As Professor Macalister remarks regarding their practices of painting the bones of the dead with red oxide: "The remarkable rite of painting the bones red should be especially noticed. . . . The purpose of the rite is perfectly clear. Red is the colour of living health. The dead man was to live again in his own body, of which the bones were the framework. To paint it with the colour of life was the nearest thing to mummification that the Palæolithic people knew; it was an attempt to make the body again serviceable for its owner's use. In this connection it is instructive to recall a familiar incident in folk tales, in which the hero, having come to grief, the flesh of his body is restored from the bones, or even from a small splinter of bone, and then resuscitated."

Mummification, indeed, is merely an elaboration of this practice, and it is plain that the Egyptian rite of mummification with all its intricate ritual was developed from the Aurignacian practice, which was its germ and seed. The Egyptians, like the Aurignacians, believed red to be the colour of life. They painted the faces of their gods red, and daubed red paint on the cheeks of their mummies. In all probability the Aurignacian, that is the Atlantean, custom of painting the bones of the dead spread along the coast of North Africa until it reached Egypt, where in course of time it took on an appearance of greater refinement, so that no longer the bones but the body was painted in the hues of life. But there is also good reason

to believe that along the entire track of Atlantean civilisation, from Egypt to Peru, a definite cult of embalm-
ment, the first signs of which we witness in late Aurignacian times in the tying up of the corpse in leather
bundles and bandages, slowly took shape until it emerged
as a definite cult with well-marked characteristics and
ritual. I believe that this cult, the Osirian, originated in
Atlantis, and spread thence all over North Africa on the
one hand and to America on the other, and that its affiliated
customs took root in most places were it was carried.

CHAPTER XVI

THE ATLANTEAN CULTURE COMPLEX

WE find then that the old belief that the great power of Atlantis founded something in the nature of ready-made colonies in Egypt, North Africa, America, and elsewhere, must give way to the much more sane and reasonable hypothesis that a species of slow cultural penetration drifted eastward and westward from the area of the now submerged continent. It is, indeed, extremely improbable that Atlantis actually founded anything in the nature of a colony. It is much more likely that the Atlantean influence, after gaining a footing on the shores of Europe, America and Africa, slowly skirted these and finally penetrated some little distance into their interiors. Indeed it is on the coast-lines of these continents that we discover the best evidences of what may be termed Atlantean influence.

Every great civilization has been distinguished by a very definite group of cultural and customary manifestations and practices, and the proof that the Atlantean civilisation was so distinguished is fairly evident. From the shores of western Europe to those of eastern America a certain culture-complex is distributed and is found on the intervening insular localities, while its manifestations are also to be discovered in great measure in North Africa and Egypt on the one hand, and in Mexico, Central America and Peru on the other. This culture-complex is so constant in the region alluded to that it is clear now that a lost oceanic link formerly united its American and European extremities.

The principal elements which distinguished the Atlantean culture-complex are the practice of mummification, the practice of witchcraft, the presence of the pyramid, head-flattening, the couvade, the use of three-pointed stones, the existence of certain definite traditions of cataclysm, and several other minor cultural and traditional evidences. The main argument is that these are all to be found collectively confined within an area stretching from the western coasts of Europe to the eastern shores of America, and embracing the western European islands and the Antilles. So far as I am aware, these elements are not to be found associated with each other in any other part of the world. This seems to supply the surest kind of proof that they must have emanated from some Atlantic area now submerged, which formerly acted as a link between east and west, and whence these customs were distributed eastward and westward respectively.

We have seen that the ancient Aurignacians of Spain and France possessed the rudiments of the art of mummification, and it is also well-known that their kindred on the Canary islands were acquainted with it in its more advanced stage. From the work of Alonzo de Espinosa, a friar of the sixteenth century, we learn that in these islands there existed a caste of embalmers who, like those of the Nile country, were regarded as outcasts. The corpse was embalmed with a mixture of melted mutton-grease and grass-seed, stones and the bark of pine-trees, the object being to give the shrunken frame the contours of life. The body was then placed in the sun until it was dried, and was later sewn up in sheepskin, which was then enclosed in pine-bark. Some of the more distinguished dead were placed in sarcophagi made of hard wood and carved in one piece in the shape of the body, precisely as were the Egyptian mummy-cases. It is also known that dressed skins were swathed round the body just as linen bands were wound round the Egyptian corpse. The Canarese custom further resembles the Egyptian in that the first incision in the body was made with a stone knife. Examination of the mummies found in the Canary Islands prove them to bear a close resemblance to those of Peru.

The beginnings of mummification are thus found among the Aurignacians of Spain and France, and its later stage among the people of the Canary Islands. If we cross the ocean to the Antilles, we find that the art of mummification had at one time flourished there. In Porto Rico the skull and bones of the dead were wrapped in cotton cloth or in baskets and preserved for worship. Again the skulls were frequently attached to false bodies made of cotton and were kept in a separate temple. The Caribs likewise made cotton images which contained human bones. Peter Martyr alludes to certain *zemis* or idols made of cotton, and one of these, discovered in Santo Domingo, consisted of a skull enclosed in a cotton covering and mounted on a body stuffed with the same material. Artificial eyes had been inserted in the eye-sockets and cotton bandages tied round the legs and arms. In Haiti it was the practice, before interring the body, to bind it with bandages of woven cloth and to place it in a grave with symbols and amulets. Las Casas and Columbus both mention that the Indians of Haiti made statues of wood in which they placed the bones of relatives, giving the statues the names of the people to whom the bones belonged. One myth of the Haitian Indians told how a certain idol, Faraguvaol, was, like the mummified Osiris, discovered in the trunk of a tree. When wrapped in cotton he was able to escape from it as the Egyptian ba or soul could escape from its mummy-swathings.

Mr. J. H. Fewkes, who has investigated the native customs of the Antilles, remarks that: "The dead were some-

AMERICAN (MAYA) FORM OF PYRAMID

times wrapped in cotton cloth, and cotton puppets or effigies of stuffed cotton cloth in which the bones of the dead were wrapped are mentioned in early writings. One of the best of these is figured in an article by the author in his pamphlet on *zemis* from Santo Domingo. . . . The figure, which was found, according to Dr. Cronau, in a cave in the neighbourhood of Maniel, west of the capital, measures 75 centimetres in height. According to the same author the head of this specimen was a skull with artificial eyes and covered with woven cotton. About the upper arms and thighs are found woven fabrics, probably of cotton, following a custom to which attention has been already called. There is a representation of bands over the forehead." Here we see a distinct reminiscence of mummy bandaging, and a great gap in the abdomen of the figure conclusively shows that the intention of the maker was to represent an eviscerated corpse.

If now we proceed further westward to the mainland of America we find abundant evidence of the practice of embalming the dead. This is, of course, more apparent in the highly civilised centres such as Mexico, Central America and Peru. The method of embalming the body differed in these several regions. In Mexico it was placed in a sedentary position inside a mummy-bundle, which was covered with embroidery, feathers and symbols. Over this was placed a network of rope, and on the top was placed a false head or mask, which provides a link with the practice of the Antilles. In Central America the body after embalment was disposed in a recumbent attitude and swathed round with bandages, almost as in Egypt. The pictures in the Mexican and Maya native manuscripts provide many representations of mummies. The Maya of Central America buried the bodies of kings and priests in elaborate sarcophagi of stone, accompanying them with canopic vessels similar to those employed in Egyptian funerary practice, and covered by lids representing the genii of the four parts of the compass, as was also the case in Egypt.

Like the Egyptians, too, the Maya associated certain colours with the principal bodily organs and with the cardinal points. In some cases colours and organs affected agree both as regards their Maya and Egyptian examples. We also find the dog regarded as the guide of the dead both in Egypt and Mexico. When a Mexican chieftain died a dog was slain, which was supposed to precede him to the other world, precisely as the dog Anubis did in the case of the dead Egyptian. A further striking similarity between Mexican and Egyptian funerary practice is the presence in Mexican manuscripts of the *tat* symbol in association with the mummy, the emblem which was believed to provide the dead with a new backbone on resurrection. This *tat* symbol, it may be said in passing, bears a strong resemblance to certain of the Azilian symbols found on painted pebbles and in caves in France and Spain.

Certain Mexican gods were actually developed from the idea of the mummy. One of them, Tlauizcalpan-tecutli, the god of the planet Venus, is shown both in the Codex Borgia and the Codex Borbonicus as a mummy accompanied by the small blue dog, the companion of the dead. On the recurrence of his festival a mock mummy-bundle was raised upon a mast, round which the celebrant priests danced. Perhaps the most instructive picture among the Mexican manuscripts in relation to this subject is that in the Sahagun MS., in which Mexican priests are depicted in the act of manufacturing the sham mummy, the mask, the paper ornaments and flags which accompanied it. Almost equally interesting is the *Relacion de las ceremonios y Ritos de Michoacan*, quoted by Seler, which contain a number of striking pictures illustrating the process of mummification in that region.

In Peru the art of mummification was widespread and the tombs of that country have furnished large numbers of mummied bodies. The dead were wrapped in llama skins, on which the outline of the eyes and mouth were carefully marked. In many other parts of America mummification was practised, but as I have already dealt with the whole evidence for this at very great length elsewhere, it would be a work of supererogation to detail it in this place.[1]

The second distinguishing element of the Atlantean culture-complex is the presence of witchcraft. It is not intended to convey the impression that witchcraft is not found in countries to which this culture-complex does not penetrate, the intention being to show that where it is discovered in connection with the other elements of the complex Atlantean culture had penetrated. In fact it seems probable that witchcraft, as a cult, originated in Atlantis. It is indeed a fertility cult, originating in a very early worship of the bull as a symbol of animal fertility, but what makes it of the greatest significance for the student of Atlantean Archæology is the fact that in its most striking aspects it is associated with those regions which were undoubtedly most affected by immigration from Atlantis—France, Spain and Mexico, and in the Aurignacian area of the two former countries. Its distribution in fact is much the same as that of the early customs which later developed into mummification.

That the Aurignacians practised it, we have the best evidence from their wall-paintings. In a rock-shelter at Cogul, near Lerida, in Spain, a painting has been discovered which represents a number of women dressed in the traditional costume of witches, with peaked hats and skirts descending from the waist, dancing round a male idol or priest, who is painted black—the "black

[1] See *Atlantis in America*, pp. 99–121.

man," indeed, of witch tradition. The scene is representative of a witches' sabbath. That the witch-cult also flourished in Mexico before and after its invasion by Cortes, is well-known. The Mexican witches, the *ciuateteo*, were supposed to wander through the air, to haunt cross-roads, to afflict children with paralysis, and to use as their weapons the elf-arrows, precisely as did the witches of Europe. The witches' sabbath was indeed quite as notorious an institution in ancient Mexico as in mediæval Europe. The Mexican witch, like her European sister, carried a broom on which she rode through the air, and was associated with the screech-owl. Indeed the queen of the witches, Tlazolteotl, is depicted as riding on a broom and as wearing the witch's peaked hat. Elsewhere she is seen standing beside a house accompanied by an owl, the whole representing the witch's dwelling, with medicinal herbs hanging from the eaves. The Mexican witches, too, like their European counterparts, smeared themselves with ointment which enabled them to fly through the air, and engaged in wild and lascivious dances, precisely as did the adherents of the cult in Europe. Indeed the old Spanish friars who describe them call them witches.

The connection between mummification and witchcraft is sufficiently clear, for the witches of Europe prized above all things a piece of Egyptian mummy-flesh as a vehicle for their magical operations, and the same practice was in vogue in America, where the hands and fingers of dead women were employed by the sorcerer for magical purposes. Moreover the Kwakiutl wizards of North-West America employed as a magical vehicle the skin and flesh of a dead man dried and roasted before the fire, and rubbed and pounded together. This was then tied up in a piece of skin or cloth and squeezed into a hollow human bone, which was buried in the ground

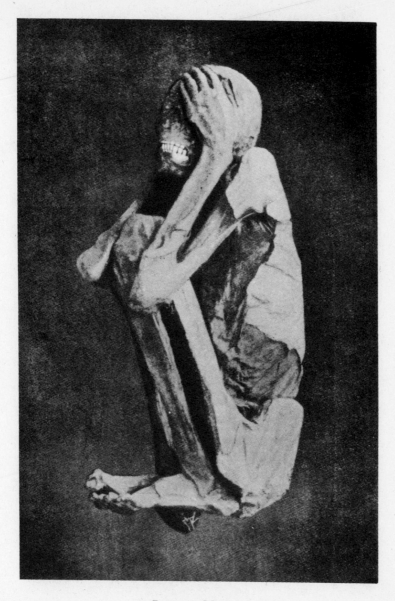

PERUVIAN MUMMY

in a miniature coffin. The relationship between European and American witchcraft is thus sufficiently clear, nor does either system show any great degree of resemblance to the sorcery cults of Asia, most of which are essentially male organisations. These similarities, when considered along with the geographical occurrence of the cult, appear much too significant to be ignored, especially when it is borne in mind that the ancient Aurignacian area was in later times one of the strongholds of witchcraft in Europe.

It would seem, too, that we have the very best possible reasons for regarding witchcraft in Europe and America as an emanation from Atlantis. In the Greek mythological tales of the Gardens of the Hesperides and of the Amazons of Hesperia, we find memories of a well-marked female cult, just as we do in the traditions of the Guanches of the Canary Islands, the last remnants of Atlantis. I have already summarized the traditional material connected with the Amazons and their invasion of Atlantis, from which it seems clear that they had a distinct association with witchcraft. They were, in short, a female cult of warlike tendencies and perhaps of cannibalistic leanings, like the more modern Amazons of Dahomey. It is significant, too, that we find the witches of Mexico behaving in precisely the same manner as the Amazons of classical tradition. In fact at one period in Mexican history a large force of Amazons or women warriors dwelling in the Huaxtec region on the Eastern coast of Mexico invaded the Mexican valley. They sacrificed their prisoners of war, and it is noteworthy that their leader on that occasion was Tlazolteotl, the chief goddess of the witches. Their principal weapon, like that of the Amazons, was the bow, and it is clear from Camargo's account of their patron goddess that she came from the classical Gardens of the Hesperides. He says that she "dwelt in a very pleasant and delectable place, where are many delightful fountains, brooks, and flower-gardens, which are called Tamoanchan, or the Place where are the Flowers, the nine-fold enchained, the place of the fresh, cool winds." This passage obviously connects the Amazons of Hesperia with those of Mexico, and the circumstance that both were armed with the bow, and the serpent-skin shield seems to clinch the matter.

Witch cults were also to be found on the European and American islands which formed links in the chain between Atlantis and the respective mainlands. Among the Guanches of the Canary Islands was found a sect known as the Effenecs, whose virgin priestesses, the Magades, worshipped in stone circles. On the Barranco of Valeron the circle in which they celebrated their rites still stands. Like the Mexicans, Aurignacians and Cretans, they engaged in symbolic dances and cast themselves into the ocean as a sacrifice to the waters which they believed would one day submerge their islands. Like the priestesses of the Mexican Tlazolteotl, too, it was their duty to baptise infants. Polyandry was in vogue among them, and it would seem that feminine rule obtained in the island. In the Antilles it is a little difficult to disentangle the native elements of witchcraft from those of the cult of Obeah, which is of African origin, but the distinct presence in these islands of priestesses of that cult shows that it must also have had a strong hold in that area.

The presence of the pyramid is a further evidence of the presence of the Atlantean complex. The evidence for this has already been referred to, and it is only necessary to say here that pyramids, either of a fully developed character or in an evolutionary form, are found closely associated with the other elements of the Atlantean culture-complex in Europe, as in the Canary Islands (in dolmen form), in the Antilles and in Mexico and Peru, as well as in the region of the Mound-builders in the Mississippi country. But we arrive now at evidence of a still more remarkable character.

The custom of flattening the head artificially is one so very peculiar that it cannot be regarded as having originated in more than one distinct area, yet we find it indubitably associated with the other elements of the Atlantean complex, whilst we do not discover it in other parts of the world to which that complex did not penetrate. Thus we discern it very clearly in the Aurignacian figures depicted in the marvellous wall-painting at Alpera, among the natives of Biscay at the present day, in the Antilles, and among the Maya and Aztecs of Central America. This type of cranial distortion seems indeed to have been a part of the specific culture which spread along the Atlantic route from Biscay to Central America. Sir Daniel Wilson remarks that Dr. Foville, "a distinguished French physician at the head of the Asylum for the Insane in the department of Seine-Inferieure and Charenton, has brought to light the remarkable fact that the practice of distorting the skull in infancy still prevails in France, by means of a peculiar head-dress and bandages; and in his large work on the *Anatomy of the nervous system* he has engraved examples of such compressed heads, one of which might be mistaken for a Peruvian sepulchral relic. The practice is probably one inherited from times of remote antiquity, and is found chiefly to characterise certain districts. Normandy, Gascony, Limousin and Brittany are specially noted for its prevalence, with some local variations as to its method and results." It is also well known that deformation of the cranium is to-day widely practised by the Basques, who occupy almost the same territory as did the Crô-Magnons in Aurignacian times.

This custom of head-distortion is also practised among the Indians of the Antilles, of whom Charlevoix says;

"They flattened their heads by art, thus reducing the size of their forehead, which pleased them greatly. To do this their mothers took care to hold them tightly pressed between their hands or between two little boards, which by degrees flattened the head, whereby the skull hardened in a moulded shape."

Now it is a well-known fact that head-flattening by means of what is known as the cradle-board was, and is, still practised among several of the tribes of the American mainland. The Maya in especial applied pressure during infancy to the forehead, as can be seen by the sloping crania of the figures depicted in their statues and bas-reliefs, and the same holds good of several of the Indian peoples of the western coast of America. I cannot find traces of any practice of the kind in the Canary Islands, and it is possible that it may have died out there, but it is not a little strange to discover a custom so pronounced precisely in the line assumed for the dissemination of Atlantean culture both eastward and westward, a practice which is by no means common in other parts of the world.

It would seem, too, that the practice of tattooing the body must be associated with the Atlantean complex.

The persistent custom of tattooing, still so prevalent among our seafaring and labouring classes, has been regarded by more than one antiquary as a relic of that remote past when, in all probability, the entire population of the British islands was so decorated. That tattooing was considered by the Romans as a practice peculiarly British is manifest from many classical passages, but especially in one from Claudian, who personifies Brittania as a female whose head is crowned with the skin of a "Caledonian monster," and whose cheeks are heavily marked with the imprints of the tattooing iron. Herodian, a Greek contemporary of Severus, is our authority for the statement that the northern Britons, whom that general

EGYPTIAN CANOPIC JARS

encountered in his campaign, did not wear garments because they did not wish to conceal the tattoo designs with which their bodies were covered.

Ample proof is, indeed, forthcoming that the tribal name "Britons" signified the "tattooed people." The Goidelic or Gaelic-speaking inhabitants of the British Isles called themselves "Cruithne" or "Qrtanoi," "those who tattoo themselves." This word, in the mouths of the Kymric-speaking sailors of Marseilles, who carried merchandise to and from Briton, became "Brtanoi," and in those of the Greek merchants of that town, Bretanoi, thus for ever associating our national designation with a foreign mispronunciation. To the Welsh, another Kymric-speaking people, Pictland was known as "Priten," and at an early era there is proof that they gave this name to the whole island, "Ynys Prydain," or "The Picts Island," that is "The Island of the Tattooed People."

That "Cruithne" or " Qrtanoi" signified "Tattooed" is clear enough from another passage in Herodian, who says that the Northern Britons tattooed upon their skins the figures of animals. This notice of the practice is doubly valuable, as it was written at least a century before the name of the Picts or tattooed people is mentioned in classical literature. It is upheld by a rendering of the early Gaelic writer Duald MacFirbis, who says that "Cruithneach (Pictus) is one who takes the *cruths* or forms of beasts, birds and fishes on his visage, and on his whole body."

This evidence, it will be seen, is entirely apart from those older derivations which drew the name "Pict" from the Latin *pictus*, "painted." But that the name Pict, in its native, and not in its Latin form, meant "tattooed" is certain. It goes back to an old Goidelic form *Qict*, and to a much more ancient Aryan root *peik*, signifying "tattooed," and that the word naturally became

confused by the Romans with their own term *pictus*
admits of no doubt. Claudius's oft-quoted statement
that the Picts were "nec falso nomine Pictos," "not
wrongly called the Painted People," simply implies that
he knew that they decorated their bodies with symbols,
and was rather surprised to find their tribal name resemble
the Latin word for a painted thing or person. "*Pictos*,"
says Rhys, "was a Celtican word of the same etymology
and approximately of the same meaning as the Latin
pictus. The Celticans applied it at an early date to the
Picts on account of their tattooing themselves, and the
Picts accepted it."

But that the word "Scot" also means "tattooed" is
less generally known. Rhys believed it to come from a
stem meaning 'cut," or "tattooed," in which derivation
he is upheld by Macbain. A passage in *Isidore of Seville*
explains "Scot" as "a word implying one having a
painted body, on which various figures have been drawn
by sharp iron and coloured stains." According to Mr.
E. W. Nicholson, of the Bodleian, there seems to have
been little or no real difference between "Scot" and
"Pict." "There was probably no greater distinction
between a 'Scot' and a "Pict'," he remarks, "than between a Saxon and an Angle: both names mean the same
thing, 'Tattooed.'" Speaking of the Picts and Scots of
Ireland, Professor Rhys remarked that "all Irish history
goes to show that they were closely kindred communities
of Cruithne, and I take it that the names Cruithne and
Scots may have been originally applicable to both alike."

But evidence of the most interesting kind has preserved
traces of the manner in which our ancestors actually did
tattoo themselves. There were Picts in France as well
as in Britain and Ireland, the Pictavi of Poitiers and
Poitou, whose custom of incising figures on their skins is
illustrated in their coinage. In a coin of the Unalli, who

inhabited the Cotentin, a head is depicted as tattooed with the design of a short sword, the hilt on the neck and the point level with the nostrils. Mr. Nicholson drew attention to this as probably associated with the name Calgacus, that of the Caledonian chief who gave battle to the Romans at Mons Graupius, and which in its native form *Calg*, means "sword." Calgacus, he thinks, may have been tattooed with the figure of a sword like the warrior represented on the coin in question.

A coin of the Aulerci of Maine shows a face the cheek of which is tattooed with a circle of dots, within which is the figure of a cock—perhaps the earliest representation of that bird as the national emblem of Gaul. On a coin of the Bodiocasses of Bayeux appears a face circled with tattoo dots, enclosing the latter A. Coins found in Jersey abound in similar figures representing tattooed faces. Frequently the designs are astronomical, depicting comets and other heavenly bodies. On one of the coins of the Continental Picts is a head, on the jaw of which a cross is incised, having a knob at each of its four ends. All these examples hail from the West of Gaul, and the tattoo designs they display are regarded by Nicholson as probably the distinguishing marks of a Goidelic or Gaelic-speaking population, and as distinguishing it from the Kymric Celts, who do not appear to have tattooed themselves.

It is known that these Pictish tribes, who were scattered over the area from North-West France to the Orkneys, were a sea-faring people of piratical tendencies. It was such a tribe, the Veneti, whom Julius Cæsar encountered in naval warfare off the Breton shores, and who were, he tells us, assisted by their kindred in Britain. Their ships were so much larger and better found than the Roman galleys that it was only after the most desperate resistance that he succeeded in overcoming them. The coasts of

North-Western France and Britain, from Cornwall to Caithness, swarmed with Cruithne or Britanni of similar type, who existed on maritime trade with each other, on fishing, and, when these failed, on plunder. These tribes, in short, were the true begetters of British maritime power, who, while Norman and Saxon were still unknown upon the sea, made voyages of hundreds of miles in vessels of considerable tonnage with sails of skin, and iron cables.

May it not be that from these hardy seafarers of the far past the maritime custom of tattooing has descended to the modern British seamen? It is noteworthy that the dress of the British sailor of Nelson's time, with its bonnet, deep collar and striped vest, is identical with the popular costume of the maritime districts of Brittany, whose sailors and fishermen are notorious tattooers. We have, of course, no evidence for the continuance of the practice during the middle ages. But it should be borne in mind that it was not then usual to record pictorially the humbler orders of society, and it is manifest that, if the custom still lingers among certain classes, it must have behind it a venerable antiquity.

So far as the origins of tattooing in Britain are concerned, it can almost certainly be traced to the ethnological association of its Celtic tribes with the Iberian race. With the Iberians the Celts mingled freely in Spain, France and Britain. It is known that the Iberians were immediately of African origin, and the ancient Egyptians put it on record that the Iberian tribes of North Africa were addicted to tattooing their bodies. Whether tattooing originated in North Africa or not, it seems probable that the custom spread thence to Asia Minor, and later to India, from where it seems to have found its way to Polynesia. However that may be, it certainly became established in Britain at an early era, so strongly, indeed, as to become the distinguishing mark of its native races, and to give its name even to the island itself.

For us, of course, "Iberian" means "Atlantean," and as tattooing in Europe certainly originated with the Iberians of Africa, it seems obvious that it must have been of Atlantean provenance. This is borne out by the fact that the Indians of the Antilles tattooed themselves in precisely the same manner as did the people of Britain and Gaul. The Guetares of Costa Rica also tattooed themselves with the figures of animals, and the Maya of Central America employed tattooing as an honorific sign, as well as head-flattening.

As we have seen, the ancient inhabitants of Spain and Gaul were tattooed. I can discover no record of the practice in the Canary Islands, but when we find the custom in vogue in three of the "links" of which Atlantis is the missing one, it would seem as though the custom of tattooing must also have emanated from the sunken continent, and have been introduced east and west along with the other features of the complex. In Britain, in particular, did it seem to linger, as doubtless it would in such an isolated area, and from that we may imply that other Atlantean imports flourished in our island until a relatively late era.

Still another custom which is of more universal adoption is to be found in connection with the Atlantean complex. This is the couvade, that strange notion, which ordains that when a child is born the father should take to his bed and there remain for days or weeks after the mother has resumed her ordinary mode of life. Diodorus Siculus assures us that it prevailed among the ancient Corsicans, and Appolonius Rhodius says that it was practised by the Iberians of northern Spain. But we find it also among the Basques of Spain and France, that is almost in the old Aurignacian region, and among the

Caribs of the West Indies as well as on the South American coast. It seems to have originated in the notion that there was a spiritual union between the father and the child, and that the latter would suffer were the sire not nursed as well as the mother. It has been traced in Europe to peoples of the Mediterranean race, that is to those races who are most closely connected with the immigrant peoples of Atlantis.

A symbolical usage, which in some manner binds together the various parts of the Atlantean complex, was the belief in the thunder-stone and its strange properties. This symbol, as the elf-arrow, or in other forms, is almost universal, and is regarded not only by primitive, but by many modern peoples as the source of tempests and seismic and volcanic phenomena, whether as the bolt of Vulcan, the lance of the Carib, or the arrow of the Mexican and Egyptian deities. But in the Atlantean region it affords yet another link between the witch and mummy cults of its peculiar culture-complex. In Mexico the planet Venus, the star of Quetzalcoatl, was regarded as the thunder-stone, and this symbol in many American and West European localities was carefully wrapped in swathings of cloth or hide precisely as the mummy is wrapped. It would seem, indeed, as if the original ideas associated with it had been fostered in some seismic region, and in any case, as has been said, it links up the witch and mummy cults with the notion of seismic instability. In some of the western Irish isles tempests were precipitated by unwinding the flannel bandages in which such sacred stones were wrapped, and in Mexico the god Hurakan, the hurricane, was the southern equivalent of the god Itzilacoliuhqui, who was merely the stone-knife of sacrifice, Quetzalcoatl, in his form of the planet Venus, wrapped up in mummy bandages. This god, like Vulcan, had been lamed through a supernatural accident, so

THREE-POINTED STONES FROM THE ANTILLES
(*After* Fewkes)

that he had obviously a volcanic significance, like the god of Mount Etna, whose volcanic scoriæ were regarded as thunderbolts.

It is difficult to believe that underlying these connections there is not some original symbolism having an application to seismic activity. Probably the thunder-stone was regarded as the very germ and essence of the tempest, the magical thing which caused ebullitions of nature, winds, earthquakes or eruptions. In another of its forms it was undoubtedly regarded as an earth-shaking implement, by means of which the gods fashioned the contours of the earth. To wrap it in bandages, however, seems to have been to render it temporarily quiescent, to have made a "mummy" of it. So long as it was confined within its swathings it was symbolically "dead" and unable to function, but once these were unwound its spirit of destruction was let loose.

Archæologists have discovered, in some parts of the Antilles, a number of strange three-cornered stones, which appear to have a close relationship with the symbol. Their geographical distribution is confined to Porto Rico, and the eastern extremity of Santo Domingo, that is to that part of the archipelago which probably formed a part of the almost vanished Antillia. These stones are usually carved in the shape of a mountain, beneath which the head and legs of a buried Titan can be observed. Says Professor Mason: "The Antilles are all of volcanic origin, as the material of our stone implements plainly shows." He proceeds to say that their shape is highly suggestive of the islands in question, and that they seem to represent mythological figures bearing the island on their backs. He points to the legend of Typheus, who was slain by Jupiter and buried under Mount Etna, and concludes: "A similar myth may have been devised in various places to account for volcanic or mountainous phenomena."

They certainly agree with the Maya conception of the
Cosmos, which alludes to the earth as supported on the
back of a great dragon or four-footed whale, and they
appear to be associated with the myth of Atlas himself,
the world-bearer connected with the story of Atlantis,
and they are further reflected in the myth of Quetzalcoatl, who, in his central American form, is assuredly the
dragon or serpent who dwelt in the sea. They certainly
seem to me to symbolise a deity, whose duty it was to
uphold the earth, but who, like Atlas, occasionally felt the
immensity of his burden and cast it from him, causing
universal destruction and catastrophe.

It would seem, too, that in these three-pointed stones
we find a combination of the idea of Atlas and that of the
world-shaping pick or hammer. Thus, in the thunder-
stone symbol, it seems, the whole significance of the
Atlantean culture-complex finds a nucleus. To it must
be referred, as to the hub of a wheel, the practice of mummification, witchcraft, and the mysteries and art of building in stone. The hammer of the thunder-god or crea-
tive deity with which he carved and shaped the earth was
indeed identical with the implement by which the early
sculptor fashioned his work. Manibozho, the god of the
Algonquin Indians, shaped the hills and valleys with his
hammer, constructing great beaver dams and moles across
the lakes. His myth says that "he carved the land and
sea to his liking," precisely as Poseidon carved the island
of Atlantis into alternate zones of land and water. Poseidon was notoriously a god of earthquake as well as a
marine deity, and it is a fair inference that he undertook
the task in question with the great primeval pick, a sharp
flint beak set in a wooden haft, the mjolnir of Thor, the
hammer of Ptah, by which the operation of land-moulding
was undertaken in most mythologies.

It would seem that this sacred pick or hammer must

have become symbolic of Poseidon in the continent of Atlantis. In all likelihood it would be kept wrapped up in linen in his temple, just as the black stone of Jupiter was preserved at Pergamos, or the arrows of Uitzilopochtli in the great temple-pyramid at Mexico. At the Kaaba at Mecca, the centre of the Mahommedan world, a similar stone is preserved wrapped up in silks, and we have seen that in the Irish islands its counterpart was swathed in flannel and preserved in a separate house.

The mythology of Mexico holds many allusions to a certain Huemac or "Great Hand," who seems to be identical with Quetzalcoatl. This figure is also found in Maya mythology as Kab-ul, the "Working Hand," a deification of the hand which wields the great pick or hammer, as is obvious in its representations in the native manuscripts. Quetzalcoatl was the skilled craftsman, the mason, who came from an Atlantic region. In his Quiche form of Tohil he is represented by a flint stone. It seems then that we have here the culture hero from a marine locality symbolised by what appears to be the central emblem of the Atlantean culture-complex. Quetzalcoatl is also the planet Venus, and this identification gives a double significance to the complex. This is by no means weakened, when we discover that this Great Hand is actually identified with Atlantis in mediæval legends, for the map of Bianco, which dates from 1436, contains an island, the Italian name of which may be translated "the Hand of Satan." Formaleoni, an Italian writer, had observed the name, but did not appreciate its significance until he chanced to stumble on a reference to a similar name in an old Italian romance, which told how a great hand rose every day from the sea and carried off a number of the inhabitants into the ocean. The legend is undoubtedly associated with the idea of earthquake or cataclysm in a marine locality, and it seems

obvious that the Great Hand was the god of this Atlantic
island, who took tribute of human lives by earthquake.
The story appears to link up with that of the Minotaur,
the bull-deity of Poseidon, who also took toll of human
lives in Crete, and with the practice of the Canary Islands,
whose priestesses, as we have seen, cast themselves into
the sea to placate the god of Ocean, as well as with
the myth of the Titans.

In Plato's account of Atlantis practically all the details
of the Atlantean complex may be discovered, and the same
holds good of the myth of Quetzalcoatl.   Not only do the
mainlands of the two continents display the clearest traces
of the presence of this culture-complex, but their advanced
island-groups are eloquent of its influence. I have
attempted to show that nowhere else in the world has a
culture-complex embracing these particular manifestations been shown to exist.   Doubtless in time it will be
possible to trace many greater or less additions to this
complex, but those already proven to have been associated
with it should suffice to make it plain that it did actually
exist and that the great likelihood is that it emanated from
a now sunken region in the Atlantic.

THE END